Fishing
Yellowstone
National Park

Help Us Keep This Guide Up to Date

Every effort has been made by the authors and editors to make this guide as accurate and useful as possible. However, many things can change after a guide is published—trails are rerouted, regulations change, techniques evolve, facilities come under new management, etc.

We would love to hear from you concerning your experiences with this guide and how you feel it could be improved and kept up to date. While we may not be able to respond to all comments and suggestions, we'll take them to heart, and we'll also make certain to share them with the authors. Please send your comments and suggestions to the following address:

The Globe Pequot Press
Reader Response/Editorial Department
P.O. Box 480
Guilford, CT 06437

Or you may e-mail us at:

editorial@GlobePequot.com

Thanks for your input, and happy trails!

Fishing Yellowstone National Park

An Angler's Complete Guide to More than 100 Streams, Rivers, and Lakes

Third Edition

RICHARD PARKS

THE LYONS PRESS
GUILFORD, CONNECTICUT
AN IMPRINT OF THE GLOBE PEQUOT PRESS

10 9 8 7 6 5 4 3

Text design by Casey Shain
All photos by Richard Parks unless otherwise indicated
Overview map by Melissa Baker © Morris Book Publishing, LLC.

ISSN: 1547-1918
ISBN: 978-1-59921-142-8

Manufactured in the United States of America

Two men have played key roles in my developing understanding of the Yellowstone country. My father, Merton J. Parks, first brought me to Yellowstone in 1947. He started Parks' Fly Shop, which I now operate, in 1953. It was under his wing that I matured as an angler and as a citizen. The late W. S. ("Scotty") Chapman first came to the Yellowstone country in 1927. There is a fair chance that he is the only man who actually wet a line in every one of the waters of Yellowstone National Park. Scotty served thirty-three years as a Yellowstone ranger. He taught my father and me a lot about the spirit of this place.

To them I dedicate this book.

Acknowledgments

One cannot produce a book of this scope without relying on the knowledge and kindness of many. John Varley, Chief of Resources at Yellowstone National Park, is the first of many people in the National Park Service, Forest Service, and various state agencies who reviewed all or part of this material. They have prevented me from making more errors than I care to contemplate and bear no responsibility for any that remain. Thank you all. My good friends Bob and Sharman Wilson of Driggs, Idaho, provided me with information and reviewed some of the material. They and Paul Brunn of Jackson, Wyoming, another informed and informative colleague, also contributed by providing lodging for me while I was on the road researching the book. Tim Bywater, friend, angler, and seasonal ranger in Grand Teton National Park, has, as always, lent support and valuable perspective. Other colleagues in the trade—Dave Kumlien, Scott Aune, Bob Jacklin, Mike Lawson, Jay Buckner, and Al Harris—were kind enough to lend me their expertise.

I appreciate the trust the editorial crew placed in me when they asked if I could write this book. It would not be in your hands without their persistence in helping me work through the complexities of getting ready for press. Again, thanks.

Contents

To Bozeman

95

91

94

89

93

North Entrance Road

90

88

Gardner

89

Yellowstone River

North Entrance

105

85

92

Gardner River

Mammoth

8

7

6

97

104

86

MONTANA

4

3

103

106

2

Gallatin River

96

102

Tower Ju

1

98

14

287

99

191

100

Heboen Lake

13

10

101

Grand Loop Road

12

Norris Junction

68

16

15

Ca

Norris Canyon Road

17

Grand Loop Road

Gibbon River

West Entrance

West Entrance Road

11

9

Grand

Madison River

Madison Junction

West Yellowstone

22

Firehole River

23

21

89

20

Grand Loop Road

19

Old Faithful

48

65

18

West Thumb

Shoshone Lake

47

49

51

63

50

Lewis Lake

Bechler River

52

IDAHO

38

53

Lewis River

34

South Entrance Road

35

26

42

32

33

27

89

24

25

28

31

Falls River

45

South Entrance

30

29

46

44

To Moran Junction

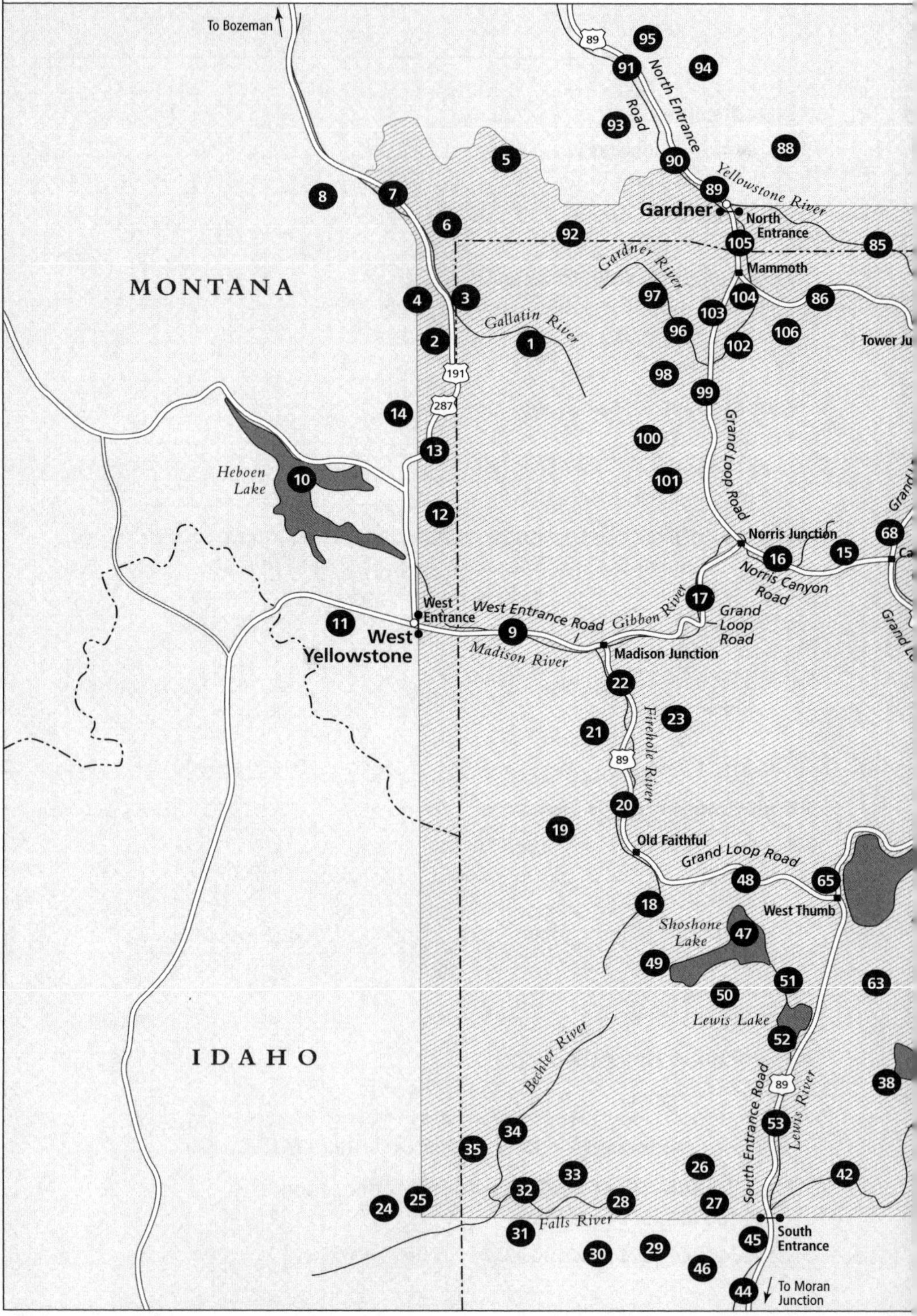

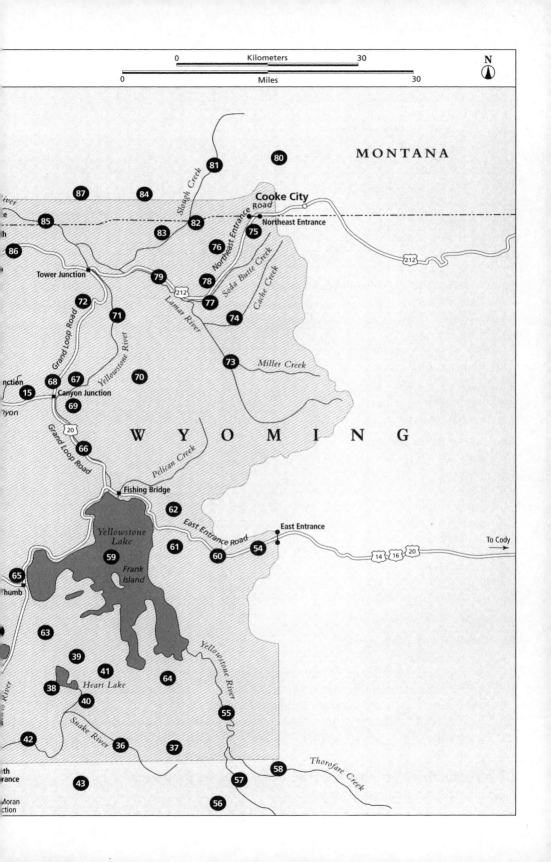

Kilometers

0 30

0 30
Miles

N

MONTANA

Cooke City

87 84 81 80

85 82 Northeast Entrance

83 75 Northeast Entrance

86 76 212

Tower Junction 79 78 Soda Butte Creek Cache Creek

72 77

71 74

Lamar River

73 Miller Creek

W Y O M I N G

15 68 67 70

Canyon Junction

69

20

66 Pelican Creek

Fishing Bridge

62

Yellowstone Lake 61 East Entrance Road East Entrance

59 60 54

Frank Island To Cody

65 14 16 20

Thumb

63

39 Yellowstone River

41 64

38 Heart Lake

40

42 Snake River 36 37 55

South Thorofare Creek

Entrance 58

43 57

Moran 56

Junction

Contents   xi

Introduction

Yellowstone Country

The sun, breaking through a low cloud, glints off the wings of a mayfly drifting down the river. Patches of snow and steam rising from a hot spring are in evidence, but the angler's concentration is on the mayfly. Without fanfare the insect drops into a hole in the water as a fish's nose breaks the surface. Spreading rings mark the spot. A careful cast and the fish rises, takes the fly, and leaps, scattering water as it feels the hook. Minutes later, the fish is released and disappears into a weed bank to sulk. The angler dries the fly and prepares to cast again, having spotted another rising fish.

Mountains, partially snow clad, surge toward the sky on the eastern horizon beyond the lake. A youngster, perhaps eight or nine years of age, winds up and inexpertly flips a folded, squarish piece of brass with red spots painted on it 45 feet out into the lake. Halfway retrieved, the lure is slammed by a fish. "I got one! Daddy, I got one!" Half cranking the reel, half backing up the beach, the fish is dragged to shore. Thrashing, the fish escapes the hook and flops back into the water. "Too big to keep anyway," consoles the father.

I stop at the top of the ridge to wring out my sweatband. Half a mile and 400 vertical feet behind me lies the river, twisting out of the canyon. Part is already shaded from the lowering sun by the canyon walls, the rest glints gold, green, steel. Ahead, cars move along the distant road. Tires scrunch gravel. A cloud of dust marks the arrival of still another car stopped half on, half off the road. Blue on the distant horizon, jagged mountains show themselves. Cameras on tripods, telephoto lenses probably capable of shooting the moons of Jupiter, waving arms, and binoculars point into the meadow 200 yards across the creek. "Do you see the wolves?" "That's just a coyote." "Look at all the buffalo; get some tape of this!" "What's that guy doing; doesn't he see the elk?" "Hey buddy, catchin' any?"

Congress established Yellowstone National Park "for the benefit and enjoyment of the people" in 1872. Yellowstone was the first national park anywhere in the world. A convergence of interests between America's infant conservation movement and the powerful financiers developing the Northern Pacific Railroad allowed passage of the legislation far ahead of its time. How far ahead? Congress did not get around to creating a National Park Service to administer such facilities until 1916.

Today, Yellowstone National Park straddles the Continental Divide at the center of the largest minimally developed ecosystem in the temperate zones of the world. Protection of the headwaters areas has allowed the preservation of an aquatic system second to none. The primary function of trout in this system is to occupy their place in the food chain, both as predator and prey. As a fringe benefit, we have one of the great sport fisheries of the world.

This book does two things. First, it describes, as candidly and accurately as I can manage, the waters of Yellowstone and their fishes. Second, it provides information on how to get to those waters. It is not intended to be a guide to fishing technique, every insect that hatches, or every rock harboring a fish. It is intended for all anglers, regardless of tackle, skill level, or age.

How to Use This Guide

I recommend that you read the preliminary sections of the book before plunging into the site descriptions. *Fishing Yellowstone* describes all waters by starting at their sources and proceeding downstream, including those streams which originate outside the park and flow into it. If you are interested in a particular watershed of Yellowstone National Park, simply turn to the appropriate section. There you'll find descriptions of that drainage's main stream and its major tributaries. Each site description includes several divisions.

Description: A physical description is given for each lake or section of stream. The general direction of flow, orientation on the ground, and relationship to landmarks is laid out. Characteristics of the bottom and cover on the banks are described. Structural features that are likely to hold fish are identified. Finally, this first division also discusses pertinent information about the regulations and seasonal patterns of the water.

The fish: The second division describes the fish to be found in each section of stream or lake. Species to be found and anticipated size ranges are discussed. Other matters of interest related to the fish also are included here.

Flies and lures: The third division takes up the question of what flies or lures to use. The names of specific fly patterns and lures are capitalized, but natural insects or categories of flies are not; for instance, hoppers on the one hand, and Dave's Hopper on the other. The lures discussed are all commonly available in the region, as are most of the flies. Something on the order of 30,000 fly patterns have been written about and/or produced over the years. Many of the patterns are redundant. One thing I tell people is that faith counts. Your favorite lure or fly is worth a try.

Despite the foregoing, some of the fly patterns listed are not common, since they are produced for my shop. The names of some of these do not reveal much about them; for this reason I describe those flies. For example, the Skinny Bugger is a damselfly nymph tied primarily with light olive marabou, including the dubbed body. The Joffe Jewel is a small yellow, white, and red marabou streamer that has proven to be particularly effective for brook trout. Both of these patterns were originated by Gardiner fly tyer Matt Minch.

All bait and lure restrictions are also dealt with in the flies and lures section.

Special equipment: A fourth division appears whenever information is provided about equipment that may prove useful for the water under discussion.

Access: The access division describes how to get to the water under discussion. This information may be very simple for those streams or lakes adjacent to a major roadway. In some cases it is more complex because there are multiple points of access to a lengthy segment of stream or shoreline. Trailheads and access points are usually discussed from the top down, just as streams are, and the points of access to lakes are described using a counterclockwise rotation.

Tributaries: The final division identifies tributaries. If the tributaries have their own description within the book, you will learn in this section where to find the information.

Brown trout on a spawning run up the Gardner River.
MICHAEL SAMPLE PHOTO

Weathered ruins of a dock on Hebgen Lake.

About Mileages, Maps, and Rocks

The sections titled "Mileage points" list the locations between which mileage was measured. I drove hundreds of miles, making notes all the way, to establish the distances between these points. With two exceptions, all of the road segments shown can be driven with an ordinary automobile. The exceptions are explicitly described both on the map and in the text. Many of the road segments can be approached from either end, so the mileage from both points are given. Your odometer may not register mileage exactly the same as mine does, so it would be a good idea to be alert to the possibility that we might disagree by a few hundred yards. Mileages along trails were either taken from posted signs or calculated using topographic maps. This means that there is more inherent uncertainty in these calculations. The same is true of the information on the altitude changes encountered on many of the access routes. They should be reasonably close, but cannot be considered exact.

The individual site maps were prepared using U.S. Geological Survey maps. The Resources section includes information on where to find the original maps.

I have tried not to use technical jargon. I haven't riddled the text with the Latin names of bugs and fish. Some words, though, mean particular things to the experienced angler. In describing the nature of stream or lake beds, I use the following terms: *muck* is very fine-grained and soft; *sand* is pretty self-explanatory; *gravel* means roundish rock less than 3 inches in diameter; *cobbles* are rounded rocks less than 2 feet in diameter; *boulders* are more than 2 feet in diameter; and *rubble* is angular rock of varying size.

Map Legend

Interstate	90	One Way Road	One Way
US Highway	89	City or Town	◯ Gardiner
State or Other Principal Road	87	Campground	▲
Forest Road	6954	Cabin or Building	▪
Interstate Highway	⇒	Peak	X
Paved Road	⇒	Mine Site	⚒
Gravel Road	⇒	Overlook/Point of Interest	◘
Unimproved Road	======⇒	National or State Forest/Park Boundary	
Fishing Site	2		
Lake, River/Creek, Waterfalls		Map Orientation	N
Bridge		Scale	0 0.5 1 Miles
Marsh or Wetland			
Trail/Route		Mileage Marker	◢
Trailhead	T	Hot Springs	
Picnic Area	╦		

The Fishes of Yellowstone Country

The Game Fish of Yellowstone National Park

Cutthroat Trout

The cutthroat trout is native to the Snake and Yellowstone river drainages. Physical isolation has encouraged the development of a number of distinct subspecies and strains of cutthroat throughout the West. In Yellowstone, as elsewhere, official and unofficial fish stocking has mixed some of these types. Most obvious is the widespread introduction of cutthroat stocks from Yellowstone Lake into parts of the Snake, Gallatin, and Madison watersheds. The cutthroat is distinguished by characteristic red markings under the jaw. Other visual clues are the relatively large dark spots, the distribution of those spots toward the tail, and an overall brownish-gold color pattern.

Grayling

Originally native to the Madison and Gallatin drainages, grayling have been functionally eliminated from their original range within Yellowstone. The only substantial surviving stocks of grayling are found in Grebe, Wolf, and Cascade Lakes. Grebe and Wolf Lakes are at the head of the Gibbon River, in the Madison drainage. They had no native fish until 1890, when they were stocked with grayling. The nearby Cascade Lake is in the Yellowstone drainage. Most efforts to expand the range of grayling within the park have not had any notable success. The most obvious physical characteristic of grayling is their very large dorsal fin with its silverspotted, iridescent purple sheen. Otherwise, the fish is silvery with small dark spots.

Brown Trout

Brown trout are native to Europe. They have been introduced into the lower Yellowstone and Gardner river systems and broadly into the Madison and Snake river drainages. An overall color pattern of brown shading to gold gives the brown a superficial resemblance to the cutthroat. However, the dark spots of the brown are more uniformly distributed along the back of the fish and are joined by red spots that are primarily distributed along the midline of the sides. There are few, if any, spots on the tail and no red markings under the jaw.

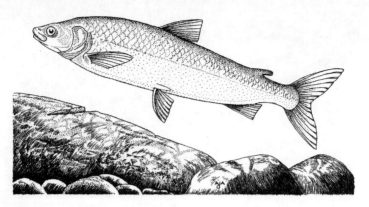

Whitefish

Whitefish still occupy all or most of their native ranges in Yellowstone National Park. They thrive in the lower sections of the Yellowstone, Gardner, Madison, Gallatin, and Snake river systems. Whitefish are dark on their backs, shading to white on their bellies. They are without spots, and very thin gill covers allow the red of the gills to show through. The scales are somewhat larger and more obvious than those of trout. A bulbous nose overhanging their lower jaw causes some to mistake them for a kind of sucker.

Rainbow Trout

Rainbow trout, like cutthroat, are native to the western United States. Their native range did not extend into Yellowstone National Park, but they were introduced there in the late nineteenth century. The characteristic feature of the rainbow is the strong reddish lateral line running along the sides of the fish, dividing a dark, often greenish, back from the white or silver belly. The rainbow is profusely speckled with small dark spots that extend onto both the head and tail. It is not unusual for rainbow to exhibit flecks of orange under the jaw.

Brook Trout

Native to the eastern United States, brook trout were introduced to Yellowstone National Park. They are a member of the char family. Two features stand out when I look at a brookie: the light markings on a dark background and their patriotic striped fins—red, blue, and white. Small red spots surrounded by a light halo are scattered along the midline of the fish. The light markings on the back look more like the tracks of a bucket of worms than the spots of browns or cutthroat.

Cutbow

Cutthroat and rainbow trout are closely related and will interbreed. The result is a fertile hybrid. Because of the probability of recrossing, there is no reliable way short of DNA analysis to positively separate cutthroat from cutbow from rainbow in those waters where both parent species exist. As a rule of thumb, the cutbow is likely to exhibit the rainbow stripe, somewhat subdued in color intensity. The cutbow is also likely to have smaller spots than the cutthroat, with a few on the head. The gold of the belly and the red of the throat slash are likely to be less prominent than on the cutthroat. The existence of the hybrid has regulatory consequences. Montana and Wyoming tend to treat the cutbow in the same way they treat the rainbow, while Idaho and Yellowstone National Park tend to treat it as if it were a cutthroat.

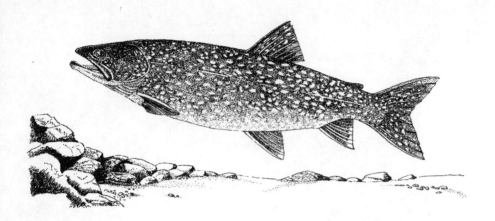

Lake Trout

Lake trout, another member of the char family, are native to eastern and northern North America. They have been introduced to Yellowstone National Park. The deeply forked tail and overall green color shading to silver are the most obvious characteristics of the lake trout. As with other char, the markings are light on a dark background, and those on the back are wormlike.

Other Fishes

Yellowstone National Park hosts nine other species of fish as well as a second hybrid. These fish are the mountain sucker, longnose sucker, Utah sucker, longnose dace, speckled dace, redside shiner, Utah chub, mottled sculpin, lake chub, and the redside shiner–speckled dace cross. The lake chub is an import to the park. A number of others have had their range expanded since David Jordan completed the first comprehensive survey of the Yellowstone fishery in 1891.

These fish play several important roles in the aquatic ecosystem. From the angler's point of view, one of the most important is their place in the food chain as forage for trout. The sculpin in particular is the inspiration for a number of fly patterns such as the Spuddler and Whitlock's Sculpin. Sculpins are also useful as an indicator of water quality as they do not do well in contaminated streams.

The Way Things Were

Ferdinand Hayden conducted the first government-sponsored, comprehensive survey of what is now Yellowstone National Park in 1871. He found approximately 40 percent of the waters in the area to be without fish. Major waterfalls on the Lewis, Falls, Firehole, Gibbon, and Gardner Rivers prevented fish from moving beyond them into those drainages. The only sportfish available were grayling, cutthroat, and whitefish. The Yellowstone drainage above the falls had neither longnose suckers nor redside shiners, though those fish were present elsewhere in the area.

How Things Got the Way They Are

People had already begun to alter the distribution of fish in Yellowstone National Park by the time Jordan conducted his survey in 1891. In fact, by 1900 the present distribution of fish was pretty much in place. Captain F. A. Boutelle and other military superintendents of the park were responsible for the introduction of brown, rainbow, brook, and lake trout to Yellowstone. Some of the plants bore no fruit. Bass introduced to the Gibbon River disappeared, as did the whitefish that had been introduced to the upper Yellowstone River. Cutthroat trout from Yellowstone Lake were widely distributed throughout the park, where they either colonized waters previously without fish or crossbred with native cutthroat strains.

It wasn't until 1936 that park policy began to work against the introduction of nonindigenous fish. One critical step was the prohibition of live bait fish. There is no doubt in my mind that the spread of chubs, dace, and shiners into many lakes of the area resulted at least in part from inadvertent or deliberate releases (dumping bait buckets) by anglers.

Fisheries policy continued to evolve and after 1955 settled into its present pattern. Native fish are to be protected. Planting of fish for the angler has been entirely replaced by management of the kill in order to protect the viability of wild, self-propagating populations. In the hope that their range will expand, safe havens are sought for grayling and certain at-risk strains of cutthroat. Waters once stocked that do not sustain reproduction or are subject to freeze-out have been allowed to return to their fishless state.

Exotics, Bucket Biology, Whirling Disease, and Other Concerns

Perhaps in a perfect world, one in which people truly could project what was best for future generations, the waters of Yellowstone would not have been planted with alien species. I really don't think that outcome ever would be likely, though. For example, I cannot believe establishing lake trout in Lewis and Shoshone Lakes (fishless at the time) was a disaster. That act has played an important role in the recovery of lake trout in their ancestral home in the Great Lakes. The wide distribution of brook trout in waters otherwise without fish may indeed have been an error, in the scientific sense. Given that current policy places as much intrinsic value in waters without fish as in waters with fish, such distribution certainly would not take place today. But brookies were integrated into the system, some time ago now, and there seems to be value in leaving them there.

It is easy to think that people are in a position to control events. Evidence suggests that accident, and sometimes even malicious intent, continues to give the lie to our hubris. I have discovered nothing that suggests anyone intended to transplant New Zealand mud snails into the waters of Yellowstone, but there they are. We are barely able even to guess what the eventual ecologic consequences may be. Chance misfortune also was in evidence when, in 1988, a researcher inadvertently killed more fish with misapplied poison in Soda Butte Creek than were lost that year to the effects of the great fires. It is equally fair to suggest that neither event had great significance for Yellowstone's trout in the long run.

Far more worrisome is the 1994 discovery of lake trout in Yellowstone Lake. My best guess is that parties unknown were unhappy with the shift in regulations that greatly restricted angler cutthroat kill in the lake. They believed they knew better than the professionals. Apparently they accomplished the deed with a few buckets and a few June or October trips back and forth between Lewis and Yellowstone Lakes, moving a critical number of lake trout into Yellowstone Lake. Given the completely balanced way in which cutthroat interact in the ecosystem as both predator and prey, the potential consequences of this act on the whole system are serious. Lake trout may destroy this delicate balance. It was a criminal act, not just in the legal sense, but in the moral sense.

Fisheries managers apparently succeeded in removing the brook trout discovered in Arnica Creek, a tributary of Yellowstone Lake. I would not be surprised to learn that the unknowns who put the lakers in Yellowstone were the very ones who introduced brook trout to Arnica Creek. While the effort to remove brown trout from Duck Lake has apparently also succeeded, cutthroat have appeared from some unknown source. The duel effort to remove all brook trout from Pocket Lake and replace them with cutthroat from Heart Lake has succeeded only in part; there is a growing population of cutthroat in the lake.

It is not certain how whirling disease was introduced to the Madison River outside of Yellowstone National Park. In the decade plus since its first discovery the parasite has spread to many other waters in the Mountain West including some in the park. The epicenter of infection appears to be Pelican Creek, (which has been closed to angling because of population collapse) Yellowstone Lake, and the Yellowstone River downstream from the lake. We can say with certainty that the disease may be spread by sloth as well as purposeful intent and even by migratory birds. The Montana Department of Fish, Wildlife & Parks has developed specific recommendations designed to inhibit the spread of whirling disease. Clean mud and aquatic vegetation off your waders, net, boat, trailer, and any other gear before leaving the stream. Dry the gear between trips. Do not transport fish or fish parts from one body of water to another. These suggestions may help decrease the spread of mud snails as well.

We do well to consider our actions. It was policy to introduce brown trout to the Firehole River. Now it is not. Policy and our understanding of the complexity of the world around us will both change. I caution against the hubris of the professional manager as much as I do against carelessness or the hubris of the amateur enthusiast. We all are responsible for the care of the great fishery we have in Yellowstone.

Regulations, Wildlife, and Courtesy

The Regulations

Yellowstone National Park was established before any of the surrounding areas attained statehood. Consequently, the park retains original jurisdiction over the fishery and the power to regulate its use.

The surrounding areas in Montana, Idaho, and Wyoming—including the J. D. Rockefeller Parkway, which connects Yellowstone with Grand Teton National Park—are regulated by their respective states. The fisheries in the national forest areas surrounding the park are administered and regulated by the states, though most other aspects of public use are controlled by the USDA Forest Service.

That means there are four sets of regulations that a widely ranging angler needs to be familiar with. However, since this book is about fishing in Yellowstone, I have not tried to explain all of the overlapping regulations. Instead, I discuss specific regulations for a given water that may differ from the standard regulations for the state or park.

Broadly speaking, Yellowstone regulations require that anglers use artificial flies or lures with barbless or crushed hooks to facilitate the release of fish. Most Yellowstone lakes and streams are catch and release; those that aren't allow a limited kill. To protect Yellowstone's birds, the use of lead sinkers has been banned. I also focus on instances in which the park boundary itself may create problems. The National Park Service and the states of Idaho, Montana, and Wyoming publish comprehensive fishing regulations that are issued free to purchasers of fishing licenses in these states. If your license vendor does not offer you a set of regulations, ask for it.

In general, you will find that the states are more likely to allow an angler to kill fish than is Yellowstone National Park. They also have longer open seasons and are less restrictive on bait usage than the park. However, there are substantial differences among Idaho, Montana, and Wyoming in philosophy and practice. It is your responsibility to understand and comply with the regulations that apply to the water you are fishing and the ground on which you stand. You can request copies of fishing regulations from the state agencies listed at the back of this book. Addresses and phone numbers are provided.

Be aware that Yellowstone National Park also requires a boat permit for all floating craft, including float tubes.

Bears, Bison, and Other Wild Things

The entire area covered by this guide is bear country. In fact, most of it is wildland and is administered under wilderness rules by either the National Park Service or Forest Service. I have not tried to replicate Yellowstone's bear management policy but have instead attempted to identify where it conflicts with the interests of anglers.

Judging from the questions I am asked in my store, many expect bears to patrol the backcountry looking for unwary hikers or anglers to eat! This is simply not the case.

There are three main ways to get into trouble with bears—with *any* wildlife for that matter. The most common, yet easiest to avoid, is the deliberate intrusion on a bear or other wild animal. A look at the emergency room log at the Lake Hospital should convince you that it makes no better sense to pet a bison than it does to ask a bear to open wide and show its teeth for the camera. Both have been done. Both have had predictable results. Critters in Yellowstone are at home; you are the visitor. There are something on the order of 25,000 elk and 3,000 bison in Yellowstone compared to about 200 grizzly and 400 black bears. You are much more likely to see an elk or bison than a bear. All the creatures, great or small, will defend their young. Viewing wildlife from a safe distance with a pair of binoculars beats a trip to the emergency room, or morgue, any day.

A surprise encounter is the most difficult to avoid. If neither you nor the bear, moose, or other animal is aware of the other's presence prior to close contact, trouble is likely. You will certainly be considered a threat, but probably not food. An animal knocking down a threat on the way out of the area is pretty routine. A bison clearing you out of his path with its horns or a moose stomping your midriff will be no better for your health than a bear slapping you upside the head. The best defense is to stay alert to your surroundings. For this and other reasons, it is a bad idea to go into the backcountry alone. Talking to a partner on the trail makes surprise encounters much less likely.

The third way in which folks commonly get into trouble with wildlife is by mishandling food. Both the Forest Service and the National Park Service have regulations for the safe handling of food. In general these rules apply in roadside camps every bit as much as they do in the backcountry. Every spring and fall we have bears moving through Gardiner and other inhabited areas. The problems can be mundane, or extreme.

I know of an instance in which a mouse decided to colonize a new Ford Explorer. After excavating a hole in the upholstery and scattering stuffing around, the mouse decided that 6-inch lengths of a new fly line were just the thing to line its nest. Snack crackers that were left in the center console may have attracted the mouse and probably contributed to the repair bill, which ran into hundreds of dollars. In an extreme case, a pair of fools set up camp in an unauthorized location, left garbage strewn about, and returned after dark to surprise a bear pillaging the place. The bear killed one and chased the other up a tree.

Leaving food around attracts animals into proximity with people. The animals become habituated to the food and the proximity. Animals that lose their fear of humans as top predator get themselves and the people they come in contact with into trouble, too often fatal trouble. The best defense is to follow the food-handling rules circulated by park rangers and never, under any circumstances, feed the wildlife. A marmot, unhappy with the withdrawal of a cookie, bit the teaser. "I just wanted a better picture," said the bitten one. Undoubtedly the teaser got no photograph.

Anglers sometimes fail to assimilate the idea that their catch, if kept, is now food.

A fast stretch of the Gardner River flows past a cedar tree. MICHAEL SAMPLE PHOTO

Proper handling is necessary for two reasons: to avoid spoilage and to prevent problems with wildlife. Rule one, in my book, for handling fish to eat is to kill and clean the fish as quickly as possible. Mechanically, cleaning fish is fairly simple. Insert a sharp knife into the fish's anal region and slit it open from anus to chin. This allows you to strip out the entrails and gills as a unit. Complete removal of the entrails and gills followed by washing the fish reduces the chances of spoilage. If possible, the fish should be stored on ice, or at least in a creel, and eaten as soon as possible.

Proper disposal of the entrails is also important. Unless you are directed otherwise by area regulations, entrails should be returned to deeper water rather than left on land. A stinking pile of fish guts is not a fun fishing companion and may very well serve to attract a bear. Hanging all your food in a tree, as required in backcountry campsites, does little good if you leave your creel sitting by the fireplace.

I also get questions about snakes. Rattlesnakes are only found in the area immediately around Gardiner. The rest of the country is elevated above their habitat range. You are unlikely to have trouble with a rattlesnake, as long as you keep your hands and feet out of places you cannot see. Garter snakes may startle you but will not hurt you. Bull snakes, which bear a passing resemblance to rattlers, are not poisonous and are not interested in you. As with the rest of the wildlife, if you leave a snake alone, it generally will leave you alone.

Following these rules will almost always keep you out of trouble with bears and other wildlife. If something does go wrong, I believe the best last-ditch defense is a

Regulations, Wildlife, and Courtesy

good pepper spray. Do not bother with the little cans; they only give you a couple of squirts at very short range. Get at least a nine-ounce spray can so that you can spare a shot or two while you're panicking and still have something left to get the job done.

One more thing: This is mountain country, and the weather can bite you just as surely as a bear. Even in summer the nighttime lows may approach freezing and drop below freezing at higher altitudes. Weather forecasts are not always reliable, but they are better than they used to be. Summer thunderstorm events are frequent. Sheltering under that big tree on the ridge could get you fried by lightning. Hypothermia is a killer. The coldest I have ever been was during a hailstorm that caught me unprepared on an August day. Weather can blow up suddenly, so never go out without rain gear.

Ethics of Backcountry and Stream

Anglers owe it to their quarry to treat them with respect. Most waters described in this book contain at least one species of fish that is regulated by catch-and-release laws. If fishing water where there is any substantial chance of hooking fish over 12 inches long, carry and use a net. I recommend flattening the barbs on hooks. Not only does this facilitate easier release of fish, which is better for them, but your flies or lures are likely to last longer.

Both the National Park Service and Forest Service have regulations governing the use of the backcountry. The resources section at the back of this book includes the addresses of Forest Service district offices and National Park Service offices where you can obtain any required permits. All camping within Yellowstone National Park must be in designated sites. Some of these sites can be reserved well in advance of your trip; others are on a first-come-first-served basis. The Forest Service prohibits overnight use of some areas, but otherwise is less prescriptive about where you can camp.

When fishing or camping, practice zero impact techniques. These ensure that the backcountry and fishing waters will stand a fighting chance of surviving our heavy use. The following guidelines should be followed to minimize our impact on the wilderness environment.

Eight Principles of Zero Impact Behavior

1. Plan ahead, prepare well, and prevent problems before they occur.
2. Keep noise to a minimum and strive to be inconspicuous.
3. Pack it in, pack it out.
4. Properly dispose of anything that can't be packed out.
5. Leave the land as you found it.
6. In popular places, concentrate use.
7. In pristine places, disperse use.
8. Avoid places that are lightly worn or just beginning to show signs of use.

A bull elk wades the Yellowstone River.
MICHAEL SAMPLE PHOTO

Guidelines for Fishing

Know and obey the regulations.

Practice catch-and-release fishing, even if the regulations do not require it. Where keeping fish is allowed, keep only what you can eat. Land a fish quickly rather than playing it to exhaustion. To release a fish caught in a stream, cradle it upright in the water facing into the current (to help water flow over the gills) until the fish recovers and swims away. In a lake, a gentle back-and-forth motion will facilitate a fish's recovery.

Lead sinkers, when ingested, are toxic to waterfowl and other wildlife. Use steel weights. Make an honest effort to recover all snagged flies, lures, and tangled line.

Respect other anglers' territory.

Unfortunately, experience suggests that it is necessary to repeat this: Keep out of other anglers' water! My first rule on selecting a fishing location is to find one that is not already occupied. If the parking area for a backcountry location is already full, think about another site. It will not always be possible to tell, of course. When I encounter other anglers, I leave the water and bypass them, leaving them room to continue fishing. Stay off the banks that other anglers are fishing. I get at least 10 feet back from the edge when passing someone. Unless specifically invited, it is never, ever, proper to fish in the same pool or area of water another angler is working.

"Well, you were changing flies, not fishing."

"It looked to me like you were just standing there."

"Hey, there was 60 feet here between you and that guy up there."

"I'm on this side, you're over there."

None of these excuses is acceptable.

Neither is it acceptable to violate the space of an angler who is using legal methods, rationalizing that you do not happen to like those methods. If you think there are good reasons why fly, spin, or bait fishing should be prohibited in a given water, take them up with the regulatory authority. Until then the other anglers have a right to fish that water, the right to expect your courtesy, and the duty to extend theirs to you.

Use common sense and practice the golden rule when selecting a campsite. There may be no regulation, but it sure is rude to pitch your tent between another party and the stream or lake. Give everyone else the courtesy of the privacy you would like to have. Some backcountry areas are heavily used by folks on horseback. Hikers should keep clear of stock on the trail and in camp. By the same token, riders should not run over hikers on the trail or in camp. Give riders the right-of-way.

Much of the area outside Yellowstone National Park hosts hunting parties after mid-September. In many cases the fishing will be past its peak by the opening of the hunting season. The angler should keep the probable presence of hunters in mind when planning a fall trip. I recommend wearing hunter orange vests when angling in the backcountry during an active hunting season.

The fishing will be better for all of us if you practice these simple principles.

The Gallatin River Drainage from Headwaters to Taylor Fork

The Gallatin River rises high on the north flank of Three Rivers Peak in northwest Yellowstone National Park. Lewis and Clark named this easternmost of the three forks of the Missouri for Albert Gallatin, then Secretary of the Treasury. The Gallatin and the tributaries described here are all mountain freestone streams with fairly steep gradients. The river flows generally northwest through fairly narrow, timbered canyons and mountain meadows that are more open but still narrow. The most significant tributaries are Fan, Bacon Rind, Specimen, and Sage Creeks.

Mileage points: Mileage from West Yellowstone, Montana, is measured from the junction of U.S. Highway 20 and U.S. Highway 191. Mileage from the north is measured from Four Corners, Montana, 5.4 miles west of Bozeman, Montana, on US 191.

1. Gallatin River, Gallatin Lake to Bighorn Pass Trailhead

Description: Gallatin Lake, at the head of the river, lies along the timberline at 8,834 feet. Due to the high altitude, small size, and steep gradient of the river as it flows out of the lake, neither lake nor river has fish. The gradient becomes less steep 5 miles below the lake. As it does, a few small nameless tributaries enter the river and so do fish. Much of this middle reach was burned to varying extent in 1988. Finally, the Gallatin enters a long, narrow meadow as it reaches toward the west and US 191. The river is still a fast-moving freestone stream here, even though it meanders a bit through an alpine meadow. The bed is mostly cobble, cut a couple of feet below the level of the meadow. Scrub willow often lines the stream bank. Stream conditions on this section of the Gallatin make it unfishable during spring runoff, which lasts until about the end of June. It will fish fairly well through the summer but tapers off noticeably by Labor Day.

The fish: There may be remnants of the native westslope cutthroat in this reach of the stream, but most of the fish are cutbows, rainbows, and Yellowstone cutthroat, with a few browns thrown in. Fairly small for the most part, in the 6- to 10-inch range, a few of these fish, particularly in the meadow sections, will reach into the 12- to 14-inch range.

Flies and lures: The flies most likely to succeed here are attractor patterns such as the Royal Wulff, smaller Stimulators, and Trudes. Useful nymphs include the Prince and Hare's Ear. Lures should be kept on the small side, under one-sixth ounce, and

Sites 1–4

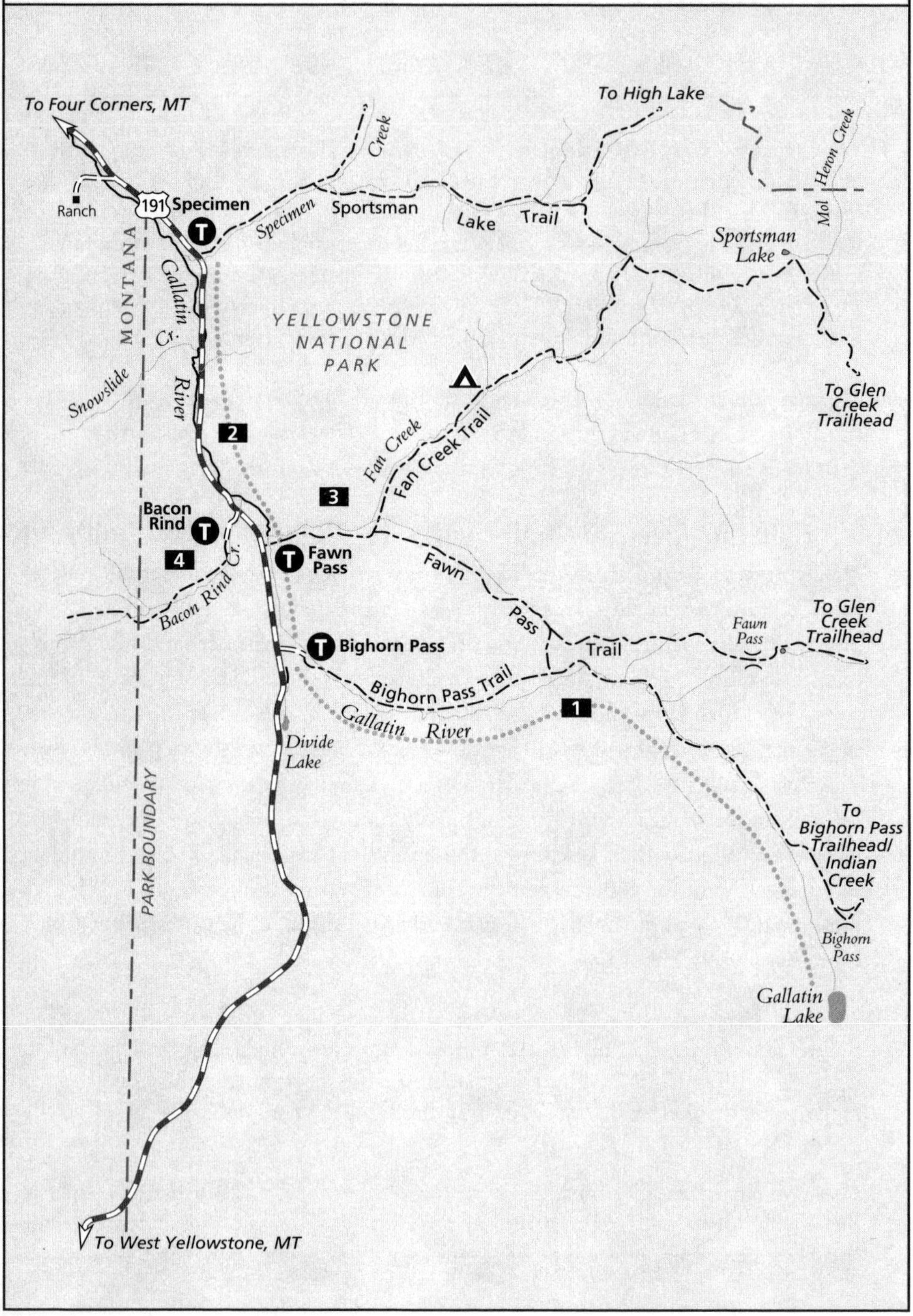

0   1   2

Miles

N

To Four Corners, MT

Ranch

191 **Specimen** Ⓣ

Specimen   Sportsman   Lake   Trail

Creek

To High Lake

Heron Creek

Mol

Sportsman Lake

MONTANA

Gallatin   Cr.

River

Snowslide

YELLOWSTONE NATIONAL PARK

⛺

To Glen Creek Trailhead

2

Fan Creek

Fan Creek Trail

3

Bacon Rind Ⓣ

4

Bacon Rind Cr.

Ⓣ **Fawn Pass**

Fawn   Pass   Trail

Fawn Pass

To Glen Creek Trailhead

Ⓣ **Bighorn Pass**

Bighorn Pass Trail

Gallatin   River

1

Divide Lake

PARK BOUNDARY

To Bighorn Pass Trailhead/ Indian Creek

Bighorn Pass

Gallatin Lake

To West Yellowstone, MT

include Mepps, Panther Martin, and Cyclone Spoon. As this section of the river is wholly within Yellowstone National Park, bait is not allowed.

Access: To reach this section of the Gallatin, take US 191 north from West Yellowstone 21 miles to the Bighorn Pass Trailhead. If you are coming from Bozeman, this trailhead is 63.3 miles south of Four Corners. The trailhead is 0.2 mile east of the highway on a dirt access road and 100 yards south of the river. Either walk to the river and work your way upstream or hike east up the trail. The Bighorn Pass Trail crosses the river a few hundred yards upstream and then parallels the river throughout its fish-inhabited portion. Cut between the trail and the river anywhere, typically a distance of about 200 yards. You are missing nothing when the trail begins to climb, soon crossing over into the Gardner drainage. There are some backcountry campsites along the trail, the first about 4 miles upriver from the road. The best fishing is found along the section between US 191 and the upper end of the meadow 4 miles east of the road.

2. Gallatin River, Bighorn Pass Trailhead to Specimen Creek

Description: Throughout this stretch the Gallatin River is a typical mountain-meadow stream. The bed is mostly cobble, from 4 to 12 inches in size. The river wanders north, repeating a pattern of going from short pitch to small pool to short pitch. The section immediately upstream from the Fan Creek confluence is braided into several channels. The fish are concentrated in the deeper waters at the heads of the pools and along the outside of the bends. The occasional larger rock, island, or timber obstruction also sets up holding water. The streambed, carved out by the annual spring runoff, is often twice the normal width of the river. The banks are abrupt, about 3 feet high, and are lined with grass, sage, or scrub willow. Dropped back casts are easy, but become expensive after you have lost a few flies. The fishing is at its best here from early July into August.

The fish: Primarily cutbow, rainbow, and cutthroat, with a scattering of browns. They run in the 7- to 12-inch range; the very exceptional fish get into the 14-inch class.

Flies and lures: If you are using lures, start with a #4 Panther Martin or one-sixth-ounce gold Cyclone. Other worthy options include the Mepps and Kamlooper in smaller sizes. The fly fisher will find a Royal Coachman Trude or Royal Wulff in a #12 or #14 the first choice. Dave's Hopper or other hopper patterns are a good August bet. Productive nymphs include the Prince and Hare's Ear.

Access: Take US 191 north from West Yellowstone or south from Bozeman. The Bighorn Pass Trailhead at the south end is 21 miles from West Yellowstone or 63.3 miles from Four Corners. Specimen Creek is 57.1 miles south of Four Corners or 27.2 miles north of West Yellowstone. The highway closely parallels this entire 6.2 mile reach of river. It is seldom more than 300 yards, often less, from any of the fairly frequent pullouts to the river. The key in choosing a section of water is to pick one of your own. I pass occupied parking spots in favor of any empty one.

Tributaries: The Gallatin is joined in this section by Fan Creek (site 3), Bacon Rind Creek (site 4), Snowslide Creek, and Specimen Creek (site 6). While Snowslide Creek does have some fish, both creek and fish are trivial. The other tributaries are described below.

3. Fan Creek *(see map on page 20)*

Description: Fan Creek is a small, fast mountain stream, with a bed that is mostly small- to medium-size cobble. It lies in a narrow valley bounded by an open meadow margin and timbered valley walls. The drainage basin is dendritic, having many branches, with the main stem trending from northeast to southwest. In May and June the stream is usually unfishable due to spring snowmelt. July and August provide the most reliable fishing. The best water is to be found in the small pools on bends, undercut banks, and just downstream of the occasional boulder. These features are concentrated in the section beginning a half mile in from the highway and

The Gallatin winds through meadows near Fan Creek.

running upstream for 2 miles. The stream becomes smaller and steeper-pitched as you ascend, and therefore less worthwhile for fishing.

The fish: Fan Creek's population is almost exclusively small cutthroat and cutbows in the 7- to 12-inch range.

Flies and lures: The best fly patterns are the Renegade, Royal Coachman, or the Prince nymph if fishing wet. The dries used most often are Dave's Hopper or Royal Coachman Trude. The most practical lures would be the smallest lures or spinners, say #2 Panther Martins or one-sixth-ounce Cyclones, though the small size of the stream argues against spin fishing.

Access: Take US 191 north 21.4 miles from West Yellowstone or 61.9 miles south from Four Corners to the Fawn Pass Trailhead. Take the Fawn Pass Trail across the Gallatin River, which divides into several channels here. A quarter mile after you cross the Gallatin, the trail begins paralleling Fan Creek. The stream usually can be located about 100 yards north of the trail, and you can leave the trail and begin fishing anytime. The trail stays on the south bank of the stream to its junction with the Fan Creek Trail, near the 2-mile marker. Continue up Fan Creek on the Fan Creek Trail to find additional fishing water.

4. Bacon Rind Creek *(see map on page 20)*

Description: Bacon Rind Creek rises on Redstreak Peak in the Madison Range and flows northeast to its junction with the Gallatin. Shedding about 2,000 feet in its first 6 miles, the upper portion of the stream rates poor to downright barren as a fishery. Only the lower couple of miles within Yellowstone National Park is worth bothering with. In this section the creek bed is composed of mostly medium-size cobble and gravel, and the stream flows through a fairly open valley. The banks are mostly grass with occasional sage or willow bushes. The best stretch is in a meadow area that begins about half a mile in from the road and extends upstream for 1 mile. Due to the small size of the creek, fish anywhere the structure of the river creates deeper water. This stream is unfishable in late May and June. It fishes best in July and August.

The fish: The fish are mostly cutbows. There appears to be a remnant population of westslope cutthroat, particularly in the upper reaches. The fish are small, in the 7- to 10-inch range, with the occasional big one reaching 12 inches.

Flies and lures: Suggested flies are grasshoppers, Royal Coachman Trudes, Renegades, and Prince nymphs. This small stream is not well suited to fishing with lures, but you could try #0 Mepps or tiny Triple Teazers.

Access: Drive north 22.1 miles from West Yellowstone on US 191 to the Bacon Rind Trailhead on the west side of the road. From Four Corners, the trailhead is 61.2 miles south. The parking area is at the end of a 0.3-mile dirt access road. The Bacon Rind Trail begins on the north side of the creek and crosses it near the upper end of the meadow before paralleling the creek for the rest of its fishable distance. Start any place that looks reasonable.

5. High Lake

Description: At 8,774 feet, High Lake lies just under the crest of the Gallatin Range. Above timberline, the surrounding terrain is a rock-and-alpine tundra bowl tipped with the lip facing south. It is a long day's hike to reach High Lake from the road, but fortunately there are backcountry campsites available here. The lake is small and can be pretty well covered from shore with fly or spin equipment. A good place to start is around the outlet to the East Fork of Specimen Creek or near the various spring inlets. Snow prevents access to High Lake until July, and the fishing is over by early September.

The fish: Cutthroat, mostly in the 7- to 12-inch range, are the only fish found in High Lake. Once in an odd while one of these cutts may reach 16 inches.

Flies and lures: A Black Gnat or Renegade is as good a bet as any for a fly. Other possibilities include a Royal Wulff, small Woolly Bugger, or Skinny Bugger. The spin angler should start with a Mepps or Kastmaster.

Access: Take US 191 north from West Yellowstone for 26.2 miles to the Specimen Creek Trailhead. Take the Specimen Creek Trail 2 miles to its junction with the Sportsman Lake Trail. Follow the Sportsman Lake Trail to its junction with the High Lake Trail and then turn left onto the High Lake Trail. If you're coming from the north, the trailhead is 57.1 miles from Four Corners. The trailhead is off the east side of the highway on a short, stubby entryway. The total hiking distance is 10.1 miles.

6. Specimen Creek

Description: Specimen Creek starts in a series of lakes along the crest of the Gallatin Range, dropping down to the Gallatin on a southwesterly course. The upper ends of both the East and North Forks are very steep and are difficult to fish. In fact, Shelf Lake and Crescent Lake, which head the North Fork, are now without fish, despite having been stocked in the past. The best waters are the lower 2 miles or so, from the road up to the confluence of the East and North Forks. The bed is mostly medium-size cobble. Find the best water where the bends result in deeper pools. The creek will be gorged with snowmelt until July. The best months to fish are July and August.

The fish: The fish are mostly smaller cutthroat and cutbows. There are some browns and rainbows in the lower part of the creek. A fish longer than 12 inches is exceptional, but there are decent numbers of fish, and they are fairly enthusiastic.

Flies and lures: If a Royal Coachman Trude will not get their interest, it is probably time to quit and go home. In August a hopper pattern is also a good bet. Specimen Creek is barely large enough to fish with lures. Try small Cyclones or Panther Martins.

Sites 5 & 6

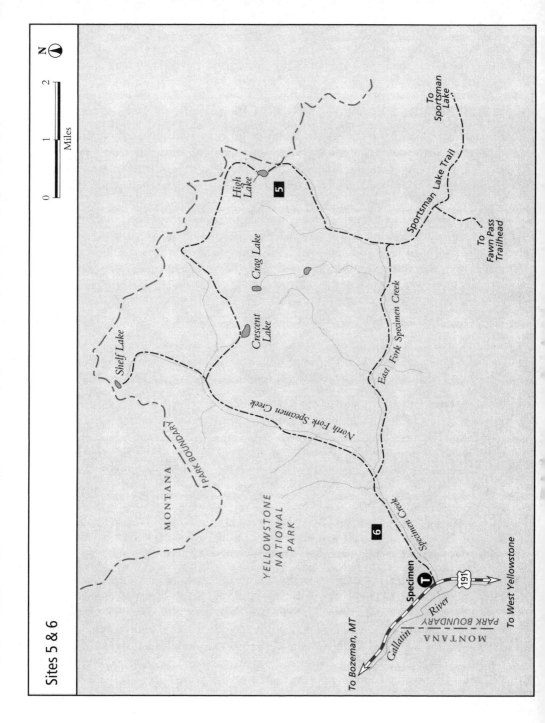

Access: Take US 191 north from West Yellowstone for 26.2 miles to the Specimen Creek Picnic Area and Trailhead. From Four Corners, take US 191 south for 57.1 miles. The best water is found in the sections where the trail and the stream parallel each other closely.

7. Gallatin River, Specimen Creek to Taylor Fork

Description: This stretch of the Gallatin River flows in a northwesterly direction through a narrow mountain valley. US 191 is on the north or east side of the river for all but the northernmost 1.5 miles. The river is a fast-moving mountain stream in an open meadow. The banks are often lined with willow patches. The meadow floor is typically about 3 feet above the bed of the river. The streambed is primarily composed of medium-size cobble. Gentle pitches alternate with short pools as the river snakes through the meadow. The best fishing opportunities are found at the heads of these pools and in the deeper water on the outside of bends. Unfishable due to spring snowmelt during most of May and June, the best months here are July and August. The lower 2.7 miles of the river are outside Yellowstone National Park, and the season in that section is open all year round, providing some fishing opportunities from March into May, before the runoff gets out of hand.

The fish: The most common fish in this stretch is the rainbow. Others found here include cutbow, cutthroat, brown trout, and a few whitefish. The average fish is in the 7- to 13-inch range, with a few exceeding 14 inches.

Flies and lures: Common flies that can be effective here include Stimulator patterns, Royal Wulffs, and Royal Coachman Trudes. Hoppers are in season from late July into early September. Stoneflies will hatch in early July, and there will be sporadic summer emergences of little golden stones. Appropriate nymphs include modest-size Bitch Creeks, Princes, and Hare's Ears. An ordinary little olive Woolly Worm is also a good bet. The spin angler should stick to the smaller sizes of Mepps, Panther Martins, Cyclones, or Kamloopers. That portion of the river outside the park is available to the bait angler, who should use stonefly nymphs, adult stoneflies, grasshoppers when in season, or worms. Be advised, though, that the river's velocity is not readily conducive to bait fishing.

Access: The southern end of this section, Specimen Creek, is 26.2 miles north of West Yellowstone via US 191. Take US 191 south from Four Corners 49.6 miles to Taylor Fork, the northern terminus. The distance from any of the frequent turnouts along the highway to the river throughout this 7.5 mile stretch is seldom more than 300 yards. The most important consideration to keep in mind along this stretch is the boundary of Yellowstone National Park. It intersects the west bank of the Gallatin 1 mile north of Specimen Creek and then follows the west bank of the river for the next 4 miles to the north. Therefore, this section of the river is subject to Yellowstone National Park regulations. A prominent sign marks the boundary as it

The Gallatin flows through a characteristic meadow on its way northwest.

Sites 7 & 8

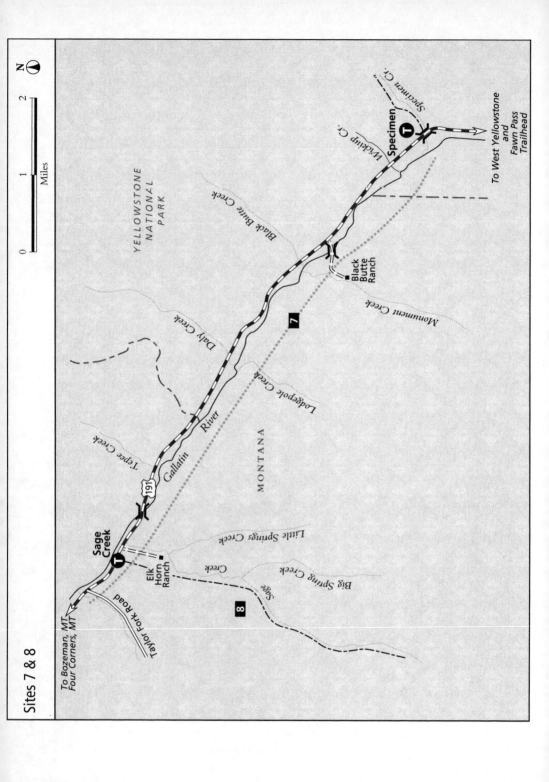

turns northeast and crosses both the river and the highway 31 miles north of West Yellowstone or 52.3 miles south of Four Corners. The remaining 2.7 miles between the boundary and Taylor Fork is on national forest land and is subject to the Montana regulations.

Tributaries: Tributaries of this section of the Gallatin include Wickiup Creek, Monument Creek, Black Butte Creek, Daly Creek, Lodgepole Creek, Tepee Creek, and Sage Creek (site 8). All are trivial and nearly fishless with the exception of Sage and Monument Creeks. Monument Creek is tiny, as are the few fish. Sage Creek is described below. This Tepee Creek should not be confused with the Tepee Creek that is a tributary of Grayling Creek in the Madison drainage. If someone reports fishing on Tepee Creek, it is almost certainly the latter.

8. Sage Creek

Description: Sage Creek is a small stream entering the Gallatin from the west. Private ranches occupy the lowest part of the creek. The most accessible section is in a tangle of willows surrounding a bed of small- to medium-size cobble. Look to the deeper water for fish. Above Big Spring Creek, entering from the south, both streams are too small to be useful. The water in Sage Creek will be very high with snowmelt from opening day on the third Saturday of May until about July 1. It will usually clear a little earlier than the main stem of the Gallatin. The fishing is finished here by the end of August. Particularly in dry years, the lower end of Sage Creek may go dry by midsummer.

The fish: Lower Sage Creek holds only a few small cutthroat and cutbows in the 5- to 8-inch range. Because of more uniform stream flows, the numbers are a little better between Big Spring Creek and Little Spring Creek.

Flies and lures: If you are using flies, try Joe's Hoppers, Renegades, or Princes fished wet. In a dry fly I would go with a #14 Royal Coachman Trude. Only the tiniest of lures would be useful here, as this stream is really too small for practical spin fishing. Live bait, particularly hoppers, is possible since Sage Creek is under Montana fishing regulations.

Access: Reach the Sage Creek Trailhead by driving south from Four Corners 49.8 miles on US 191. This point is 33.5 miles north of West Yellowstone, on the west side of US 191. The pack trail bypasses the first ranch before heading southwest up the creek.

The Madison River Drainage

Madison Junction to Hebgen Dam

The Madison is the middle of three rivers (along with the Gallatin and the Jefferson) that join to form the Missouri River. Lewis and Clark named the river after James Madison, President Thomas Jefferson's Secretary of State, who later became the fourth president of the United States. Madison Junction, where the river is formed by the confluence of the Gibbon and the Firehole, is also the purported birthplace of the national park concept. Yellowstone National Park was said to have been hatched as a consequence of campfire discussions of the Washburn party in 1870, as they completed the first serious exploration of the area since the heyday of the mountain-men fur trappers of the 1820s and 1830s. From its source, the river flows west into Montana and the lake impounded by Hebgen Dam. In addition to the Firehole and Gibbon Rivers, the Madison drainage picks up several other tributaries in this section.

Mileage points: There are a number of mileage control points for this chapter. The West Entrance road between Madison Junction and the West Entrance station defines that section of the Madison River inside Yellowstone National Park. Mileage on U.S. Highway 20 is measured between its junction with Idaho Highway 87 and the traffic light in West Yellowstone at its junction with U.S. Highway 191. Mileage on US 191 is measured between this same traffic light and Four Corners just west of Bozeman. Mileage on U.S. Highway 287 is clocked between its junction with US 191 north of West Yellowstone and Hebgen Dam.

9. Madison River, Madison Junction to Madison River Bridge

Description: The Madison is born a substantial river via the joining of the Firehole and Gibbon Rivers. Most rivers of the region carry water derived primarily from melting snow. The Firehole and Gibbon, and therefore the Madison, predominantly carry water discharged from Yellowstone's thermal vents. The bed varies considerably as meadows with sandy bottoms alternate with long riffle sections characterized by bottoms of cobble and gravel. There are frequent weed beds in the channels. The river is typically 75 or more feet wide with a fairly flat bottom. There are a few deeper pools and runs. The river's course for the first 13 miles is westerly before turning north a mile and a half before reaching the boundary of Yellowstone National Park. Fishing this lower section can be confusing because the river straddles the park boundary line for a mile before turning west again to enter Hebgen Lake.

Since Montana and Yellowstone Park have not coordinated their seasons it is imperative that you are sure of your location. The Montana season runs from the third Saturday of May through November 30. The Yellowstone season runs from the Saturday of the Memorial Day weekend through the first Sunday of November. That large portion of the Madison inside the park is restricted to fly fishing only. In both jurisdictions browns and rainbows are catch and release, except that outside the park junior anglers under fifteen may keep one rainbow.

The opener will usually find the Madison high and off color, with marginal fishing at best. Because the Gibbon and Firehole headwaters are at or near the altitude of the central plateau, these streams, and therefore the Madison, crest in late May or early June. The Madison will fish well in June, become substantially more difficult from July through September, and then improve again until the end of the season. During the early weeks of the season, the better water is found in the first 8 miles of river from Madison Junction down to the monster riffle that starts near the head of Riverside Drive. Fish along the margins of riffles, around rocks, and in the channels between weed beds. The fall season is dominated by the search for migrants in the Barns Pools and a couple of other runs.

The fish: The dominant fish in the Madison are brown trout, rainbow trout, and whitefish. You may find, although rarely, a brook trout or, even more rarely, a grayling. Besides the resident fish, there are seasonal runs of spawners coming up out of Hebgen Lake in the spring and fall. The resident fish are typically in the 8- to 14-inch range with an occasional fish reaching 18 inches. The migratory spawners are more often 16 to 20 inches with occasional lunkers over 24 inches. The less common whitefish are typically 12 to 16 inches long. Any brook trout is likely to be under 12 inches. A grayling is not likely at all, but would probably be under 10 inches in length.

Flies and lures: All but a few hundred yards of this section are under Yellowstone National Park's fly-fishing-only regulation. That portion of the river outside the park may be fished with lures and even bait. Effective fly patterns vary with the season. In the spring, basically the month of June, try Blue-Winged Olives, Pale Morning Duns, and Elk Hair Caddis fished dry. Hare's Ear, Prince, and stonefly nymph patterns are good wet fly choices. For the fall spawners running up out of Hebgen Lake, try big streamer and nymph patterns such as the Woolly Bugger and Brooks Stone nymph during late September and October. Good lures for that portion outside the park include the Mepps, Cyclone, and Rapala.

Access: Access to this 19-mile section is excellent, with the upper 13 miles seldom more than 200 yards from the road. There are numerous parking spots, virtually all of them available for the angler.

9a. Firehole/Gibbon Confluence

To reach the confluence of the Firehole and Gibbon Rivers at Madison Junction, take the West Entrance Road 14.1 miles east from the West Entrance to Madison Junction. Turn right (heading south) toward Old Faithful on the Grand Loop Road

A cow elk bows her head to the water along the Madison River.
MICHAEL SAMPLE PHOTO

and drive for 100 yards to the Madison Picnic Area. Park at the south end of the lot. Alternatively, take the West Entrance Road 14 miles from the West Entrance to the Madison Junction Campground and use the parking areas near loops A, B, or C. The entrance to the campground is 0.1 mile west of Madison Junction. In either case, the confluence of the Firehole and Gibbon Rivers is a couple of hundred yards south on a line between the parking area and National Park Mountain.

9b. Mount Haynes Overlook and Wheelchair Fishing Access

Take the West Entrance Road 3.5 miles west from Madison Junction or 10.6 miles east from the West Entrance to the Mount Haynes Overlook and Fishing Access (barrier free). There are few places where wheelchair access to streams is practical in Yellowstone National Park or anywhere else. A boardwalk here ends in a useful fishing platform overhanging 70 feet of riverbank. The parking area, only about 100 feet from the river, is equipped with appropriate curb ramps.

9c. Gneiss Creek Trailhead and 7 Mile Bridge

Often in the early part of the season the Madison will be high and unfordable, making it difficult to access the less heavily fished north side of the river. Drive west from Madison Junction for 6.5 miles to the 7 Mile Bridge. If coming from West Yellowstone, take the West Entrance Road 7.6 miles to the bridge. In either case, park on the north side of the road at the east end of the bridge at the Gneiss Creek Trailhead. This trail closely parallels the Madison for 0.8 mile downstream. Walk downstream on the trail to reach less fished water. The bridge doesn't help the angler fish the upstream side because that area is a closed waterfowl nesting zone in the spring.

9d. Riverside Drive

At one point, where the West Entrance Road pulls away from the river, a section of the old entrance road has been retained as Riverside Drive. To access Riverside Drive from the west, go 4.8 miles from the West Entrance. To access Riverside Drive from the east, drive 8.2 miles toward West Yellowstone from Madison Junction. The drive runs north of the West Entrance Road. Park in any unoccupied pullout in this 1.1-mile section to fish one of the biggest riffles in the park.

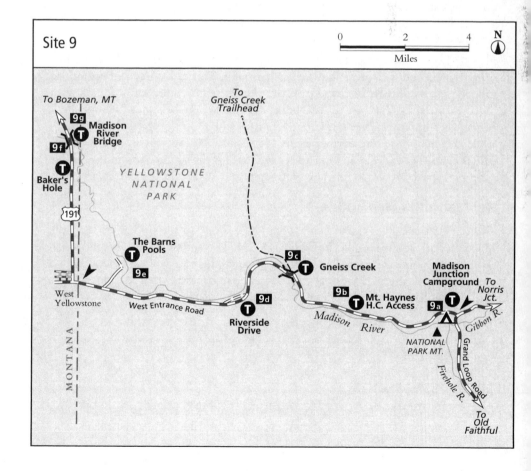

9e. The Barns Pools

The Barns Pools are possibly the most notorious section of the Madison within the borders of Yellowstone National Park. During the fall spawning run, these pools host a subculture of those anglers who pursue lunker browns. Although this is the closest river access to West Yellowstone, the river cannot be seen as you enter the park on the West Entrance Road because it has turned north away from the highway and is out of sight here. Go east from the West Entrance 0.6 mile and turn left onto the gravel Barns Pools Road, marked only by a stop sign. If coming from Madison Junction, drive 13.5 miles west and turn right. Take the gravel road 1.1 miles to the stream bank of the Upper Barns Pool, then turn left at the Y 1 mile from the West Entrance Road, and drive for another 0.5 mile to the Lower Barns Pool. The Barns Pools are the site of a series of riffle-runs stretching downstream from these two points. Start fishing at the head of the upper pool and work downstream. If you and your party have this stretch of river to yourselves, you can coordinate your efforts any way you'd like. If you are there with the fall crew, join the party and conform to the pool protocol, which has everyone taking a turn fishing through the stretch and staying in order.

9f. Baker's Hole Campground

From West Yellowstone, drive 2.9 miles north on US 191 to Baker's Hole Campground and turn right into the campground. This is a Forest Service campground right on the Madison where the river leaves Yellowstone National Park. Fish in either direction. It is wise to have both Montana and Yellowstone National Park fishing licenses, as the river straddles the border with more squiggles than a snake's track. If coming from the north, Baker's Hole is 81.4 miles south of Four Corners. This is a well-signed location with a left-turn lane for the southbound traffic. Hard-sided campers are required for those wishing to stay overnight at the campground.

9g. Madison River Bridge

Take US 191 3.8 miles north from West Yellowstone to the bridge crossing the Madison. Park at either end. The bridge is 80.5 miles south of Four Corners on US 191. At this point the river flows through something of a willow swamp with a muck and sand bottom that holds little attraction to fish other than migrants in season. Hebgen Lake begins just downstream; how far depends on the reservoir level.

Tributaries: Two substantial tributaries join the Madison in this section. The Gibbon and the Firehole Rivers, covered in later chapters, join at Madison Junction to form the Madison.

10. Hebgen Lake

Description: Hebgen Lake is impounded behind PPL's (formerly the Montana Power Company's) Hebgen Dam. A long, narrow lake with three main arms,

A fishing platform, on the right-hand bank, is helpful for anglers with disabilities.

Hebgen is oriented on an east-west axis. Each of the arms receives one or more tributary streams. The east end of the lake has fairly flat, willow-lined shores. As you approach the dam, the banks steepen, the lake deepens, and the valley narrows into a canyon. The west shore, west of the South Fork Arm, has heavy timber right to the water's edge. The upper eastern ends of the arms tend to be willow swamps. The north shore is more open with some willow, boulders, and even sage on the fairly steep bank. The flanks of most of the Madison Arm are dry lodgepole pine woods.

Like most Montana lakes, Hebgen is open to fishing year-round. It generally freezes over sometime in December with ice-off in early May. The first month after the spring thaw is usually productive with streamers fished close to the surface or by shallow trolling. Being sheltered from the prevailing winds, the South Fork Arm and the western shore of the lake provide excellent high-summer opportunities for the float-tube angler. Fish, particularly the browns, tend to move in close to shore and then up the tributaries again in the fall. Ice fishing is possible during mid- to late winter.

The fish: The major fish in Hebgen are rainbow and brown trout. There are some cutthroat, as well as a number of nongame fish. Brook trout and grayling are rare but

The docks at Rainbow Point, Hebgen Lake.

are occasionally found here. For the most part, the fish will run in the 14- to 20-inch range. On occasion, either species may produce a specimen up to 28 inches in length.

Flies and lures: During the early and late season, the fly fisher should concentrate on Woolly Buggers fished in the top 5 feet of water. Late July to early September mark "Gulper Season," when the best bet is a small Blue-Winged Olive dry fly. Cream Midges and gray mayfly patterns are also potential winners. Top lures here include the Flatfish in silver and frog finishes and gold Rapalas. In winter try marabou jigs and Swedish Pimples. The general Montana bait regulations apply.

Special equipment: Hebgen is a big lake, and using large motorized craft makes sense here. The float-tube user should keep a keen eye on the weather and not wander too far from shore. The motorboater should be alert to the possible presence of low-profile folks in tubes, leaving them plenty of room to fish safely. Check locally for ice conditions in winter before venturing onto the ice.

Access: With a paved highway within a few hundred feet along the north shore and gravel forest access roads to the arms and along the south and west shores of the lake, getting to Hebgen Lake is straightforward. The only complicating factor is private land. About two-thirds of the shore is public land. A simple guideline can help you determine where private land lies: If it looks like somebody's yard, it is.

10a. Lake Access

Drive north from West Yellowstone on US 191 for 8.6 miles and turn left onto US 287. If coming from the north, drive 75.7 miles south of Four Corners and turn right onto US 287. Driving 6.1 miles farther to the west on US 287 brings you to the first public lake access point on the north shore. Most of the shoreline from this point west to the dam is public. If eastbound on US 287 from the Ennis, Montana, area, the access is 7.6 miles east of Hebgen Dam. This first access can only be used to launch hand-carried craft, as there is no ramp. It is exposed to wind and wave action, so caution is in order. The highway is in close proximity to the lakeshore from here to the dam. There are numerous pullouts along this stretch that provide pedestrian access to the lakeshore.

10b. Kirkwood Ranch and Marina

Take US 287 for 11.3 miles to the west from its junction with US 191 to the Kirkwood Ranch complex. Alternatively, if coming from the west, Kirkwood is 2.4 miles east of Hebgen Dam. Kirkwood Ranch has a full-service marina that offers boat rentals and launching service for large craft. Also available are a commercial campground, motel, and small store.

10c. Hebgen Dam

Drive 13.7 miles west on US 287 to Hebgen Dam. At this point you are 49.3 miles south of Ennis. Public access to the dam itself is restricted by the operator for safety reasons. Pedestrian access to the lakeshore is permitted as posted.

Sites 10 & 11

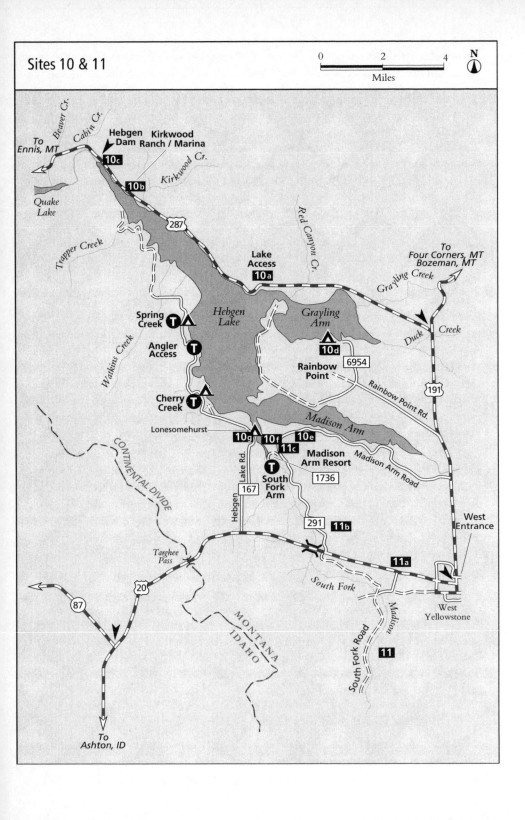

0   2   4
Miles

N

To Ennis, MT

Beaver Cr.

Cabin Cr.

Hebgen Dam

Kirkwood Ranch / Marina

Kirkwood Cr.

10c

10b

Quake Lake

Trapper Creek

287

Red Canyon Cr.

Lake Access
10a

To Four Corners, MT
Bozeman, MT

Grayling Creek

Spring Creek

Angler Access

Watkins Creek

Hebgen Lake

Grayling Arm

10d

6954

Rainbow Point

Duck Creek

191

Cherry Creek

Madison Arm

Lonesomehurst

10g   10f   10e

11c

Rainbow Point Rd.

CONTINENTAL DIVIDE

South Fork Arm

Madison Arm Resort

1736

Madison Arm Road

West Entrance

Hebgen Lake Rd.

167

291   11b

11a

Targhee Pass

South Fork

West Yellowstone

20

MONTANA
IDAHO

South Fork Road

Madison

11

87

To Ashton, ID

10d. Rainbow Point

Rainbow Point is the USDA Forest Service campground and boat launch area on the Grayling Arm. Take US 191 north 5 miles from West Yellowstone or 79.3 miles south from Four Corners and turn west onto the Rainbow Point Road. Caution! This road is surfaced with a layer of deep, loose, small gravel. It's almost like hydroplaning on an inch-deep puddle and dusty beyond belief. Turn right onto Forest Road 6954 at the four-way junction 3.3 miles west of US 191. Take the left leg of the Y 5.1 miles west of US 191 to enter the campground or the right leg to access the public boat ramp. The ramp is provided with a dock but no other services, and the turnaround area is somewhat cramped for really large boat trailers. Because bears frequent the area, the Forest Service requires overnighters to sleep in hard-sided campers.

The center road at the four-way junction is a private access road. Turn left on Forest Road 610 and drive 1.3 miles to reach the Madison Arm and access the main body of the lakeshore. This road runs along the shore for 5.4 miles, onto the Horse Butte Peninsula. The bad news is that this is the windward shore, often pounded by surf.

10e. Madison Arm Loop

Take the Madison Arm Road to access the south shore of the Madison Arm, Madison Arm Resort and Marina, and the east shore of the South Fork Arm and South Fork of the Madison River. One end of the Madison Arm Road meets US 191 at a point 3.5 miles north of West Yellowstone or 80.8 miles south of Four Corners. The other end meets US 20 at a point 4.5 miles west of West Yellowstone—9.2 miles east of the ID 87 junction. The road is gravel with many curves. There are a couple of obvious points of pedestrian access to the shore of the Madison Arm between US 191 and the Madison Arm Resort. Drive 5.7 miles west from the junction with US 191 to reach the commercial facilities of the Madison Arm Resort. The resort has a campground, cabins, small store, and launch facilities for trailered boats. The resort is 6.3 miles from US 20 if coming from the west. The Madison Arm Road is listed as Forest Road 291 on some maps.

10f. Forest Road 1736, South Fork Arm

Take US 20 west 4.5 miles from West Yellowstone and turn north onto the Madison Arm Road. Drive 4 more miles north and turn left onto FR 1736. This is a dirt two-tracker that lurches and twists over to the confluence of the South Fork of the Madison with the South Fork Arm. Fish up the South Fork or launch a tube to fish the upper pool of the South Fork Arm.

10g. Forest Road 167, Hebgen Lake Road

Starting in West Yellowstone, drive west 7.4 miles on US 20 and turn north (right) onto FR 167, the Hebgen Lake Road. This road provides the only vehicle access to the west shore of Hebgen Lake and its South Fork Arm. To reach FR 167 from the

The boat ramp at Lonesomehurst, at the mouth of the Madison Arm of Hebgen Lake.

west, drive 6.3 miles over Targhee Pass on US 20 from its junction with ID 87. There are a number of options on FR 167:

1) Go 3.7 miles north on FR 167 and turn right into the Lonesomehurst Boat Launch area. Lonesomehurst is a Forest Service area with some campsites, a boat ramp, and dock, but no other facilities.

2) Find the Cherry Creek Campground at the end of a 0.9-mile access road which leaves FR 167 to the right 5.1 miles north of the US 20 junction. The Cherry Creek road is easy to miss, as it is not well signed. A small boat can be hand-launched here, but there is no boat ramp.

3) A parking area for anglers is on the lake side of the road 8.2 miles from the US 20 junction. This access overlooks a small bay that may be of particular interest to float-tube anglers.

4) The Spring Creek Campground access is 9.2 miles from US 20. A drive of 0.5 mile brings you to the lakeshore campsites. Small craft can be hand-launched at this point.

Tributaries: Besides the Madison itself, Hebgen Lake receives several other tributaries. Of these, Grayling Creek (site 13), Duck Creek (site 12), and the South Fork of the Madison (site 11) are the most significant.

The Madison River flows through much of the part of Yellowstone National Park that was burned by forest fires in 1988.

11. South Fork of the Madison *(see map on page 38)*

Description: The South Fork rises in a series of springs on the west flank of the plateau that makes up the main mass of Yellowstone National Park. The South Fork generally flows north until it loses itself in the South Fork Arm of Hebgen Lake. The upper 10 miles or so are characterized by a medium-size cobble streambed and a series of riffles and pools. The occasional deadfall dam also makes pools. These pools and the holes under cut banks are the best fishing waters. The banks are mostly willow-lined. The bed becomes finer-grained as you approach the lake, and the timber common in the upper section gives way entirely to willow. Open June 15 through November 30, the South Fork generally is fishable throughout its season. Migrating spawners may be in the lower end in the fall. Fishing in the upper section is best in midsummer.

The fish: The resident fish in the South Fork are mostly browns in the lower end and brook trout in the upper reaches, with a mix in the middle. Spawning rainbows and browns will come into the lower end of the stream during spring and fall. The resident fish are typically under 10 inches in length. Spawners may run more than 20 inches.

Flies and lures: The South Fork will fish best with dry flies. Pale Morning Duns or Blue-Winged Olives will come closest to matching hatches in the morning and evening. Hoppers are probably the best bet in high summer. In the smaller upper water, any basic attractor such as a Royal Coachman Trude or Royal Wulff should do just fine. Spin anglers should try small spoons or spinners. The Panther Martin, Mepps, Cyclone, and Triple Teazer come to mind as good bets.

Access: Access to the South Fork of the Madison is remarkable. With the exception of about 3 miles starting at the US 20 bridge and extending upstream through a ranch residential area to the South Fork Road bridge, the stream is within a few hundred yards of a road and mostly flanked by public land.

11a. South Fork Road

Access the upper section of the South Fork by driving west from West Yellowstone on US 20 for 2.1 miles and turning left onto the South Fork Road. If coming from the Idaho side, drive 11.6 miles east from the ID 87 junction and turn right. Once on the South Fork Road, bear right at the T junction 0.7 mile from the start. Ignore the private drive to the left and the right fork of the next Y to go straight ahead across the bridge 1.1 miles from the highway. Turn left at the next junction, 1.3 miles from the highway, beginning your ascent toward the South Fork of the Madison. The road comes again into close proximity with the stream about half a mile upriver and thereafter is seldom as much as 100 yards away for more than 3 miles. The road deteriorates as you go south, though it remains drivable. Park in any unoccupied spot off the road and fish in either direction.

The banks of the South Fork of the Madison River are brushy in places.

11b. Madison Arm Road

Drive west 4.5 miles on US 20 from West Yellowstone and turn north (right) onto the Madison Arm Road. It's a left turn off US 20 9.2 miles east of the ID 87 junction if you are coming from the Idaho side. After the first mile the Madison Arm Road periodically approaches the South Fork of the Madison, and each of these points provides access to the stream, which is on your left, for approximately the next 2 miles. Fish either upriver or down from any of these access points.

11c. Forest Road 1736

Drive west from West Yellowstone 4.5 miles on US 20 and turn right onto the Madison Arm Road. From the Idaho side, take US 20 east 9.2 miles from the ID 87 junction and turn left onto the Madison Arm Road. Take the Madison Arm Road 4.3 miles north to FR 1736, a dirt two-track on your left. This road corkscrews through the scrub vegetation to the confluence of the South Fork with the South Fork Arm. Fish upstream on the South Fork.

12. Duck Creek

Description: The streams in the Duck Creek drainage often seem confused. They know where they came from, off the Gallatin Range. They know where they are going, into the Grayling Arm of Hebgen Lake. In between, both they and the map makers have sometimes seemed to lose their way. All of the water flowing under the highway bridge bearing the sign "Cougar Creek" is actually Maple Creek. Cougar Creek proper has a dry channel connecting it to Maple Creek, but, in fact, the stream sinks into the ground before joining Maple Creek. It is possible that the connection was severed by the 1959 earthquake. The fishable sections feature a gentle gradient. The bottom is often mud or sand with ponding and weedbeds. The banks are generally willow-lined in the lower reaches, with a mix of grass and willow in the upper sections. With one exception, Richards Pond, the tributary waters in this complex are not very useful to the angler as they harbor few fish.

With the exception of streamside travel along Duck and Richards creeks to Richards Pond, Yellowstone National Park's Bear Management Plan prohibits access to most of this area. This is another boundary-area situation with differing seasons for Montana and Yellowstone Park. Because the streams originate on the southern flank of the Gallatin Range at relatively low altitude, they are generally fishable whenever they are open.

The fish: Brown and brook trout dominate the population in these waters, though reports suggest that the proportion of rainbows derived from Hebgen Lake is increasing. There is a remnant westslope cutthroat population in Cougar Creek above the Gneiss Creek Trail. Grayling were planted in this section of Cougar Creek in 1993 and again in 1994 as part of the grayling restoration effort. The stream is effectively closed to angling by the Bear Management Plan, and it is unclear how the fishery has fared. At one point Duck Creek and Richards Pond had an awesome reputation as a source of large brown and brook trout. Reports suggest that while a larger fish is still possible, it is more likely that any caught will be under 10 inches in length.

Flies and lures: This is classic stillwater fishing. The fly fisher should look to scuds, damselfly nymph patterns, and midges, unless a specific hatch has fish moving to the surface. Common hatches here are small mayflies and caddis. On the other end of the scale, a Woolly Bugger, particularly in the fall and in the evening, may entice larger fish. The spin angler should try Panther Martins or Triple Teazers. A small Rapala could be just the ticket during October.

Access: Access to Duck Creek outside of Yellowstone National Park is limited by private land that is divided into residential lots.

12a. Gneiss Creek Trail

Reach the north end of the Gneiss Creek Trail by driving north 9.8 miles from West Yellowstone on US 191, turning right into the trailhead parking area. The trailhead is on the left 74.5 miles south of Four Corners on US 191. Drive east from the West

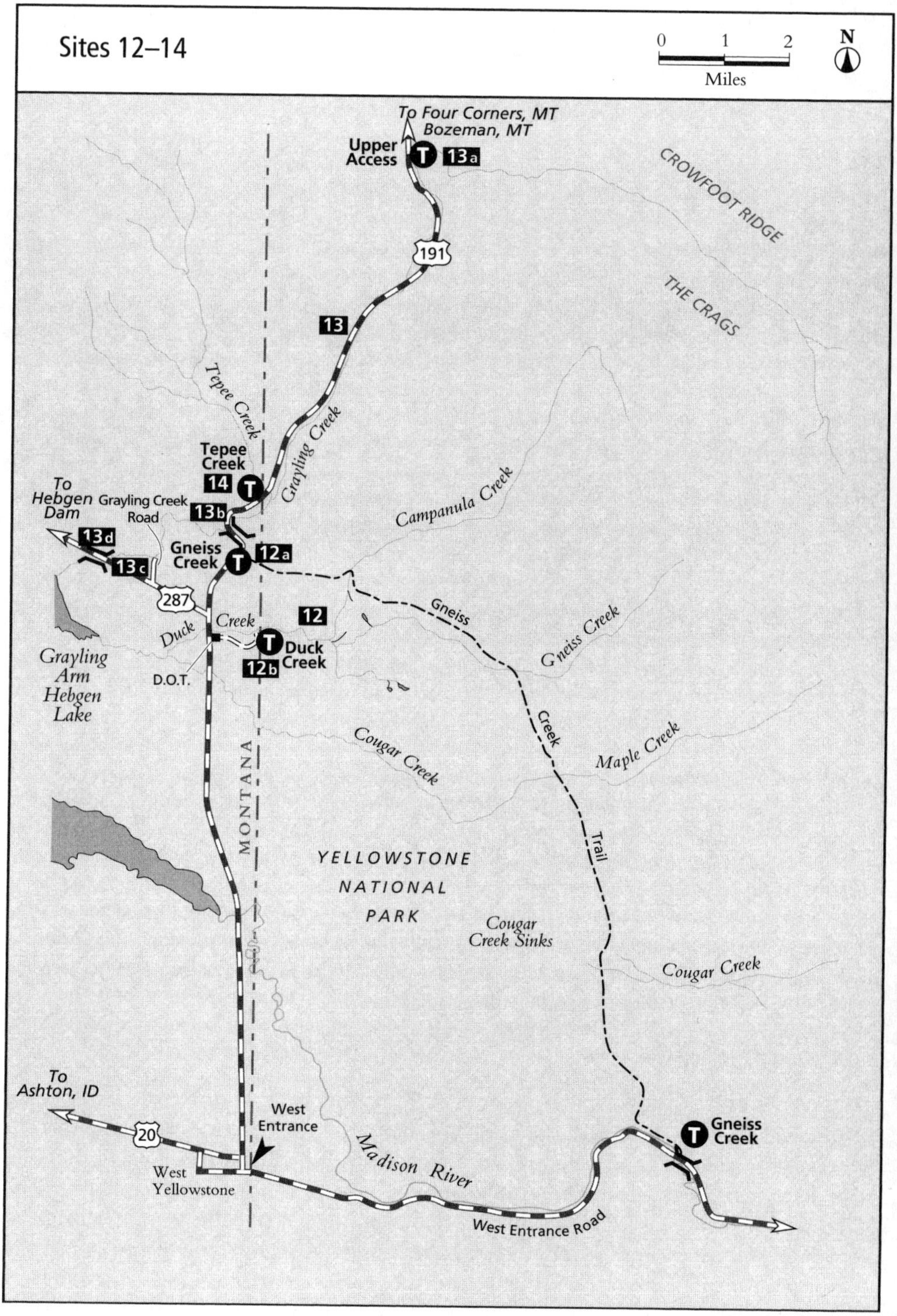

Sites 12–14

0   1   2
Miles

N

To Four Corners, MT
Bozeman, MT

Upper
Access   **T** **13a**

CROWFOOT RIDGE

THE CRAGS

191

13

Tepee Creek

Grayling Creek

Tepee
Creek
14 **T**

Campanula Creek

To
Hebgen   Grayling Creek
Dam   Road
13d   **13b**
13c   Gneiss
Creek   **T** **12a**

Gneiss

Gneiss Creek

287

Duck Creek   **12**

D.O.T.   **T** Duck
12b Creek

Creek

Maple Creek

*Grayling
Arm
Hebgen
Lake*

Cougar Creek

Trail

MONTANA

Cougar Creek Sinks

YELLOWSTONE

NATIONAL

PARK

Cougar Creek

Cougar Creek

To
Ashton, ID

West
Entrance   Gneiss
T Creek

20

Madison River

West
Yellowstone

West Entrance Road

The banks of Duck Creek are one part of the drainage not closed to travel under Yellowstone's Bear Management Plan.

Entrance 6.5 miles to the 7 Mile Bridge and park at the trailhead on the left, just beyond the bridge, to access the east end of the trail. The trailhead is on the right 7.6 miles west of Madison Junction on the West Entrance Road. The Gneiss Creek Trail arcs around the foot of the Gallatin Range from the 7 Mile Bridge east of West Yellowstone on the Madison to US 191 north of West Yellowstone. In the process it cuts the upper reaches of most of the Duck Creek tributaries. The Bear Management Plan mandates that the streams can only be fished in those areas where the trail crosses or closely parallels the creeks.

12b. Duck Creek

Take US 191 north 8.3 miles from West Yellowstone and turn right into the Montana Department of Transportation Section House. This is a private road that serves a rural housing area along Duck Creek. There are many driveways and some forks in what eventually becomes an unimproved two-track. At each of these forks, keep to the right. Take the right-hand fork 0.3 mile in and take the next right-hand fork 0.6 mile in on this road. The road comes up to the Yellowstone National Park boundary 0.8 mile from US 191 and then takes an abrupt left turn for the remaining 0.2 mile before ending in a turning circle overlooking Duck Creek. The main track up Duck Creek goes along the edge of the higher, drier ground. The Bear

Management Plan allows travel only along the stream corridor. It is just more than 1 mile east, upstream, to the confluence of Campanula, Gneiss, and Richards Creeks, which form Duck Creek. Any of this is fishable if you are willing to fight the willow swamp and bog bottom. When facing upstream, Richards Creek is the extreme right-hand tributary. Continue up Richards Creek about an additional mile and a half to its headwaters in Richards Pond.

Tributaries: The most significant tributary to Duck Creek is Maple Creek, discussed above. Campanula and Gneiss Creeks, Duck Creek tributaries, and Cougar Creek are all small, as are the fish found in them. Richards Creek connects Richards Pond to Duck Creek; it, too, is small. Maple Creek, as already described, is called Cougar Creek where it crosses US 191.

13. Grayling Creek (see map on page 45)

Description: Grayling Creek is a fairly steep, medium-size stream. It rises on the crest of the Gallatin Range and flows west nearly to the border of Yellowstone National Park before turning abruptly southward on its way to Hebgen Lake. The bed is mostly medium- to large-size cobble with some deadfall dams in evidence. Short meadows lined with willow are separated by steeper, more heavily timbered sections until the stream emerges from its own valley into the Madison basin. The last couple of miles of stream are flatter, with a fine-grained bottom in what amounts to a willow swamp. Much of the most fishable part of this stretch is on a private ranch. Grayling Creek is high and unfishable during most of May and well into June, July in some years. The best time to fish the stream is from late June or early July through the middle of August. The most productive spots are the structural pockets formed by rocks and deadfall, or the deeper slots next to the occasional cut bank. The lower 3 miles or so of the creek is outside Yellowstone National Park. On that water, Montana regulations and licenses apply. The park boundary crosses the creek about 10.8 miles north of West Yellowstone.

The fish: The bulk of the fish in Grayling Creek are cutbows. Particularly in the lower reaches there may be some browns, and in the upper reaches there are substantial numbers of westslope cutthroat. There are some Yellowstone-strain cutthroat, but it has been a long while since anyone has caught a grayling. The fish run in the 8- to 12-inch range, with an outside chance a larger fish will be caught in the lower half of the creek. The average size decreases the farther one goes up the creek away from US 191.

Flies and lures: Good flies for Grayling Creek include the Royal Coachman Trude, Royal Wulff, and bead-head Prince. Grasshopper imitations, when in season, are another good bet. Because the stream is small and steep, the best lures will be smaller sizes of Mepps, Panther Martin, or Cyclone. A Triple Teazer can also be a good choice. Bait is allowed in that short section of the creek outside Yellowstone National Park.

Access: The best sections of Grayling Creek are easily reached from US 191, which closely parallels the stream for several miles. Three bridges on US 191 and one on US 287 cross Grayling Creek. The upper section of Grayling Creek is off the trail network, making it more difficult to reach.

13a. Upper Access

To reach the upper section of Grayling Creek, drive 17.7 miles north on US 191 from West Yellowstone or 66.6 miles south from Four Corners on US 191. Park in the unmarked pullout on the east (creek) side of the road. Grayling Creek rushes down to the road from the east at the bottom of a steep-walled canyon about 50 feet deep. Bushwhack up the creek. The lower 3 or 4 miles provide relatively less finicky fish of somewhat larger sizes. In the next 3 to 4 miles, the fish become progressively fewer and smaller, eventually disappearing altogether.

13b. Grayling Creek Bridge (US 191)

After running south along US 191 for about 7 miles and crossing it twice, Grayling Creek cuts west into a little canyon while the road zigs east over the creek and up a hill. Drive north on US 191 10.3 miles from West Yellowstone or south 74 miles from Four Corners and park at the bridge. Fish downstream into the canyon, a section that is somewhat out of the way, if no one has beaten you to it.

13c. Grayling Creek Road

From West Yellowstone take US 191 north 8.6 miles to its junction with US 287 and turn west on US 287. This junction is 75.7 miles south of Four Corners. Drive 1.1 miles on US 287 and turn right (north) onto the Grayling Creek Road. Grayling Creek Road is 12.6 miles east of Hebgen Dam, and the turn is to the left. Grayling Creek Road accesses private property that controls lower Grayling Creek. A drive of 0.5 mile brings you to the bridge that marks the end of the public road and the beginning of the no-trespassing signs. While it is legal to fish up the creek, the gate hung with a rubber chicken and a BAD JUJU sign suggests fishing downstream from the US 191 bridge instead.

13d. Grayling Creek Bridge (US 287)

Take US 191 north to the US 287 junction and turn west onto US 287. Drive 2.3 miles west to the bridge over Grayling Creek and park at the bridge. Grayling Creek Bridge is 11.4 miles east of Hebgen Dam. Fish downstream toward Hebgen Lake. Fishing here tends to be poor except in the latter part of September or October when there is some possibility of encountering migrant fish from the lake. Take care along this section of the creek. There is a willow swamp with quicksand to ensnare your back casts and trap your feet.

Tributaries: Tepee Creek (site 14) is the only significant tributary to Grayling Creek.

Most good fishing spots along Grayling Creek can be reached from U.S. Highway 191.

14. Tepee Creek (see map on page 45)

Description: Tepee Creek rises on the southeast flank of the Madison Range and flows generally southeasterly to its junction with Grayling Creek. For practical purposes, only the lower 2 miles of stream are of much use to anglers. The bed is mostly medium to large cobble with some deadfall thrown in. The stream is typically about 10 feet wide. The banks are a mix of timber, willow, and grassy areas. The best places to look for fish are the structural pockets formed by larger rocks and deadfall.

Most of Tepee Creek falls under the general Montana regulations; hence it opens the third Saturday of May and closes November 30. It is unlikely to be fishable prior to mid-June due to the spring runoff. Fishing improves from mid-June to mid-July but tapers off almost to nothing by the end of August or early September. The lower 600 yards of the creek are inside Yellowstone National Park, and this section falls under the park's regulations.

The fish: Tepee Creek's fish are the same cutbow and cutthroat mix found in Grayling Creek. Few fish reach, much less exceed, 10 inches.

Flies and lures: An attractor pattern, say a Royal Wulff or Royal Coachman Trude, is likely to be the best choice. Early-season anglers fishing before the runoff has ended should try Prince or rubber-legged Hare's Ear nymphs. In summer a grasshopper pattern is an obvious and productive alternative. Tepee Creek is barely big enough to make spinning practical. Try the smallest sizes of Mepps or Cyclone spoons. Most of the creek is outside Yellowstone National Park so bait, such as worms, technically is legal. Unfortunately, there is no practical legal route by which to get bait to the stream, as the only access that makes sense is inside the park.

Access: To reach Tepee Creek drive 11.3 miles north on US 191 from West Yellowstone. A small unmarked pullout on the left (west) side of the road sits adjacent to the culvert carrying Tepee Creek under the highway. If coming from the north on US 191, this pullout is on the right 73 miles south of Four Corners. About 200 yards of lower Tepee Creek is between US 191 and Grayling Creek. No more than 400 yards upstream is the west boundary of Yellowstone National Park. Only the lower 2 miles of creek amount to much.

The Gibbon River Drainage

The Gibbon River rises on the south flank of the Washburn Range, flowing out of Grebe Lake. The Hayden survey of 1872 named the river for General John Gibbon, who was then touring in the park. After flowing west to Wolf Lake, the river splashes over Virginia Cascade and oozes into Norris Geyser Basin. Hooking around Norris Geyser Basin proper, the river takes a southerly course through Elk Park, Gibbon Meadows, and the Gibbon Canyon before plummeting 88 feet over Gibbon Falls. Its final act bends back to a westerly course to join with the Firehole River, forming the Madison River, at Madison Junction. The stream passes near Ice Lake, which was stocked repeatedly up until about 1960. The lake is subject to freeze-out and has no substantial inlet. The outlet is not large enough to permit either consistent spawning or migration. While the last surveys turned up no fish, a couple of anglers reported catches of rainbows in 2005.

Mileage points: There are several mileage control points for the Gibbon. Norris Junction and Canyon are at either end of the Norris-Canyon Road. Mammoth, Norris Junction, and Madison Junction are on the Grand Loop Road.

15. Grebe Lake

Description: Grebe Lake is about three quarters of a mile across and nearly round. The north shore was timbered before the 1988 fires. Anglers can wade along much of the north and east shorelines, but the marshy bank and soft bottom around the south shore make wading difficult there. The outlet of the Gibbon River is at the west end of the lake. There are several backcountry campsites available, making Grebe Lake a popular overnight destination as well as a practical day hike.

The lake is normally very high when the season opens at the end of May. Some years, though the ice may be off the lake, the trail can still have up to 18 inches of snow plugging up your access. By mid-June the water level of the lake will be down some and the trail passable. The fish will be hungry and particularly concentrated near the outlet. Results are usually excellent for about a month, then taper off through the summer.

The fish: Grebe Lake was without fish when Yellowstone National Park was established in 1872. Rainbow and grayling were introduced during the 1890s and were stocked periodically until the 1950s. The rainbows run 8 to 18 inches. The grayling are likely to be under 14 inches, but this remains the most reliable spot in the Yellowstone area to catch this dramatically colored western native.

Flies and lures: Unless there is an obvious hatch, the best choices in flies are likely to be Prince nymphs, A. P. Blacks, or Woolly Buggers, the latter fished very slowly

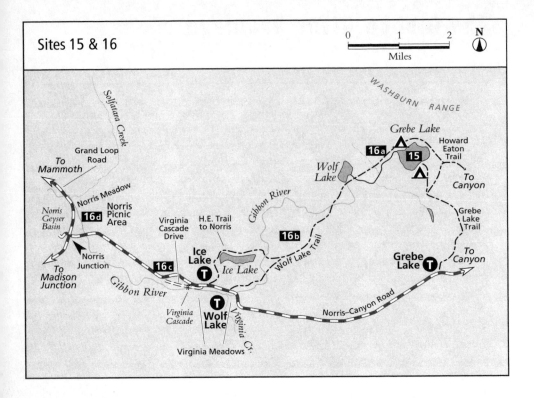

(Map labels:)
Solfatara Creek
WASHBURN RANGE
Grand Loop Road
To Mammoth
Norris Meadow
Grebe Lake
16a
15
Howard Eaton Trail
Wolf Lake
To Canyon
Norris Geyser Basin
16d
Norris Picnic Area
Gibbon River
Grebe Lake Trail
Virginia Cascade Drive
H.E. Trail to Norris
16b
To Madison Junction
Norris Junction
16c
Ice Lake
T
Ice Lake
Wolf Lake Trail
Grebe Lake
T
To Canyon
Gibbon River
Virginia Cascade
Wolf Lake
T
Virginia Cr.
Norris–Canyon Road
Virginia Meadows

as a leech. Dry fly patterns will run to Adams and Black Gnats. The spin fisher should try Mepps and black Rooster Tails first.

Special equipment: A float tube can be very useful on Grebe Lake. It is a 3-mile hike, which may sound difficult with a float tube. The good news is that the trail is quite level, most of it being an old fire road, making walking easy.

Access: Take the Norris-Canyon Road 8.4 miles east from Norris Junction or 3.6 miles west from Canyon Junction to the Grebe Lake Trailhead. The trail is a broad cut through mostly burned timber damaged in the 1988 fires. The trail forks about 2.5 miles in, the left branch going directly to Grebe Lake and the right branch intersecting the Howard Eaton Trail east of the lake. The right fork is actually the best choice if you are heading toward the north shore or outlet area of the lake; simply head west on Howard Eaton Trail at the intersection. There are several backcountry campsites on the lake. The Howard Eaton Trail connects to Cascade Lake and Canyon to the east and to Wolf Lake and the Ice Lake Trailhead to the west.

16. Upper Gibbon River, Grebe Lake to Norris Meadow

Description: The Gibbon River rises as a series of springs around and in Grebe Lake at the southern base of the Washburn Range in central Yellowstone National Park. Typically about 15 feet wide, the bed is mostly medium-size cobble between Grebe and Wolf Lakes. Structural pockets around the larger rocks and the occasional pool, sometimes formed by deadfall, present the best fishing opportunities. The area was subject to intense burning during the 1988 fires. The bank is lined with many snags for the first quarter mile below Grebe Lake; thereafter, the stream winds through an open meadow area with a relatively low gradient and finer-grained bottom.

The stream picks up speed as the gradient steepens below Wolf Lake. Pocket water predominates, with some cascades, until the river hits Virginia Meadows. The gradient picks up again as the river pitches over Virginia Cascade, and pocket water predominates for about the next mile. The final 3 miles of this segment are again flatter in the Norris Junction Meadow down to the bridge at the entrance to the Norris Campground.

The Gibbon is generally high and off-color when the season opens at the end of May. The water drops into fishable condition by about June 10 most years. This section of the river stays cool during the summer and provides good fishing for most of the season. After Labor Day the fish are less active. Fishing is likely to be quite poor in the meadow section near the Norris Campground unless there is a substantial hatch triggering rising fish.

The fish: The upper part of this stretch of the Gibbon is populated by rainbows along with a few grayling out of Grebe or Wolf Lakes. A cascade section near the

Grebe Lake, the headwaters of the Gibbon River.
NATIONAL PARK SERVICE PHOTO

east end of Ice Lake marks the upper limit for brook trout. From there down to Norris Junction, the population is primarily brookies, though at the lower end browns become part of the catch. The rainbows will run mostly in the 8- to 12-inch range, topping out at about 16 inches. Brookies range between 5 and 11 inches, most of them about 8 inches. The grayling are likely to be under 10 inches, but there are a few, particularly early in the year, that run upwards of 14 inches.

Flies and lures: Attractor dry fly patterns such as a Royal Coachman Trude or Royal Wulff are excellent first choices for the fly fisher. Good nymph patterns would include the Prince and rubber-legged Hare's Ear. Good spinning lures include smaller Panther Martins, Mepps, and Cyclone spoons.

Access: About half of this section is fairly easily reached from the roads at Norris Junction or off the Norris-Canyon Road. Access above Virginia Meadows requires taking one of the trails or bushwhacking along the creek.

16a. Grebe Lake to Wolf Lake

Drive east from Norris Junction 8.4 miles or west from Canyon 3.6 miles to the Grebe Lake Trailhead on the Norris-Canyon Road. Follow the Grebe Lake Trail to its junction with the Howard Eaton Trail and then turn west (to the left) on the latter. The trail skirts the north shore of Grebe Lake for just over a mile and then follows the north bank of the Gibbon to Wolf Lake. Start anywhere, and fish in whichever direction you prefer.

16b. Wolf Lake to Virginia Meadows

There are three access points to this segment that eventually merge:
1) Driving west 8.1 miles from Canyon or east 3.9 miles from Norris Junction on the Norris-Canyon Road brings you to the head of Virginia Meadows. There is a large pullout on the south side of the road 100 yards west of the culvert that carries the Gibbon under the highway. Park, cross the road, and bushwhack up along the stream. A cascade section about 1 mile upriver divides the brookie water from the rainbow water. Continuing on upriver is hard work. There is no regular trail, and the fires have left a lot of deadfall in the canyon. That means that the rainbows dominating this section of river are less wary of anglers than those fish downriver of this point.
2) The pullout described above is also the parking place for the Wolf Lake Trailhead. There is no sign for the trail. The trail parallels the stream for several hundred yards, crosses the river, and heads east until it intersects the Howard Eaton Trail a couple of hundred yards after the latter crosses the Gibbon, 1 mile from the trailhead. It is 3 miles from here to Wolf Lake.
3) The Ice Lake Trailhead is signed. Locate the trailhead by driving 8.5 miles west from Canyon on the Norris-Canyon Road. The trailhead is on the

A minor ledge creates a small pool on the Gibbon.

north side of the highway. It is 3.5 miles east of Norris Junction. Take the trail 0.5 mile to its junction with the Howard Eaton Trail at the nearly fishless Ice Lake and turn right to the east. The trail joins up with the Wolf Lake Trail after crossing the Gibbon River 1 mile from its start, making this route to Wolf Lake 4 miles long.

16c. Virginia Cascade Drive

Take the Norris-Canyon Road east 1.7 miles from Norris Junction to the western end of the Virginia Cascade Drive. This is 10.3 miles west of Canyon. Virginia Cascade Drive is a one-way segment of the old road, which provided close access to the Gibbon River below Virginia Cascade and the lower end of Virginia Meadows. This road segment reopened in 2001 after being closed for several years because of a landslide. The exit end is 3.7 miles east of Norris or 8.3 miles west of Canyon. At the west end the road is about 0.5 mile north of the river. A pullout about halfway through overlooks the lower end of the canyon headed by Virginia Cascade.

16d. Norris Meadow

There are several access options for the Norris Meadow:
1) It's an obvious and short walk to the stream from the Norris Campground. Access to the Norris Campground is 0.8 mile north of Norris Junction on the Grand Loop Road or 20.8 miles south of Mammoth.
2) A large pullout on the east side of the Grand Loop Road (beside the meadow), just south of the Norris Campground, is 0.7 mile north of Norris Junction or 20.9 miles south of Mammoth.
3) Taking the Norris-Canyon Road 0.2 mile east from Norris Junction or 11.8 miles west of Canyon brings you to the bridge across the Gibbon and a pullout.
4) Take the Norris-Canyon Road 0.3 mile east from Norris Junction and turn left into the Norris Picnic Area. If heading out from Canyon, drive 11.7 miles to the west; the picnic area access will be on the right.

Tributaries: There are four principle tributaries to the Gibbon River in this section. None are of significance or use to anglers. The maps don't even show names for the upper three, though the stream joining from the south in Virginia Meadows appears to be named Virginia Creek. Solfatara Creek is the largest of the lot and enters the Gibbon from the north at the Norris Campground. Its upper reaches are heavily impacted by thermal activity, and it has never been a stream that held fish in any numbers.

17. Lower Gibbon River, Norris Geyser Basin to Madison Junction

Description: In the 15 miles from Norris Junction to its confluence with the Firehole River, the Gibbon exhibits three different personalities.

From the bridge carrying the Grand Loop Road across the river at the Norris Campground, the river hooks around the north and west sides of Norris Geyser Basin. In this section the river increases in width from 15 to 25 feet to a typical 25 to 40 feet. The bottom alternates between sandy-bottomed pools and short freestone

Site 17

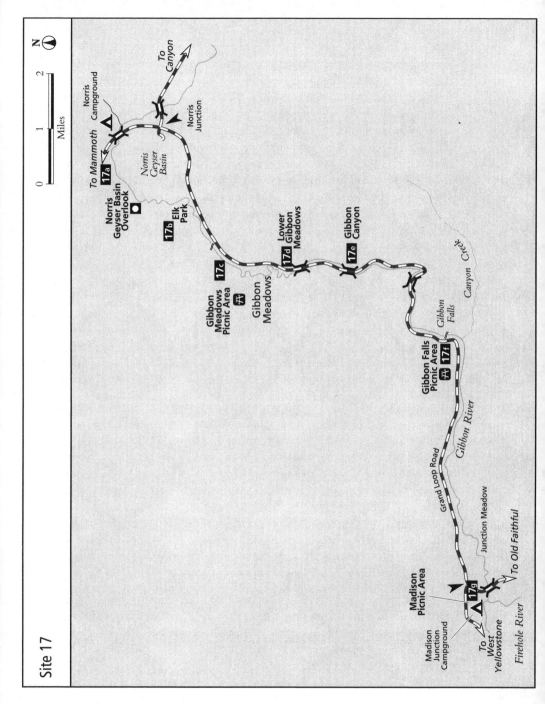

stretches punctuated with a lot of burned deadfall. The best places to find fish are in the heads and tails of the pools and around the structure in the freestone stretches.

In its second guise the Gibbon River is a meandering meadow stream with a sandy to small-gravel bottom and open grassy banks. These banks are often under-cut by the river. The shallow sandbars at the heads and tails of pools and the deep pools on the outside of the bends establish some structure to the river. The only other structural features of note are the occasional timber obstruction and the rather more frequent submerged clods of broken-off and sunken sod. Without a substan-tial hatch to make fish active, these meadows are very difficult to fish. There are three meadows: Elk Park, Gibbon Meadows, and what I call Junction Meadow, just upstream from where the Gibbon merges with the Firehole.

The third aspect of the Gibbon's split personality is a brawling, freestone-and-bedrock, pocket-water river. The mile-long Gibbon Cascades separates Elk Park from Gibbon Meadows. Over 7 miles of the Gibbon Canyon separates Gibbon Meadows from Junction Meadow. As with most pocket water, the shoreline struc-ture is the best bet for fishing during the early season. With dropping water levels the fish move into the deeper, mid-channel pockets.

On opening day the Gibbon usually is too high and off-color to fish. It generally will be in fishable condition by the end of the first or second week of June. The mead-ows are most likely to produce good fishing during the last two weeks of June and the first week of July. Norris Geyser Basin and other hot springs pump in hot water, mak-ing July and August poor fishing months here. In October spawning trout out of Hebgen Lake reach up through Junction Meadow nearly to the base of Gibbon Falls.

The fish: At the upper end of this section the fish are mostly brookies. In Elk Park, however, the population has shifted toward brown trout, which are definitely in the majority through Gibbon Meadows and down through the Gibbon Canyon. Below Gibbon Falls a substantial number of rainbows are added to the mix, but by this point the brook trout have mostly disappeared. Throughout this stretch there is a small chance the angler will hook grayling, and at the lower end, particularly in Junction Meadow, the river holds a few whitefish. The pocket-water fish will run to the smaller end of the 6- to 14-inch range. The meadow fish may reach over 20 inches on occasion but will average closer to 14 inches. Neither the brook trout nor the grayling can be expected to attain much more than 11 inches here.

Flies and lures: The pocket-water sections will fish best with attractor dries such as a Royal Wulff or Royal Coachman Trude. The Prince nymph or Hare's Ear are good choices for the wet fly angler. In the meadows the best bet is to wait for a hatch, which often can be matched with a #18 Pale Evening Dun. What you hope for is an emergence of the much larger brown drake.

The 88-foot Gibbon Falls marks the division between the fly-fishing-only regu-lation area down to the confluence with the Firehole, and the standard artificials-only regulation applying to the rest of the drainage. In the section above the falls, the spin angler should try smaller Panther Martins, Triple Teazers, or Kamlooper spoons.

Access: There are seven primary access points along this stretch of the Gibbon River.

17a. Norris Geyser Basin Overlook

The upper part of this stretch of river, around the northern and western flank of Norris Geyser Basin, is most easily reached from an unmarked but prominent pull-out overlooking the basin. To reach this overlook, drive north on the Grand Loop Road 1.5 miles from Norris Junction and turn left into the pullout where the road goes around a sharp right corner at the top of a long hill. If you're coming from the north, the overlook is on the right and pretty much straight ahead, where the road jogs left; this pullout is 20.1 miles south of Mammoth. The slope down to the river was burned in 1988, so you have a clear view of the stream below. This view of the river eventually will be obscured by the regenerating pines. Once reaching the river, fish in either direction.

17b. Elk Park

Drive south from Norris Junction 1.9 miles and park on the right in the long pull-out alongside the river. You will find this pullout on your left 13.8 miles north of Madison Junction. Fish upriver or down, being careful not to encroach on water being fished by other anglers.

17c. Gibbon Meadows Picnic Area

Take the Grand Loop Road 3.3 miles south from Norris Junction and pull into the Gibbon Meadows Picnic Area to access the upper end of Gibbon Meadows or the lower end of the Gibbon Cascades. The drive is 10.5 miles north from Madison Junction to reach the picnic area, which is equipped with tables and a pit toilet.

17d. Lower Gibbon Meadows

The center and lower end of Gibbon Meadows are best accessed from a series of pullouts just south of the Artist Paint Pots access road. These pullouts are between 4.2 and 4.4 miles south of Norris Junction or 9.4 to 9.6 miles north of Madison Junction on the Grand Loop Road. Take care to park completely off the roadway as these pullouts can also become congested with wildlife watchers.

17e. Gibbon Canyon

The Grand Loop Road closely follows the river from Gibbon Meadows nearly to Madison Junction, more than 7 miles. Gibbon Falls is 8.8 miles south of Norris Junction or 5 miles north of Madison Junction. There are three bridges along this stretch of river. In no case is the river much farther than 100 yards from the road. It often is wise to cross one of the bridges to start fishing upstream on the side opposite the road, reducing the possibility of conflict with other anglers. In general, the sections upstream from the lowest bridge and downstream from Gibbon Falls fish better than the middle section.

Gibbon Meadows.

17f. Gibbon Falls Picnic Area and Canyon Creek

The former site of the Gibbon Falls picnic area is found 9.2 miles south of Norris Junction or 4.6 miles north of Madison Junction. The picnic area has been turned into the construction yard for work rehabbing the road in the Gibbon Falls area, but as of 2006 it was possible to park here on the east side of the road. The base of Gibbon Falls is a few hundred yards upstream. Canyon Creek enters the Gibbon from the east just downstream from the construction yard.

17g. Madison Picnic Area

The best access to the lower end of Junction Meadow is the Madison Picnic Area. It is found 0.1 mile south of Madison Junction on the Grand Loop Road, heading toward Old Faithful. Turn right into the picnic area and park in the middle of the lot. Walk across the Grand Loop Road to fish up into the meadow. If traveling from the south, the picnic area is 15.8 miles north of Old Faithful. Turn left into the picnic area just after crossing the Gibbon River bridge. This picnic area has a restroom that is heated and can handle more than one user at a time.

Tributaries: The only significant tributary in this stretch of river is Canyon Creek, just below Gibbon Falls. The fish are few and small. In the early 1990s an effort was made to reintroduce grayling to Canyon Creek but without notable success. Yellowstone National Park is now attempting to remove the browns and rainbows in Canyon Creek and replace them with westslope cutthroat.

The Firehole River Drainage from Madison Lake to Madison Junction

From its source in Madison Lake, hard up against the Continental Divide under Trischman Knob, the Firehole flows northward to its confluence with the Gibbon. The source of the name is not clear. Mountain men often called mountain valleys "holes," as in Jackson Hole or Gardners Hole. A few early sources imply that the "fire" part of Firehole was prompted by a forest fire or its aftermath. More often, the columns of steam and hot rocks of the great geyser basins are cited as the inspiration for the name. I like Jim Bridger's story of the stream that ran so fast it started fire by friction.

The Firehole seldom is too muddy to fish. The season opener on Saturday of Memorial Day weekend usually finds the Firehole at or near its annual crest. Its color at this time resembles tea brewed with pinewood tannin. The stream is very cold south of Old Faithful. The geyser basins pour millions of gallons of hot water into the stream. As a result, by the end of June the Firehole has heated up to the point where fish are lethargic. The river does not cool off again until sometime in September. October is an excellent time to find consistent hatches and migrating browns. The entire river is restricted to fly fishing only.

Mileage points: All the mileages in this section are measured on the Grand Loop Road from West Thumb, Old Faithful interchange, or Madison Junction.

18. Firehole River, Madison Lake to Biscuit Basin

Description: The 3-mile-long meadow stretching north downstream from the Firehole's source in Madison Lake ends as the river pitches into a canyon. The river drops more than 200 feet in the next 0.5 mile. The Firehole is fishless above this canyon section. The upper Firehole typically is about 15 feet wide, with a bottom of medium-size cobble. With the exception of a couple of small meadow sections, the banks are lined with lodgepole pine. Just south of Old Faithful the river enters another canyon section, called Kepler Cascades, which isolates the fish populations above from those below.

The river is closed to fishing from the bridge 1.5 miles east of Old Faithful downstream through Upper Geyser Basin to the bridge at Biscuit Basin, 1.7 miles north of Old Faithful. Between the Geyser Basin discharge and the confluence of the Little Firehole with the Firehole, the river more than doubles in volume by the time it reaches Biscuit Basin. Passing under the Biscuit Basin footbridge is the full-size, 60-foot-wide Firehole. There are two basic bottom types in this section: Small gravel and sand, often with weed beds, alternate with a cobble-strewn bottom of old hot spring

The canyons in the upper section of the Firehole contrast sharply with the flatter lower stretches of the river. MICHAEL SAMPLE PHOTO

deposits. The latter can make for difficult wading because the bottom seems fine until you step in a defunct thermal vent or trip over an unseen deposit ledge.

South, above Old Faithful, the Firehole is cold all season. Fishing generally is best here from mid-June through August. In Biscuit Basin, the river fishes well in June and again from mid-September until the end of the season.

The fish: Above Kepler Cascades the fish are all brook trout. By the time the river emerges from the Upper Geyser Basin into Biscuit Basin, the population has shifted to a mix of browns and rainbows. The brook trout are typically under 10 inches in length and often are smaller. The browns and rainbows are mostly in the 6- to 12-inch range, though larger fish are present. The best of the day is likely to be under 16 inches. The rare, occasionally caught monster can exceed 25 inches and 5 pounds.

Flies and lures: The entire Firehole River is restricted to fly-fishing only. Above Old Faithful, attractor patterns, such as the Royal Coachman Trude or Prince nymph, are all one really needs. During the early season in Biscuit Basin, the best bets are Woolly Buggers, Prince nymphs, and Hare's Ear nymphs. By mid-June there are hatches of mayflies and caddis that prompt the use of smaller Pale Morning Duns

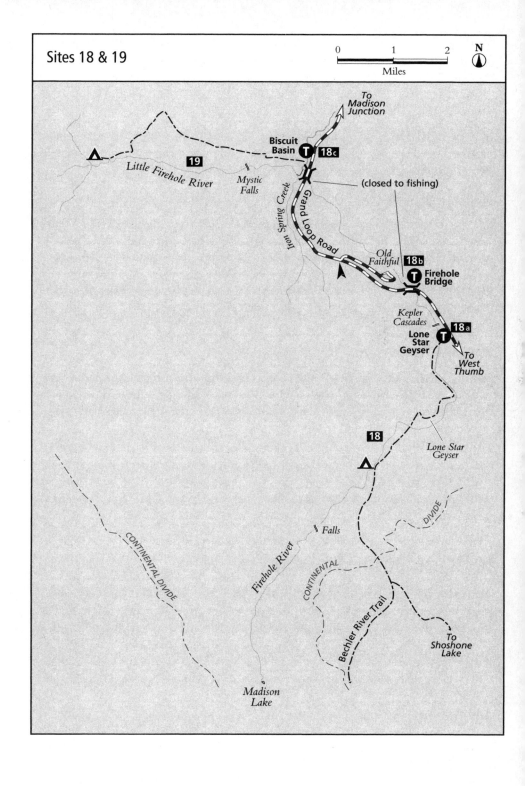

Sites 18 & 19

0   1   2
Miles

N

To
Madison
Junction

Biscuit
Basin **T** 18c

19

Little Firehole River

Mystic
Falls

Iron Spring Creek

Grand Loop Road

(closed to fishing)

Old
Faithful 18b

T Firehole
Bridge

Kepler
Cascades

Lone
Star
Geyser **T** 18a

To
West
Thumb

18

Lone Star
Geyser

DIVIDE

CONTINENTAL DIVIDE

Firehole River

Falls

CONTINENTAL

Bechler River Trail

To
Shoshone
Lake

Madison
Lake

and Elk Hair Caddis in dries, and smaller Pheasant Tail or Hare's Ear nymphs in wet flies. When fishing picks up again in the fall, the best bets are the Pale Morning Dun or Blue-Winged Olive, both in a size #18. Use Pheasant Tail and Hare's Ear nymphs in a #16 or #18 when the fish are not rising. Afternoons may turn out a hatch of small caddis, for which an Elk Hair Caddis or Royal Coachman Trude in a #16 or #18 is the best match.

Access: There are three primary access points along this stretch of the Firehole River. All of them are located off the Grand Loop Road.

18a. Lone Star Geyser Trail

The upper Firehole is best accessed from the Lone Star Geyser Trail. Drive 2.6 miles east from Old Faithful on the Grand Loop Road and turn right into the trailhead. If coming from West Thumb Junction, drive 15.2 miles and turn left. The trail closely follows the river, crossing a couple of times before Lone Star Geyser. There is a backcountry campsite near where the trail leaves the river and heads toward Shoshone Lake and the Bechler River. Fishable water ends about a mile upstream from the campsite.

18b. Firehole Bridge

Take Grand Loop Road east 1.5 miles from Old Faithful to the bridge over the river, which is 16.3 miles west of West Thumb Junction. Fish upstream into the Kepler Cascades area. Remember, the river downstream of this point is closed to fishing.

18c. Biscuit Basin

Go north from Old Faithful 1.8 miles and turn left into the Biscuit Basin parking lot. From Madison Junction, drive south 14.2 miles to Biscuit Basin, on your right. Fish upstream from the footbridge that connects the parking lot with the thermal area. The river is closed to fishing upstream from the highway bridge.

Tributaries: The Little Firehole River (site 19) and its tributary, Iron Spring Creek, are the only significant tributaries in this reach of river.

19. Little Firehole River Drainage *(see map on page 63)*

Description: The Little Firehole River rises in a meadow 4 miles west of Biscuit Basin and flows east to the Firehole. It drops off the plateau over Mystic Falls and picks up Iron Spring Creek only a couple of hundred yards upstream of its confluence with the Firehole. The lower section of the stream is characterized by a deep, sandy-bottomed channel. The banks are grass-covered now but were heavily timbered before the 1988 fires. Look for fish in the holes on bends, around tree roots, and near deadfall dams.

Mystic Falls, 70 feet high, represents the stream's leap off the plateau. Only a mile upstream from its outlet, this falls-and-cascade zone separate the lower river from the river atop the plateau. The Little Firehole has cut a deep, steep canyon for 2 miles back into the rim. The stream here is typical boulder pocket water.

The three main forks of the Little Firehole all come together within yards of each other on the east side of the Little Firehole Meadows. This water is much flatter, with a small-gravel bottom and open, grassy banks. The best places to find fish are the deeper waters on the outside of bends and under the corners where one riffle blends into the next pool.

Iron Spring Creek also rises on the plateau, south of Black Sand Basin, leaving the creek with a northerly course to its junction with the Little Firehole. The most fishable section is its lower 1.5 miles, just upstream from Biscuit Basin. Like the comparable section of the Little Firehole, the bottom is mostly sand and gravel but also has some of the hot-spring-deposit bottom typical of the Firehole itself. The banks are mostly open and grassy. For fish, look to the deeper holes around the corners, behind rocks, under cut banks, and adjacent to deadfall.

All of this water will be high, tea-colored, perhaps a little muddy, and barely fishable on opening day. By the end of the first week of June, it usually is more manageable. The Little Firehole is not much affected by hot spring discharges, so it stays fairly cool all summer. This attracts fish from the Firehole into the lower mile of the stream. As the overall temperature cools off in the fall, most of those fish go back into the main river. Much like the Firehole, Iron Spring Creek is at its best in June, late September, and October.

The fish: Below Mystic Falls on the Little Firehole and along comparable cascades on Iron Spring Creek, the streams exhibit the population pattern of the Firehole: Browns and rainbows predominate, though some brook trout are found there. Above Mystic Falls the Little Firehole holds transplanted cutthroat. The resident fish in these streams run in the 5- to 10-inch range. The fish that migrate to cooler water are generally larger. They average 10 to 16 inches and on occasion may exceed 22 inches.

Flies and lures: During the early season, start with a bead-head Prince. Other good choices in wet flies are Woolly Buggers and Hare's Ears. In June try Pale Morning Duns during caddis hatches. In high summer flat-water hopper patterns such as the Letort Hopper and flies imitating other terrestrials, like ants and beetles, are the best bet. Both streams' small size argue against using lures even though they are legal. Go ultralight if you try spinning.

Access: The fishable section of Iron Spring Creek is generally within 400 yards of the Grand Loop Road, between Biscuit Basin and Old Faithful. Any available pullout will do for access if someone else has not gotten there first. The Little Firehole is best accessed from the Biscuit Basin parking area, which is 1.7 miles north of Old Faithful or 14.2 miles south of Madison Junction on the Grand Loop Road. The Mystic Falls Trail takes off from the west end of Biscuit Basin, but it is not much help in reaching the canyon section of the stream, which is an isolated bushwhack. However, the trail comes close enough to the river to be useful about 5 miles west of Biscuit Basin and follows it for the remaining mile to a backcountry campsite in the Little Firehole Meadows.

Tributaries: Other than Iron Spring Creek, this system does not have significant tributaries.

20. Firehole River, Biscuit Basin to Sentinel Creek

Description: Low-gradient meadow sections alternate with steeper and faster riffle segments throughout this 8-mile reach of the Firehole River. The stream's width (25 to 75 feet) and depth vary widely. The bottom is usually bedrock or solid hot-spring deposit overlaid with frequent patches of small- to medium-size cobble. Slower sections have a finer-grained bottom of gravel or sand with frequent weed beds. Watch your footing: The Firehole is neither slippery nor difficult wading, but extreme and abrupt changes in depth are common. The banks are typically open. Timber comes down to the river in several locations, but, except for a couple of miles between Biscuit Basin and Midway Geyser Basin, it seldom encroaches directly on the river for more than a few yards at a time.

The Firehole opens with Yellowstone National Park's general fishing season on the Saturday of Memorial Day weekend. A short section 200 yards either side of the Midway Geyser Basin footbridge is closed to fishing. For the opener, count on high (at or near crest) and tea-colored but fishable water. Clarity improves as the river drops throughout June. By the end of June or early in July, the temperature rises as the cold water from snowmelt decreases in proportion to the hot-spring inflow. This makes the Firehole a bad bet in July, August, and until mid-September. The river comes alive again in the fall.

The fish: Rainbow trout predominate in this section of the Firehole. Browns are possible anywhere but are more common in Biscuit Basin and other meadow sections. The fish usually run between 8 and 12 inches, the typical top-end fish perhaps 17 inches. Extraordinary fish are known to exceed 25 inches. The Firehole is fished intensely by experienced folks, and as a consequence the fish are also experienced. They require precision performance on the angler's part.

Flies and lures: During the early part of the season, I would start with a Prince nymph or Woolly Bugger. By mid-June the caddis and mayflies are hatching, so shift to Pale Morning Duns and Elk Hair Caddis. Hare's Ear and Pheasant Tail nymphs are best bets for fishing wet. Fall fishing generally requires #16 and smaller Blue-Winged Olives dry or Pheasant Tails wet. Small attractor patterns such as a Royal Coachman Trude are useful in the riffle sections.

Access: The upper, southern 4 miles of this section are generally within sight of the Grand Loop Road, and even when the water's not visible, it's no more than a few hundred yards away behind the trees on the west side of the highway. Numerous parking pullouts provide ready access to the river. From Midway Geyser Basin to the mouth of Sentinel Creek at the north end of this stretch, the river is typically a mile from the highway.

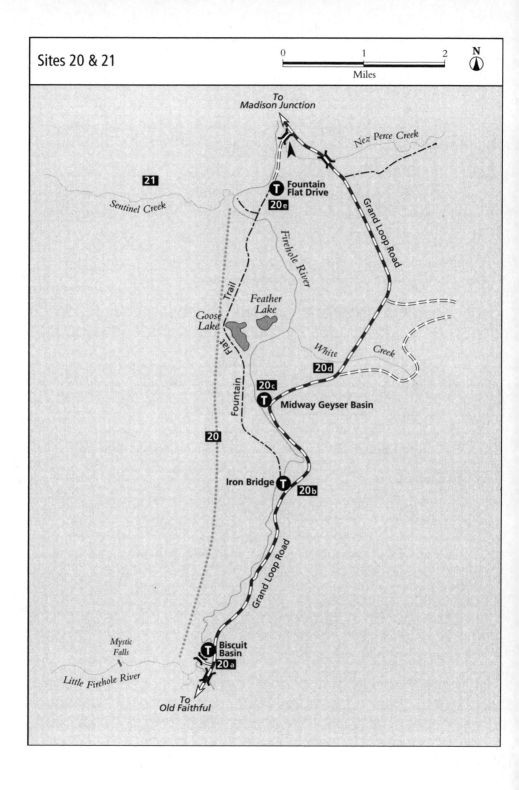

Sites 20 & 21

0   1   2

Miles

N

To
Madison Junction

Nez Perce Creek

21

Sentinel Creek

Fountain
Flat Drive

20e

Firehole River

Feather
Lake

Grand Loop Road

Goose
Lake

Trail

White

Creek

20d

Fountain

20c

Midway Geyser Basin

20

Flat

Iron Bridge

20b

Grand Loop Road

Mystic
Falls

Biscuit
Basin

20a

Little Firehole River

To
Old Faithful

20a. Biscuit Basin

To reach Biscuit Basin from Old Faithful, drive 1.8 miles north on the Grand Loop Road and turn left into the Biscuit Basin parking area. From Madison Junction, go 14.1 miles south and turn right at the sign. Fish or walk downstream into the Biscuit Basin Meadow, which is reputed to hold the largest resident fish in the entire Firehole system. They are also some of the hardest to catch.

20b. Iron Bridge/Freight Road

The "Freight Road" used to run from above Midway Geyser Basin to well below Lower Geyser Basin to get administrative traffic away from the tangle of tourist traffic on the Grand Loop Road. It now survives only as a biking/hiking trail. Drive 4.2 miles north from Old Faithful and turn left onto the short road leading to the parking area and historic bridge. It is on your right 11.7 miles south from Madison Junction. Fish either upriver or down on either side of the river.

20c. Midway Geyser Basin

The Grand Loop Road pulls away from the river at Midway Geyser Basin. A large parking area and a couple of toilets make this a convenient place to start a day. It is also the uppermost of the three logical points of access to the isolated river segment. Midway is on the west side of the Grand Loop Road 5.7 miles north of Old Faithful or 10.2 miles south of Madison Junction. Walk downstream on either side of the river. There are no real trails here, so it is best to stay along the edge of the timber on drier ground. This is particularly true in June when some areas are flooded. In any case, the meadow ground tends to be spongy and difficult to walk on.

20d. White Creek

White Creek is primarily hot-spring discharge water, and it is not itself suitable for fishing. It does provide a route to get from the Grand Loop Road to the Firehole in the center of the isolated section. There isn't much parking; a wide shoulder on the west side of the highway is about it. Take the Grand Loop Road north from Old Faithful 6.6 miles and park opposite the Firehole Loop Road entrance. From Madison Junction it is 9.3 miles south to the Firehole Loop Road. Timbered higher ground parallels the south bank of White Creek. Walk west down White Creek along the margin of the timberline to the Firehole River. Fish in either direction but be aware that if moving upstream, you're more likely to run into people coming down from Midway Geyser Basin.

20e. Fountain Flat Drive

Fountain Flat Drive is the access to Sentinel Creek and the lower end of the isolated section of the Firehole. Drive north from Old Faithful 10.2 miles and turn left onto Fountain Flat Drive. From Madison Junction the turn is to the right, 5.7 miles south

Water in all its forms—frozen, liquid, and gaseous—
dominates this landscape along the Firehole River.

on the Grand Loop Road. Take the Fountain Flat Drive 1 mile to its terminus and park. Walk 0.5 mile on the trail to the Firehole River at Ojo Caliente Spring. A bridge crosses the river here and makes it easy to fish upstream on either side. When fishing downstream you're likely to run into people who have fished up from the parking area.

Tributaries: The only significant tributary in this section is Sentinel Creek (site 21). There are two fair-size lakes, Goose Lake and Feather Lake, which do not have clear surface connections to the river. Goose Lake has some rainbows. Feather Lake used to hold fish but is now probably fishless. Feather Lake has left its name on the angler's nomenclature of the Firehole network. The large meadow between the mouth of White Creek and Midway Geyser Basin is generally referred to as Feather Lake Flat. If interested in fishing Goose Lake, the best approach is probably to take a bicycle from either end of the Fountain Flat Trail. The shortest pedestrian access is to start at Midway Geyser Basin and hike downriver to where it makes a big bend to the right. Cross the river by the big island, climb the 30-foot hill to the bike trail, and hike a final 300 yards west on the trail to the lake. This route is just shy of a mile but will seem longer in waders, particularly if you carry a float tube.

21. Sentinel Creek *(see map on page 67)*

Description: Sentinel Creek flows east to join the Firehole River. The lower 3 miles of the stream are characterized by a sandy or gravel bottom between steep grassy banks. Overall, the creek is seldom more than 10 feet and often only 4 or 5 feet wide. Key fishing structures to look for are the holes on the outside of the many bends and the pools formed by deadfall jammed in the channel. Upstream, the creek comes off the plateau rim and cascades over a vertical drop of more than 150 feet. The stream is fishless above the falls.

The very high spring flow levels argue for waiting until mid-June to fish Sentinel Creek. In July and August there are often fish from the Firehole taking shelter from the heat of the river in the relatively cooler water of the creek. Action picks up again after mid-September.

The fish: Sentinel Creek hosts a mixed bag of brown, rainbow, and brook trout. The brook trout become more common as you go up the creek. The resident fish is typically 5 to 10 inches in length. The summer fish out of the river are more commonly 12 to 16 inches.

Flies and lures: My first choice is a bead-head Prince. There may be a mayfly or caddis hatch; typically, a Blue-Winged Olive or Partridge Caddis is the best match. In summer a flat-water hopper pattern such as a Green Letort often is the best bet. While lures are legal, the stream really is too small to fish comfortably with spinning gear. If you choose to try, the best choices will be the smallest of Panther Martins, Mepps, or Triple Teazers.

Access: The access to Sentinel Creek is from the parking area at the end of the Fountain Flat Drive (access point 20e). Drive 5.7 miles south from Madison

Junction or 10.2 miles north from Old Faithful on the Grand Loop Road. Turn west onto the Fountain Flat Drive and continue 1 mile to the parking area. A small grove of pine trees on the point of a big bend in the Firehole, about half a mile upstream, is directly opposite the mouth of Sentinel Creek. Hike up to the grove, cross the Firehole, and fish upstream on Sentinel Creek.

22. Firehole River, Sentinel Creek to Madison Junction

Description: The lower 6 miles of the Firehole flows north to its confluence with the Gibbon at Madison Junction. Flatter sections with weed beds are common in the first couple of miles of this stretch, but even here riffles begin to predominate. The bed becomes paved with much larger cobble as the gradient increases. Finally, the river pitches over the cascades of the Firehole into Firehole Canyon, 2 miles up from Madison Junction. Firehole Falls is 40 feet high and marks the upper limit of fish moving upstream from the Madison River. Much of the bank on the east side of the river has little vegetation or is backed up against the Grand Loop Road. The west bank is more timbered. The canyon walls are close in the lower end.

The Firehole fishing season opens with the start of the park season on Memorial Day weekend. It is fly fishing only. The river is high and tea-colored but usually is fishable when the season opens. The canyon in the lower 2 miles has a

Bison and thermal activity on a winter day along the Firehole River.
MICHAEL SAMPLE PHOTO

The Firehole River Drainage from Madison Lake to Madison Junction   71

stonefly hatch in early June. Like the rest of the river, July and August are not good bets for fishing. Migrating spawners move upriver into the area below Firehole Falls later in the year. A few will make it into the river by the end of September and be available to the angler through October.

The fish: Above Firehole Falls the population is primarily rainbow with some brown trout thrown in. Below the falls the brown trout fraction increases, and whitefish are added to the mix. They average 8 to 12 inches. The bigger resident fish top out at about 18 inches. The fall migrants from Hebgen Lake average 15 to 17 inches and on occasion exceed 25 inches.

Flies and lures: The Firehole is restricted to fly fishing only. Above the cascades the best choices are Woolly Buggers, or Prince nymphs during the first week of the season. Below the cascades, especially below the falls, bead-head stone patterns—Sparkle Brooks Stone or Sparkle Golden Stone—are often good choices. During the remainder of the June season, the Royal Coachman Trude or Elk Hair Caddis, backed up by a Stimulator or other adult stonefly pattern, are effective flies in the riffle water. The slower sections are likely to produce best with Pale Morning Duns or smaller Elk Hair Caddis in dries and Prince or Hare's Ear nymphs in wets.

Access: Only at the upper and lower ends is this reach of river more than 100 yards from the Grand Loop Road or some other road. There are numerous pullouts; pick one with as few other anglers in sight as possible.

22a. Fountain Flat Drive/Nez Perce Picnic Area

The upper end of this section is reached from Fountain Flat Drive. Take the Grand Loop Road 10.2 miles north from Old Faithful and turn left onto Fountain Flat Drive, which is also reached by taking the Grand Loop Road 5.7 miles south from Madison Junction and turning right. The Nez Perce Picnic Area is on the right 0.1 mile from the highway. There is a toilet there. There are a couple of other parking areas on the right in the next mile before the road ends in the trailhead for the bike trail. Park and fish upriver toward the mouth of Sentinel Creek.

22b. Firehole Canyon Drive

A section of the old Grand Loop Road through the Firehole Canyon has been preserved as a one-way scenic loop. The entrance to the Firehole Canyon Drive is 15.4 miles north of Old Faithful or 0.5 mile south of Madison Junction on the Grand Loop Road. The first pullout, 0.3 mile from the start, provides access to the lower 0.5 mile of the river by working downstream. Park in either of the next two pullouts to fish the remainder of the river below Firehole Falls, which is 0.9 mile from the entrance. The exit back to the Grand Loop Road is 2.2 miles from the beginning.

22c. Madison Picnic Area

The final section of the Firehole, from its confluence with the Gibbon upstream into the bottom end of the Firehole Canyon, is accessed from the Madison Picnic Area.

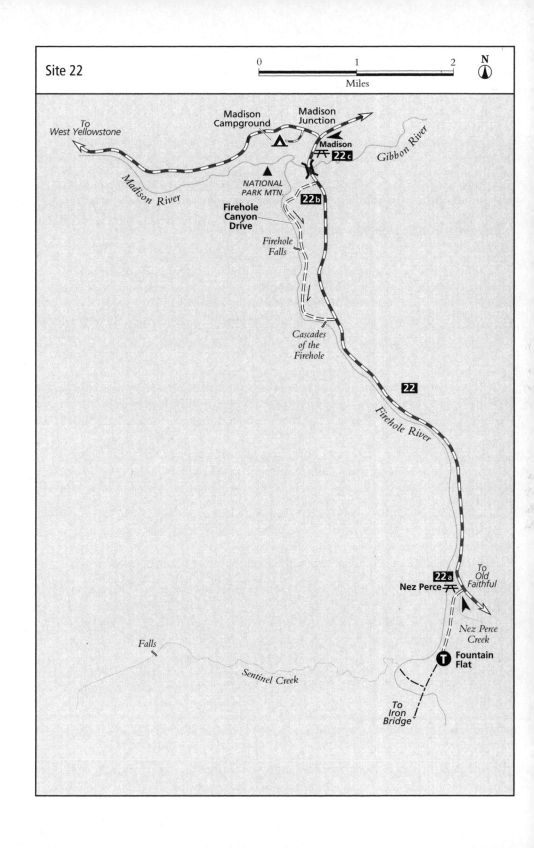

Site 22

0   1   2

Miles

N

To West Yellowstone

Madison Campground

Madison Junction

Madison **22c**

Gibbon River

Madison River

NATIONAL PARK MTN.

Firehole Canyon Drive

22b

Firehole Falls

Cascades of the Firehole

22

Firehole River

22a
Nez Perce

To Old Faithful

Nez Perce Creek

Falls

Fountain Flat

Sentinel Creek

To Iron Bridge

Located on the Grand Loop road just 0.1 mile south of Madison Junction or 15.9 miles north of Old Faithful, this picnic area is provided with a large heated restroom. This makes it a dandy place to change into and out of waders on those spring and fall days when the weather stinks but the fishing does not. Park at the south end of the lot. Look toward National Park Mountain to the southwest, and you will see the junction of the Firehole and Gibbon. Hike across the meadow and fish upstream.

Tributaries: Nez Perce Creek (site 23) is the Firehole's largest tributary below Biscuit Basin and the only one of importance in this section.

23. Nez Perce Creek

Description: Nez Perce Creek rises near the center of Yellowstone National Park in Mary Lake and flows west to join the Firehole River. It is the largest of the Firehole tributary streams. Typically 15-feet wide in its more fishable sections, it spreads out in its final mile to 25 and even 30 feet. As it does so, it loses depth and holding water. The bed is mostly medium-size cobble. The banks are fairly open and grassy with about a 2-foot drop to the water. Occasional deadfall adds to the structure created by bends and cobble bars. Only occasionally does timber come to within 25 feet of the creek bank. These structural features are the best places to find fish.

Nez Perce is usually fishable on or within a week of the season opener. Like the Firehole, it tends to warm up and produce less well in high summer, though it is never as warm or as dead as the Firehole becomes. Lures are allowed. It is important to note that Nez Perce Creek is major grizzly country, and the Bear Management Plan restricts travel in the area prior to June 16. Fall fishing on Nez Perce Creek takes a backseat to the Firehole. The first 5 miles going upstream from the Nez Perce Bridge is the best water.

The fish: The bulk of the fish in Nez Perce are browns in the 6- to 10-inch range. Rainbows are more common in the lower couple of miles, and brook trout show up as one goes up the creek. Resident fish seldom exceed 14 inches. The lower section gets some refugees from the summer heat in the Firehole. These fish may reach 18 inches.

Flies and lures: During the early part of the season, it is hard to beat a Prince nymph. As the waters drop, Elk Hair Caddis and Royal Coachman Trudes become useful dries. During the summer a Dave's or Letort Hopper would be a good choice. The spin angler must consider the small size of the creek and fish with light lures. Mepps, Panther Martins, and Triple Teazers are good choices.

Access: There are numerous pullouts along the Grand Loop Road in the Lower Geyser Basin.

23a. Nez Perce Picnic Area

The lower segment of Nez Perce Creek is readily accessible from the Grand Loop Road. Take the Grand Loop Road 5.7 miles south from Madison Junction, or 10.2 miles north if coming from Old Faithful, and turn onto the Fountain Flat Drive.

Site 23

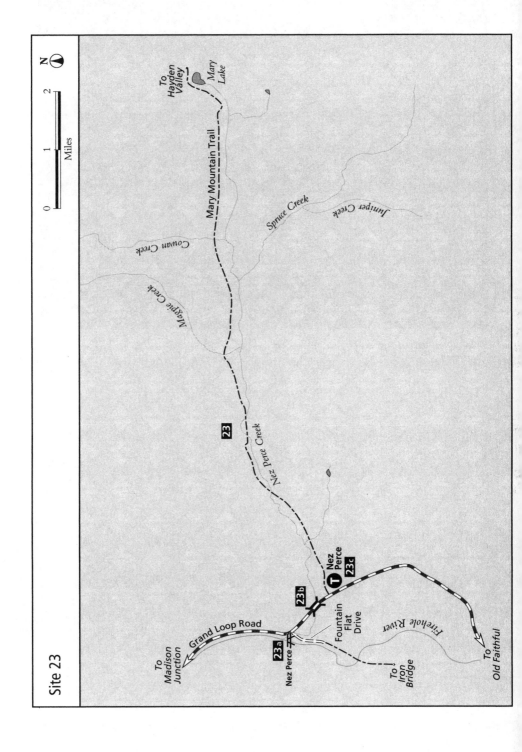

A lower stretch of the Firehole.

This road immediately crosses Nez Perce Creek, and a stub road turns right into the Nez Perce Picnic Area.

23b. Nez Perce Bridge

Driving south 6.2 miles from Madison Junction or north 9.7 miles from Old Faithful brings you to the Nez Perce Bridge. Park at the bridge and fish either upstream or downstream. Because of probable bear activity, the upper section of the creek is closed 1 mile upstream from the bridge prior to June 16. Consult the Bear Management Plan.

23c. Nez Perce/Mary Mountain Trail

The Mary Mountain Trail runs from the Nez Perce Trailhead to Hayden Valley on the Yellowstone River side of the divide near Canyon. It is closed until June 16 and open only to day-use travel thereafter. Find the Nez Perce Trailhead 6.5 miles south of Madison Junction or 9.4 miles north of Old Faithful on the Grand Loop Road. The trailhead is on the east side of the road. The trail and creek first approach each other 1 mile east of the trailhead. Thereafter the trail and creek are seldom more than 100 yards apart.

Tributaries: Magpie and Spruce Creeks are the Nez Perce's largest tributaries. They are both small, a long hike upstream (too far for a day trip), and marginally populated by trivial fish.

Cascade Corner

The Falls River, a tributary of the Henry's Fork, and Robinson Creek, part of the Warm River drainage, drain the southwest corner of Yellowstone National Park. This section of the park is often referred to as "Cascade Corner" due to the numerous waterfalls that drop off the plateau toward the Snake River Plain of southeastern Idaho. The Falls River officially received its name from the Hayden survey in 1872, but it actually had been pegged by trapper Osborne Russell much earlier. His 1838 journal notes it as the "falling fork." Army scouts were using the name Robinson Creek by 1898, apparently naming the stream for an Idaho rustler shot in the vicinity in 1887.

Mileage points: Mileage on U.S. Highway 20 is measured from its junction with Idaho Highway 87 on the north and Idaho Highway 47 in Ashton, Idaho. Mileage on Reclamation Road is also measured from Ashton on the west to Flagg Ranch, Wyoming, on the east end, where the road meets U.S. Highway 89 just south of Yellowstone's South Entrance. At its western end Reclamation Road is identified as Ashton–Flagg Ranch Road. At its eastern end it is simply signed as Grassy Lake Road. In between it is often marked Forest Road 261. I will refer to it throughout its length as Reclamation Road.

To access the west end of Reclamation Road, take ID 47 east from its junction with US 20 in Ashton for 1 mile to the Idaho Highway 32 junction, then take ID 32 south for 0.9 mile to its junction with Reclamation Road. Heavy snowfall in the Calf Creek Hill area often closes Reclamation Road to through traffic until July 1; check with the Ashton Ranger Station for the road's condition. Cave Falls Road is identified as Green Timber Road at its western end where it joins ID 47. Thereafter, it is variously referred to as Cave Falls Road or Forest Road 582. I will use Cave Falls Road in all instances.

Robinson Creek and Horseshoe Lake

24. Robinson Creek

Description: Robinson Creek rises on the edge of the lava plateau along the western flank of Yellowstone National Park. Almost immediately cutting into canyons, Robinson Creek winds toward the southwest to join Warm River, which soon joins the Henry's Fork. Mostly 15 to 25 feet wide, its bed is hard lava rock overlaid with small cobble and the occasional boulder. The riverbed is interrupted by minidams of rockfall or deadfall trees. During the 1970s the USDA Forest Service, in conjunction with the Youth Conservation Corps, augmented the natural structure by installing fifty or more plunge-pool, log-check dams. These obstructions provide the fish-holding structure.

Most of Robinson Creek is in Idaho, outside the park. The Idaho general season and regulations apply. Saturday of Memorial Day weekend is the opening day, and the season closes November 30. Idaho limits the kill of cutthroat and cutbow in this region to two fish; neither of them can be between 8 and 16 inches in length. High water, perhaps not quite fishable, can be expected on opening day, but Robinson Creek is seldom truly muddy and drops fairly quickly through June. The early season is slow going for the angler but will pick up as the water drops. Summer and fall fishing are usually quite good until after the end of September.

The fish: The fish are rainbow, cutthroat, cutbow, and brook trout, mostly in the 10- to 14-inch range. The proportion of rainbows is greater in the lower portion of the creek, and the average size of fish shrinks in the upper reaches. Recent reports suggest that the remnant cutthroat population has been almost completely displaced by brookies. Furthermore, the fish population in the part of the creek nearest the park boundary may have been depressed by a forest fire in the region several years ago. The upper end of Robinson Creek primarily contains brook trout under 8 inches. Robinson Creek fish are neither particularly sophisticated nor numerous. The good news is that in the fall, brown trout from the Henry's Fork move up the creek for several miles looking for spawning water. These fish run 12 to 15 inches.

Flies and lures: Nymphs tend to be most effective in the early season; bead-head Prince, Hare's Ear, and modest-sized stonefly nymphs come to mind. Attractor dries such as Royal Coachman Trudes or Royal Wulffs generally are satisfactory through the summer and early fall. Hoppers are also a reasonable choice most of the summer. The average size of the angler's patterns should shrink late in the season. Lures should be kept to the smaller sizes of Mepps, Panther Martins, or Kamlooper Spoons.

Access: There are only four reasonable access points to over 10 miles of Robinson Creek. While a couple of bushwhacks are possible off the Snow Creek Road, they are very difficult. The key intersection is the junction of the Cave Falls Road with ID 47 east of Ashton. From the Ashton junction of ID 47 with US 20, take ID 47 east through town 6.3 miles to the Cave Falls Road. If coming from the West Yellowstone area, this junction is 63 miles from West Yellowstone via Ashton or 60 miles via Forest Road 294 (Mesa Falls Road).

24a. Robinson Creek Road (Forest Road 241)

You can reach this road from both its ends. If coming from the south or west, take ID 47 east from Ashton 6.3 miles to its junction with the Cave Falls Road, known also at this end as Green Timber Road. Turn east, to the right, and go 5 miles to the local road called 4500 E. Turn left, heading north, onto 4500 E. (which is FR 241 at its northern end on some maps) and drive 2.3 miles to the Robinson Creek Bridge. Fish in either direction but be aware that public land ends about a mile downstream.

Robinson Creek flows from Yellowstone
National Park into Idaho.

Sites 24 & 25

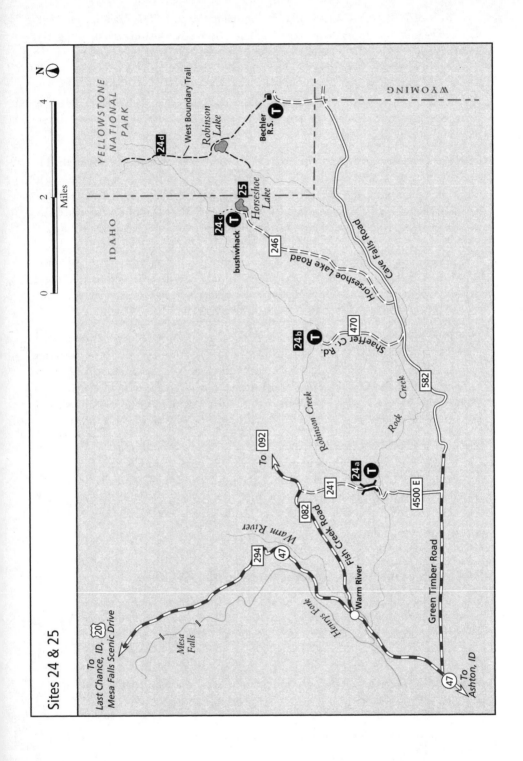

If coming from the north via US 20, say from West Yellowstone, take FR 294 from its junction with US 20 just south of Last Chance, Idaho. This intersection is 23.4 miles south of the ID 87 junction. The sign here identifies the road as the Mesa Falls Scenic Drive. FR 294 has been recently repaved, but it is narrow. It traverses open range, so watch out for cattle on the roadway. A few miles north to the next junction the road improves dramatically as it becomes ID 47. Turn left onto Forest Road 082 at Warm River (heading northeast) 20 miles south of the FR 294/US 20 junction. Follow this road, also known as the Fish Creek Road, 4.1 miles and turn right onto the Robinson Creek Road. At this end the road is identified as FR 241. A final 2.1 miles takes you to the Robinson Creek Bridge. Rock Creek, big enough here to fish, joins Robinson Creek a few yards upstream from the bridge, providing a fishing alternative.

24b. Shaeffer Creek Road (Forest Road 470)

Follow the Cave Falls Road 9.9 miles east of the ID 47 junction to the Shaeffer Creek Road (FR 470). Watch your mileage carefully because Shaeffer Creek Road, to your left (heading north), is unsigned. There is a sign stating that Robinson Creek is a couple of miles to the north. Turn left onto FR 470, which passes the Rock Creek Girl Scout Camp before continuing north to the end, 2.5 miles later, perched above Robinson Creek. Fish in either direction. Migrating fall browns are known to make it this far up Robinson Creek but probably not much farther.

24c. Horseshoe Lake Bushwhack

Drive east on the Cave Falls Road 10.9 miles to its junction with the Horseshoe Lake Road (Forest Road 246). Take the Horseshoe Lake Road 5.5 miles to its practical end just off the northwest corner of the lake. An anglers' track continues north down a draw into the Robinson Creek Canyon for another 0.5 mile to the stream. Fish either up or down but be mindful that the park boundary is less than a mile upstream. Pay attention to your landmarks, as this is neither a marked nor maintained trail.

24d. West Boundary Trail

Take the Cave Falls Road east from its junction with ID 47 for 17.1 miles and turn left onto the Bechler Ranger Station Road. Drive 1.5 miles to the ranger station and trailhead area. Park in one of the designated areas at the trailhead. Take the West Boundary Trail north for 4.1 miles to Robinson Creek. This is the only access point for the creek within Yellowstone National Park. The fishing is likely to be better by working downstream simply because there is more water. The west boundary of Yellowstone National Park is a bit over a mile downstream. The trail passes by Robinson Lake 2 miles north of Bechler Ranger Station. This lake is in an advanced stage of eutrophication—its low level of dissolved oxygen in the water favors the growth of aquatic plants—and is without fish.

Tributaries: "Rock Creeks" generally are so named because they have steep beds that are full of rocks. However, this Rock Creek, Robinson Creek's most significant tributary, is named for one Richard W. Rock, a hunter, Indian scout, and wildlife entrepreneur who lived in the area and was widely believed to have acquired some of his inventory on the sly from within Yellowstone. Rock Creek is physically very much like Robinson Creek and is fished the same way, with the same methods and equipment. Horseshoe Lake (site 25) has no obvious surface connection to either Robinson or Rock Creeks, although it lies between them.

25. Horseshoe Lake *(see map on page 80)*

Description: It takes some imagination to turn the battered, upside-down L shape of this lake into a horseshoe. The long side of the L runs north to south and is about a quarter-mile long. The lake is no more than 300 yards at its widest. The shore is mostly timbered with a mix of pine and aspen, and the bottom of the lake is mostly rocky. The south end of the L is marshy and has quite a few lily pads. Unlike the creeks, the lake is open for fishing all year.

The fish: Horseshoe Lake is stocked with rainbow trout and grayling. The fish run 10 to 16 inches in length.

Flies and lures: Concentrate on still-water patterns. Woolly Buggers, leeches, Skinny Buggers, and flies that imitate various midge pupa can be good choices. The spin angler should start with Rooster Tails or Kastmasters. Other solid choices include Rapalas, Mepps, and Swedish Pimples.

Special equipment: A float tube could be very useful on Horseshoe Lake. Motors are not allowed.

Access: Take the Cave Falls Road 10.9 miles east from its junction with ID 47 to the Horseshoe Lake Road (FR 246). Turn north on the Horseshoe Lake Road, following it 5.3 miles to the lake. There are a couple of obvious places to park along the lakeshore.

The Falls River Drainage

The Falls River and its major tributaries generally flow west or southwest from the southwest flank of the great volcanic plateau that forms the core of Yellowstone National Park. They merge in Idaho with the Henry's Fork of the Snake River. The upper reaches of this drainage—most of the course length of these streams is found within the park—were without fish prior to human intervention.

26. Beula Lake

Description: Beula Lake is generally considered to be the headwaters of the Falls River even though it has one substantial inlet and also seasonally receives water

A bull moose feeds in the Falls River.
MICHAEL SAMPLE PHOTO

from nearby Hering Lake (site 27). The immediate shoreline of the lake appears to have been spared serious impact from the 1988 fires that burned along its western and northern flanks. The bottom varies with areas of sand, cobble, and muck, with muck particularly characterizing the deeper areas. The eastern shoreline shelves slowly, allowing an angler with chest waders to get some distance offshore. At 107 acres, Beula Lake is larger than most Yellowstone lakes. The trail meets the lake at its southwestern corner, and Falls River flows out of its northwestern corner. The inlet stream comes from the southeast. Backcountry campsites, a relatively short access hike, and its location in one of the less-used areas of Yellowstone make this lake quite popular.

The best fishing takes place here as soon as the snow is off the road and trail, around mid-June. In recent years the road has been closed for bear-management purposes until June 1 regardless of road condition. Concentrate on the areas around the inlets and outlets and along the more sheltered western shore. Wading or a float tube will be required to reach the fish cruising off the eastern shore. Productivity drops off after mid-July, and fishing can be poor after mid-September.

The fish: Originally fishless, Beula Lake was heavily planted during the 1930s and 1940s with cutthroat fry and fertile eggs taken from Yellowstone Lake. Good reproductive opportunities and the catch-and-release rule combine to provide the angler with excellent opportunities for finding fish in the 12- to 16-inch range.

Flies and lures: Good wet fly patterns are midge pupa, Skinny Bugger, Prince, and Hare's Ear nymphs. An Adams, Blue-Winged Olive, or Pale Morning Dun will match most of the surface hatches. Beetles may be the best bet for terrestrials, particularly later in the season. Unlike most lakes in the park, Beula Lake does not have a large population of leeches, reducing the effectiveness of patterns like the Woolly Bugger. On the other hand, the worst enemies of the numerous cutthroat fry are their grown-up relatives. Try a white Zonker or Kiwi Skunk. The Spin-a-Lure, Krocodile, Kastmaster, and larger Mepps spinners are the leading choices for the spinning angler.

Special equipment: Chest waders or a float tube are particularly useful on Beula Lake.

Access: To reach Beula Lake take Reclamation Road 9.6 miles west from Flagg Ranch or 39.7 miles east from Ashton. Park at the trailhead on the north side of the road and follow the Beula Lake Trail. The hike is 3 miles, the first 0.5 mile or so being mostly uphill but much flatter thereafter.

Tributaries: The unnamed inlet stream is fishable for a couple of miles upstream. It is likely to be best early in the season. Hering Lake (site 27) has a substantial spring outlet to Beula Lake; otherwise, the tributaries are small intermittent flows and springs.

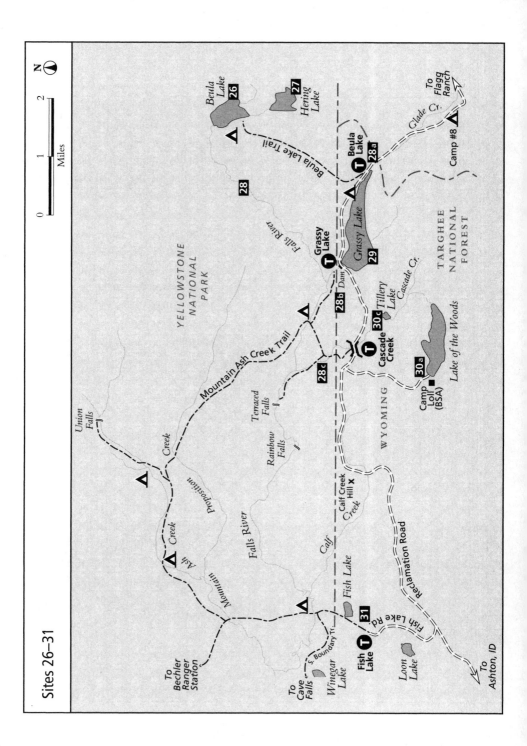

27. Hering Lake *(see map on page 85)*

Description: Hering Lake lies just south of the nearby Beula Lake and in the same fold of the plateau that contains Beula. The 1878 Hayden survey named the lake after Rudolph Hering, who had been part of the 1872 survey team. Hering Lake is without substantive surface inlets and only an intermittent but obviously annual outlet to Beula Lake. The shoreline is heavily timbered. The bottom is mostly cobble and sand, only turning to muck in the deepest part of the lake. The west side of the lake drops off much more quickly than the remainder. Snow usually makes the lake inaccessible until about July 1. Fishing is best in July and tapers off thereafter. Extended periods of drought often shrink the lake to the point that fish are no longer able to spawn or migrate in from Beula Lake. This probably accounts for the spotty reputation of the lake.

The fish: The fish of Hering Lake are cutthroat averaging in the 11- to 14-inch range. Individual fish of more than 18 inches have been taken. U.S. Fish and Wildlife Service researchers were surprised in 1973 to find a healthy population of fish from at least five different spawning years in a lake then widely believed to be fishless and without any stocking record. Environmental upset, particularly periods of drought that desiccate the one inlet stream that can support spawning, can create wide swings in population. The most consistently productive fishing areas are along the western shore, where the depth increases quickly, and along the northeastern shore, where intermittent tributaries and spring seeps supply most of the lake's water.

Flies and lures: Absent any evidence to suggest otherwise, the angler's first choice in a fly should be a scud pattern, say, a Troth Dark Shrimp. Hatches here include mayflies and caddis, so an Adams is also a good bet. Nymphs should run to the Hare's Ear and Pheasant Tail. Lure anglers should try the Spin-a-Lure, Kastmaster, and Panther Martin.

Special equipment: A float tube can be very useful.

Access: The only really practical access to Hering Lake is from the Beula Lake Trail. From Flagg Ranch, south of the South Entrance to the park, drive west for 9.6 miles on the Reclamation Road. Park at the Beula Lake Trailhead and hike in. Upon reaching Beula Lake, turn back south along the lakeshore for another 0.25 mile to Hering Lake.

28. Upper Falls River, Beula Lake to Mountain Ash Creek
(see map on page 85)

Description: For the first half of the stretch from Beula Lake to Mountain Ash Creek, the Falls River drops slowly toward the southwest. Along the way it picks up some significant tributaries and a much increased flow. There are a couple of pocket-meadow sections, one about a mile below Beula Lake and the other around the confluence with Grassy Creek, a half mile below Grassy Lake. The remainder of the banks are timbered. The bed is mostly small to medium cobble and sand. The meadow areas have a lot of willow overhanging the river. The next 2 miles of stream drop rapidly, losing 500 feet in elevation in a tight canyon. There are two major waterfalls, Terraced Falls and Rainbow Falls. The remaining 6 miles of the reach are in the Falls River Meadows. As the meadows above, these meadow stretches are often willow-lined with a fine-grained bottom that can make fishing difficult. In the meadow sections the best water is in the deeper holes around the outside of bends and the corners at the tops of pools. In the canyon sections the key water is the pockets around rocks and deadfall.

Falls River usually is in full flood on opening day. The good news is that by early July, the river falls back into fishable shape, stoneflies will be emerging in the canyons, and Pale Morning Duns will be effective for greedy fish in the meadows. The bad news is that hordes of mosquitoes and deerflies will be feeding on you. The

The Falls River is a tributary of the Henry's Fork of the Snake River.

water drops steadily throughout the summer, though discharges from Grassy Lake for downstream irrigation may change flow levels unexpectedly. The fish become increasingly wary and hard to find as the season advances. Late July through early August is also berry season, which is good for your grazing but also attracts bears with the same idea. Late August and early September have good hatches, and the biting flies have mostly gone. September can be very good but technically demanding, while October is generally slow and subject to nasty weather.

The fish: From Beula Lake downstream to some cascades just above the confluence with Grassy Creek, the population is exclusively cutthroat. Below this cascade section the population is a mix, primarily cutbows with some cutthroat and rainbows and some fugitive brook trout from Fish Lake. The fish in the canyon sections mostly run in the 8- to 12-inch range. The meadow fish, including some of the brookies, can reach up to 18 inches.

Flies and lures: Early season flies include the Pale Morning Dun and Golden Stone. Later in the season, brown drakes and then gray drakes emerge, and the angler will need to imitate them. High summer in the meadows also produces hoppers, ants, and beetles. Effective nymph patterns include the Prince, Hare's Ear, and olive Hare's Ear. The lure fisherman will find small- to medium-size Mepps, Panther Martins, and Kamlooper spoons useful.

Access: There are four major access routes for this section of Falls River. All of them are reached from Reclamation Road.

28a. Beula Lake Trail

Drive west 9.6 miles from Flagg Ranch on Reclamation Road, 39.7 miles east from Ashton, to the Beula Lake Trailhead. Park at the trailhead and hike 3.5 miles to the outlet of Beula Lake. Work your way downstream.

28b. Grassy Lake Dam

Take Reclamation Road west from Flagg Ranch for 11.3 miles to Grassy Lake Dam. A short (0.2 mile) access road drops down to the trailhead at the base of the dam. This access road is 38 miles east of Ashton via Reclamation Road. The South Boundary Trail heads west down Grassy Creek to its confluence with Falls River, then parallels Falls River for about a mile before heading over the divide toward Mountain Ash Creek. There is a backcountry campsite just after the trail crosses Falls River.

28c. Cascade Creek

Drive west on Reclamation Road 13.3 miles to the Cascade Creek Bridge. The trailhead is on the north side of the road at the west end of the bridge. Take Reclamation Road east 36 miles from Ashton to reach Cascade Creek. The trail follows Cascade Creek for 1 mile as it descends to its confluence with Falls River and then down

Falls River an additional 0.5 mile to Terraced Falls. Fish in either direction once on the river.

28d. Fish Lake *(see site 31)*

Fish Lake is described in site 31, but it also provides access to the upper river. Officially Forest Road 048, the Fish Lake Road is found by driving east from Ashton 29.6 miles on Reclamation Road. This junction is 19.7 miles west from Flagg Ranch, but its location to the west of Calf Creek Hill makes it more likely that access will be gained from the Idaho side earlier in the season. The junction is signed for both Fish Lake and Loon Lake. The Loon Lake Road forks left off the Fish Lake Road 0.3 mile from Reclamation Road. It is 1.5 miles to the trailhead, just short of Fish Lake itself. This is as rough a road as is passable with an ordinary passenger car—crooked, rutted, narrow all the way, and puddled after any rain. Park at the end of the road and hike north on the trail 1.1 miles to meet the South Boundary Trail and Falls River. Fish in either direction. This is the best access to Falls River Meadows. There is a backcountry campsite near where the trail crosses the river.

Tributaries: The principle tributaries to Falls River in this reach are Grassy Creek, Cascade Creek (site 30), and Calf Creek. Calf Creek is not particularly significant, and the most important aspect of Grassy Creek is Grassy Lake (site 29). The only other water of interest in the area is Fish Lake (site 31).

29. Grassy Lake *(see map on page 85)*

Description: Grassy Lake lies in a high valley closely girded by a lodgepole pine forest that generally comes right to the high-water line. The dam plugging the west end of the valley is 118 feet high. Built in the late 1930s, Grassy Lake is 2 miles long and just under 1 mile wide at its widest. A storage dam holding irrigation water for land downstream in Idaho, the lake fills in the spring and is drawn down 50 or more feet by fall. The bottom is mostly cobble with an occasional stump (from the trees cut to make way for the lake) sticking up here and there.

Wyoming allows fishing on the lake all year, but the road is closed to vehicle traffic until June 1. During the winter, snow-machine access is allowed to those wishing to fish through the ice. Summer fishing on the lake is best the month after the road opens. Fish may be inshore again in the late fall, but watch out for the weather. The best fishing areas are the western end of the lake in the vicinity of the Grassy Creek inlet on the south shore, and the stump field at the eastern end of the lake. Be particularly alert to the possibility of fish working midges in the shallows.

The fish: For years the principle fish in Grassy Lake was the cutthroat. Some rainbows came over from Lake of the Woods through a diversion of Cascade Creek from Tillery Lake to Grassy Lake. This naturally resulted in some cutbows as well. Around 1971 Wyoming made one plant of lake trout. These fish are now well established. The cutthroat and rainbows run in the 14- to 18-inch range. The lake trout are typically 18 to 28 inches; the record here is twenty-four pounds.

The water of Grassy Lake is drawn down in the latter half of the fishing season.

Flies and lures: The Kiwi Skunk, white Zonker, and Woolly Bugger are good streamer choices. Hatches don't appear to be very consistent, but if one occurs and gets the fish to rising, do the obvious thing. Small Adams, midges, and Serendipities should cover that angle. Good lures include Rapala, Flat Fish, Kamlooper spoon, Spin-a-Lure, and Krocodile. Try marabou jigs or Swedish Pimples when fishing through the ice. Bait fishing is allowed.

Special equipment: There isn't much in the way of boat ramps, and the road isn't well suited to hauling trailers up here, but a hand-launched boat, canoe, or float tube could be very useful.

Access: The only access to Grassy Lake is via Reclamation Road. Drive 9.5 miles west from Flagg Ranch to the head of the lake. The road follows the lakeshore closely for 0.25 mile past a couple of campsites and then climbs up away from the lake until it reaches the dam. These campsites are provided with bear-proof provision boxes but no toilets. The nearest toilet is at Camp #8, 2 miles back to the east along upper Glade Creek. The lake can also be accessed from either end of the dam, which is 37.8 miles from the Ashton end of Reclamation Road. The west end of the dam seems to be the best place to launch a boat from a trailer.

Tributaries: There are only two significant tributaries to Grassy Lake, neither of them providing much fishing. Grassy Creek itself is just big enough to provide spawning opportunities for cutthroat and rainbows. A diversion ditch carries water from the Cascade Creek drainage to Grassy Lake, but it only runs for part of the year. While not exactly a tributary, there is 0.5 mile of Grassy Creek between the dam and Falls River. This is closely hemmed in with timber and willow. Its population is mostly cutbows. The amount of discharge from the dam determines whether it will be approachable and fishable.

30. Lake of the Woods and Cascade Creek *(see map on page 85)*

Description: Lake of the Woods is in an east-west seam of a mountain valley. Heavy timber comes right down to the lakeshore in most places. The banks are fairly steep, except at the lake's eastern and western ends. Some maps, particularly the older 1/250,000-scale series, indicate that the lake drains from its western end, but that is wrong. It actually discharges east through Cascade Creek to Falls River. The upper 2 miles of Cascade Creek alternates between timber and willow meadow. The Tillery Lake diversion dam creates a pond bigger than the occasional beaver ponds. After crossing Reclamation Road, the remaining 1.5 miles of Cascade Creek is mostly timbered as it drops down a short canyon to its junction with Falls River. In the flat sections, the bottom is mostly small cobble, pea gravel, and fine material. Medium to large cobble dominates the steeper sections.

Lake of the Woods is open April 1 through October 31, but much of that time the lake will not be accessible. The road does not open for the summer season until June 1. Fishing here is best in June and tapers off thereafter. Cascade Creek will fish best in July and August. Productive fishing areas in Lake of the Woods are around the few points and in the outlet end of the lake. Cascade Creek offers some beaver ponds; otherwise, stick to the structure around bigger rocks, the deeper holes on the bends, and around deadfall.

The fish: Rainbow are the principle fish in the Cascade Creek–Lake of the Woods system. In the lake they average around 14 inches. The fish in Cascade Creek are more likely to run in the 8- to 12-inch range. Particularly in the lower end of Cascade Creek, you will also catch some cutthroat and cutbows.

Flies and lures: Both white and black Marabou Muddlers as well as Woolly Buggers are good choices for Lake of the Woods. In Cascade Creek I would start with an attractor dry; a Royal Coachman Trude is likely to be effective. In high summer a hopper also is a good bet. The spin angler should try larger Panther Martins, Mepps, or Kamlooper spoons in Lake of the Woods. Go much smaller in Cascade Creek, perhaps a small Cyclone spoon or Triple Teazer, along with small spinners. Bait is allowed until Cascade Creek enters Yellowstone National Park a quarter mile downstream from the road.

Special equipment: The only boat launch on Lake of the Woods is at Camp Loll. This is a public ramp, but try to stay out of the way of any Boy Scouts in residence. Due to the limited access, a float tube may not be terribly useful.

Access: The only road access to this system is via Reclamation Road.

30a. Lake of the Woods

From Flagg Ranch, take Reclamation Road 13.8 miles to Camp Loll Road. Turn left onto Camp Loll Road and drive 2.4 miles to its end at the Boy Scout camp on the west end of Lake of the Woods. The Camp Loll Road is 35.5 miles east of Ashton via Reclamation Road. Some maps show a road to the eastern end of the lake, but that road no longer exists. Camp Loll is a busy Boy Scout camp during the summer season. There is very limited public parking at the end of the road.

30b. Cascade Creek *(see site 28c)*

From Flagg Ranch, drive 13.3 miles west on Reclamation Road to the Cascade Creek Bridge. The road parallels the creek for 0.25 mile before reaching the bridge. The trailhead for the trail down Cascade Creek to Terraced Falls on Falls River is to the right, at the west end of the bridge. Park at the trailhead and either fish downstream or take the trail, which pulls away from the creek before rejoining it after about a third of a mile. Some maps show a road from here to the east end of Lake of the Woods. This road was closed some years ago and is not even a good trail now.

30c. Tillery Lake

From Flagg Ranch, go 12.3 miles (37 if coming from Ashton) on Reclamation Road to the Tillery Lake Road. This is a 0.25-mile stub road heading south to the Tillery Lake diversion dam. Fish the pond or work upstream on Cascade Creek.

31. Fish Lake *(see map on page 85)*

Description: Fish Lake is nearly round. The southeast side is up against a hill, and timber surrounds the lake from its southern point, up and around to its northeastern edge. The remainder of the shoreline is open and often marshy along the edges. An intermittent discharge channel runs off north to Falls River. At its widest point the lake is about 300 yards across. The bottom is mostly muck, although it is firmer along the southeastern shore.

While the Wyoming season allows fishing from April 1 through October 31, it is unlikely that you will be able to get in here before June. Fish Lake is best for about two weeks right after the ice goes off, is at least fair for another couple of weeks after that, and then rates mediocre until late fall when the fish come inshore again. The fall angler in particular should try fishing around the intermittent inlet stream on the south shore.

The fish: While rainbow and cutbow are said to be present in Fish Lake, apparently its biggest attraction is the possibility of running into a large brook trout. Some of these fish are reputed to exceed 20 inches. However, it seems such fish are more often talked about than seen.

Flies and lures: Damselfly nymphs such as the Skinny Bugger, scuds, and leech patterns are good choices here. Also, it is almost never wrong to try an Adams dry fly.

In the fall try a Joffe Jewel for one of the big ones. The lure angler should start with a Mepps. Other good choices include Rooster Tails and Little Cleos. Bait is allowed.

Special equipment: Fish Lake is a short hike without a lot of hills, which makes it a good location for backcountry float-tube fishing.

Access: The only practical access to Fish Lake is Fish Lake Road, off of Reclamation Road. Take Reclamation Road 29.6 miles east from Ashton to Fish Lake Road, then take it to the north (turn left). From Flagg Ranch, Fish Lake Road is 19.7 miles down Reclamation Road, on the right. Ignore Loon Lake Road, which splits off to the left 0.25 mile in. Drive 1.5 miles to the end of the road at the Winegar Wilderness boundary. This road has to be the worst track I took my Honda on while researching this book. Hike north on the Fish Lake Trail, 0.7 mile to the lake. Fish Lake is on the Idaho side of Calf Creek Hill, which in most years isn't passable until sometime in July.

32. Falls River, Mountain Ash Creek to Cave Falls Campground

Description: Falls River, already a substantial stream, is further augmented by the flow of Mountain Ash Creek. The first mile of river course—probably not much more than 0.5 mile laterally—is meadow water much like the rest of the Falls River Meadows. The bed has a fairly fine-grained bottom of sand and small cobble. There are also occasional patches of clay. The banks are grass or willow-lined. Then the timber closes in, and the river becomes wider, shallower, and steeper in gradient. The bottom of the river, for the remaining 6 miles or so, is mostly lava rock pocked by holes and frequent small ledges that create miniature waterfalls. Other bottom features include small gravel bars and large cobble. The key waters for the angler are the structural pockets formed around the boulders, the plunge pools below the ledges, deeper water caused by deadfall, and the occasional gravel bar.

The short section of Falls River between the Yellowstone National Park boundary and Cave Falls Campground that is subject to Wyoming regulations is open April 1 through October 31. The odds are good that the road will not be open until about the time the park season opens on Saturday of Memorial Day weekend. It is also a safe bet that the river will be too high to fish effectively until at least late June, when the first thing to look for throughout this reach is a stonefly hatch. The balance of the summer is dominated by successive mayfly hatches and grasshoppers. Fishing slacks off markedly in early October.

The fish: Most of the fish in this section are cutbows. There are, of course, some rainbows and cutthroat as well, plus a few brookies that have escaped from Fish Lake. The fish run in the 8- to 14-inch range, except for the smaller brook trout. In the meadow section the average is more likely to be 12 to 16 inches.

Flies and lures: Effective fly patterns include Royal Wulffs, Stimulators, Pale Morning Duns, and, later in the season, brown and gray drakes. Productive nymphs include the Prince, Hare's Ear, and Brook's Stone. Panther Martin, Mepps, and

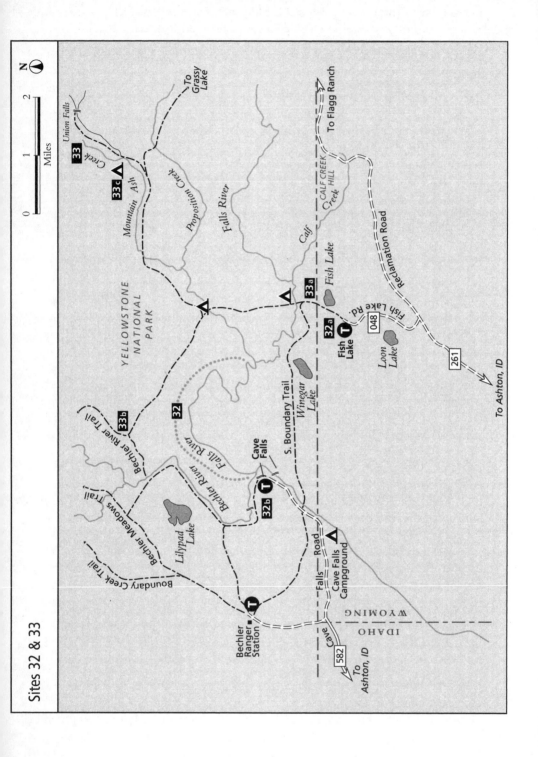

Sites 32 & 33

Cyclone spoons are among the best choices in lures. Wyoming allows the use of bait in the short section outside the park.

Access: There are two logical points of access to this stretch of river.

32a. Fish Lake Road

Access to the reach of river just downstream from the confluence with Mountain Ash Creek is best achieved by taking Reclamation Road to Fish Lake. Drive 29.6 miles west from Ashton on Reclamation Road and turn left (heading north) onto the Fish Lake Road (Forest Road 048). From Flagg Ranch, drive 19.7 miles west on Reclamation Road to Fish Lake Road, on the right. Drive 1.5 miles to the turnaround at the end of Fish Lake Road. A cautionary note here: This road is just barely passable with an ordinary passenger car. Hike about 1 mile to the South Boundary Trail junction. Hike west on the South Boundary Trail for another mile and then strike north down the intermittent outlet of Winegar Lake to the Falls River. An additional 0.5 mile down Falls River brings you to its confluence with Mountain Ash Creek. Fish downstream from there.

32b. Cave Falls Trailhead

Take ID 47 6.3 miles east from Ashton and turn right on the Cave Falls Road (Forest Road 582). Drive east 18.7 miles on Cave Falls Road to the Cave Falls Campground. From Cave Falls Campground, Falls River is closely paralleled by the Cave Falls Road for 1.4 miles to the trailhead. Fishing the first 0.4 mile of Falls River up from the trailhead is straightforward. Early in the season it may prove impossible to cross the mouth of the Bechler River to continue ascending Falls River. I strongly caution you not to take silly chances wading this river if it is dangerously high. Once the water drops to a safe level, fish up past the confluence with the Bechler or consider wading across Falls River to work its south side.

Tributaries: The major tributaries in this section are Mountain Ash Creek (site 33) and the Bechler River (site 34).

33. Mountain Ash Creek

Description: The streamlets that combine in the vicinity of Union Falls to form Mountain Ash Creek come off the southwest quadrant of the Pitchstone Plateau and flow southwesterly to their eventual merging with Falls River. After Bechler River, Mountain Ash Creek is the largest contributor to the flow of Falls River. Union Falls is unusual, as a major tributary joins Mountain Ash Creek literally in the middle of the waterfall. The mile or so below Union Falls is fairly steep and fast, mostly big cobble bottom in a rocky canyon with timbered banks. The lower 6 miles of stream has a much more moderate gradient and finer-grained bottom. The banks remain mostly timbered with small meadow areas here and there. The stream is mostly about 30 feet wide.

In a typical season, Mountain Ash Creek reaches a fishable water level early in July. The key waters are the deep corner pools along the edges of gravel bars, around deadfall, and boulder pocket pools. The stream usually fishes well through the summer and into early fall. It is without fish above Union Falls, and the tributary streams are, for the most part, not worth exploring.

The fish: Mountain Ash Creek and its tributaries are populated by cutthroat and cutbows. In the lower reaches of Mountain Ash Creek, these fish range from 10 to 14 inches, with an occasional larger fish. The farther upstream you go, the smaller the fish.

Flies and lures: Early in the season, start with Pale Morning Duns. Later, try hoppers, small Golden Stones, attractor dries like the Royal Wulff, and then bigger drakes such as the Blue Dun. Effective nymph patterns include the Hare's Ear, Prince, and Pheasant Tail. Spin anglers should try smaller Cyclone spoons, Mepps, Panther Martins, and Triple Teazers.

Access: Three main access routes approach Mountain Ash Creek.

33a. Fish Lake

The shortest route is via Reclamation Road and Fish Lake Road. Drive 29.6 miles east from Ashton, and turn left onto Fish Lake Road. Drive 1.5 miles to the end of the road. Fish Lake Road is a rough dirt two-track, just barely passable with a car. From the end of Fish Lake Road, hike a bit over 2.5 miles to Mountain Ash Creek and fish either upstream or downstream. There is a backcountry campsite here where South Boundary Trail joins the Mountain Ash Creek Trail. While only 19.7 miles from Flagg Ranch, snow on Calf Creek Hill will often necessitate approaching Fish Lake from the Idaho side until mid-July.

33b. Mountain Ash Creek Trail/West

Take Cave Falls Road 17.1 miles east from its junction with ID 47 to the Bechler Ranger Station Road. Turn left onto the ranger station road and drive to the trailheads at the ranger station. Park and take the Bechler Meadows Trail to its junction with Mountain Ash Creek Trail. Cross the Bechler River at Rocky Ford and continue east on the Mountain Ash Creek Trail to its junction with the Fish Lake Trail on the banks of Mountain Ash Creek. This hike is an aggregate distance of about 7 miles. Fish either upstream or down. You can start from the Cave Falls Trailhead, but the walk in from Bechler Ranger Station is 0.3 mile shorter if you use the Bechler Meadows Trailhead.

33c. Mountain Ash Creek Trail/East

From Flagg Ranch, take Reclamation Road 11.3 miles west to Grassy Lake Dam. Turn right to find the trailhead at the base of the dam and park. Hike the Mountain Ash Creek Trail 6 miles, more or less, to Mountain Ash Creek. A campsite on the way to Union Falls is about 0.5 mile upstream, and a second one is downstream at the ford about halfway between the Union Falls Trail junction and the Fish Lake Trail junction. The trail follows the creek between these two points.

Tributaries: Proposition Creek is the largest tributary to Mountain Ash Creek. It is not a major fishery. The upper ends of the tributaries have cascades and falls that prevent fish from entering them.

The Bechler River Drainage

The Bechler River heads along the Continental Divide, crossing the Madison Plateau. It and its tributaries flow south or southwest toward their eventual junction with the Falls River. The 1872 Hayden survey named the river for their cartographer, Gustavus R. Bechler. It is likely that Cave Falls on the Falls River and Bechler Falls on the Bechler River acted as barriers, so that the entire Bechler drainage was fishless in 1872. Reports from as early as 1891, however, indicate that somebody had planted fish in this stream, and at some point, while records only indicate the planting of cutthroat, rainbow were also introduced, resulting in the cutbow hybrid.

34. Bechler River

Description: The Bechler River is formed by the confluence of the Phillips, Gregg, and Ferris Forks at Three Rivers Junction. Of these streams only Gregg Fork has any fish to speak of. From Three Rivers Junction downstream to Colonnade Falls, a stretch of between 4 and 5 miles, the river drops southwesterly through a canyon section with timbered banks and a rocky bottom. The river is typically 25 to 40 feet wide. After pitching over a series of falls, the last being Colonnade Falls, the river flattens considerably. The banks remain timbered and the bottom rocky nearly to the point where the steam acquires Ouzel Creek. At this junction the timber starts to break up, the bottom is more often composed of smaller material, and the stream begins to meander across Bechler Meadows. Only 3 miles as the crow flies, the river must meander close to twice that distance between Ouzel Creek and Boundary Creek. At the junction with Boundary Creek, the timber is back, the bottom is again mostly lava rock and cobble, and the gradient steepens. The river width, due in part to shallowing, doubles to 60 feet, more or less. The Bechler zigs, zags, and pitches over Bechler Falls in the next 3 miles before losing itself in the Falls River.

August and September are the best months for fishing. Late fall is usually not very productive. July is often challenging for the angler due to mosquitoes and other biting insects that often get to you before you find the fish. On opening day the Bechler is usually too high to fish. The river drops steadily through the summer, usually becoming fishable sometime in July. The canyon sections add stoneflies to the mayflies and caddis more common in the meadows. High summer also brings grasshoppers, ants, and beetles to the attention of the fish. In the canyon sections, the pockets around rocks and ledges are the obvious and best places to fish. In the meadows, look for rising fish holding around the outsides and upper corners of the pools. By August the Bechler is crystal clear. Stealth tactics and precision presentations are absolutely required in the meadows.

The fish: Above Colonnade Falls the population is strictly cutthroat, mostly in the 6- to 11-inch class. Below Colonnade Falls the fish show the behavior and appearance of rainbow, though they may be cutbows; only a DNA test can determine this for sure. The Bechler Meadows in particular harbor some much larger fish, up to 22 or even 26 inches, but these fish are not pushovers for the angler. The bulk of the fish remain under 18 inches. Once the river tips over into the faster water below Boundary Creek, the chances for a larger fish drop off again.

Flies and lures: In the rougher water of the canyon sections, an attractor pattern, say a Royal Wulff or Prince nymph in a #12 or #14, works as well as anything. The flat water of the meadows demands sophistication in pattern as well as presentation. Try a Pale Morning Dun, Griffith's Gnat, Jasid, or Green Letort dry; or a Hare's Ear, olive Hare's Ear, Serendipity, or Pheasant Tail nymph wet. The lure angler should start with something fairly small, say a fluorescent red and gold Kamlooper spoon. Other good bets are Mepps and Panther Martins.

Access: There are two practical access points to the Bechler. The Cave Falls Trailhead is best to access the river directly between Cave Falls and a point about 0.5 mile above Bechler Falls. The Bechler Meadows and Bechler River Trails are more useful for all points substantially north of Bechler Falls. Someone looking for a long, multinight backcountry experience should consider entering or leaving Cascade Corner via the Lone Star Trailhead near Old Faithful. The backcountry campsites near the junction of Boundary Creek, Colonnade Falls, and Three Rivers Junction are the most interesting to the angler.

34a. Cave Falls Trailhead

Take the Cave Falls Road 20.1 miles east from its junction with ID 47. Park at the trailhead facility and take the trail up the Falls River. It is 0.4 mile to the confluence with the Bechler River. The trail closely parallels the Bechler for 3.8 miles to Rocky Ford, where the Bechler River Trail crosses the river and heads north. An angler track follows the river, while the main trail cuts west to meet the Bechler Meadows Trail, which originates at the Bechler Ranger Station.

34b. Bechler Ranger Station

Drive 17.1 miles east on the Cave Falls Road from the ID 47 junction. Turn left onto the Bechler Ranger Station Road and drive the 1.5 miles to the ranger station trailheads. Take the Bechler Meadows Trail to access Bechler Meadows and the upper reaches of the Bechler River. It is 3.5 miles to the meadows, 5.5 miles to Bechler Ford, 8.6 miles to Colonnade Falls, and 13 miles to Three Rivers Junction. Even in the meadows the trail is seldom more than 0.5 mile from the river and closely follows it above the Ouzel Creek confluence.

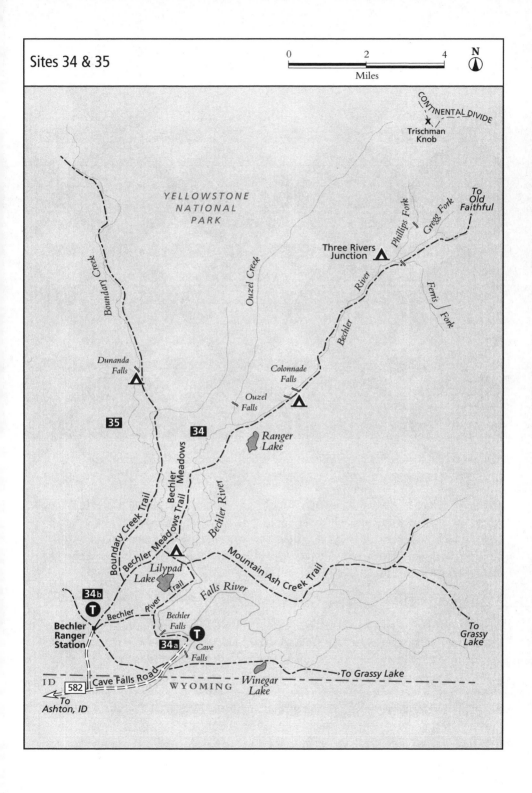

Sites 34 & 35

0   2   4

Miles

N

CONTINENTAL DIVIDE

✕ Trischman
Knob

YELLOWSTONE
NATIONAL
PARK

To
Old
Faithful

Boundary Creek

Ouzel Creek

Three Rivers
Junction ⛺

Phillips Fork

Gregg Fork

Ferris Fork

Bechler River

*Dunanda
Falls* ⛺

35

*Colonnade
Falls* ⛺

*Ouzel
Falls*

34

*Ranger
Lake*

Bechler Meadows Trail

Boundary Creek Trail

Bechler Meadows

Bechler River

⛺

*Lilypad
Lake*

Bechler   River   Trail

Mountain Ash Creek Trail

Falls River

34b
🅣

**Bechler
Ranger
Station**

*Bechler
Falls*

🅣

*Cave
Falls*

34a

To
Grassy
Lake

Bechler   River   Trail

Cave Falls Road

582

ID

WYOMING

*Winegar
Lake*

To Grassy Lake

←To
Ashton, ID

On a timbered section of the Bechler River, the water flows quickly through riffles.

Tributaries: Gregg Fork is the only headwater stream that holds any fish, and they are few and small, not worth the hike. Phillips Fork, Ferris Fork, and most of Ouzel Creek are without fish due to large falls near their lower ends that prevent upstream migration. Boundary Creek (site 35) is fishable in its lower 6 miles below Dunanda Falls. Neither Lilypad nor Ranger Lakes produce fish.

35. Boundary Creek *(see map on page 99)*

Description: Boundary Creek flows south, parallel to the park boundary, to its confluence with the Bechler River. The lower 6 miles or so of the creek, from Dunanda Falls downstream, is fishable. Virtually all of this is in the Bechler Meadows, where the stream has a small-gravel to sand bottom, sometimes overlaying clay patches, and grassy banks. The low gradient means slow, clear, technically challenging water, particularly for the angler who is sight-fishing for the larger fish. Lots of meandering means deeper water on the outside of bends and at the upstream corners of pools; these are the best areas in which to look for fish. Generally too high to fish in June, the season really starts in July and runs well into the fall. The earlier part of the season is plagued by mosquitoes and biting flies.

The fish: Boundary Creek, like the Bechler River, is host primarily to rainbow trout. Some fish appear to be pure cutbow or cutthroat, but without DNA testing there is no way to be sure. Most of the fish run in the 10- to 14-inch range, but there are a few fish in the 18- to 22-inch range.

Flies and lures: In the early season the best choice is the Pale Morning Dun; later, try using brown drakes and then grasshoppers and gray drakes. Good nymphs include Prince, olive Hare's Ear, and Pheasant Tail. The flat water often requires the use of micro-midges such as the Cream Midge, Jasid, Midge Pupa, Brassie, and Serendipity. The spin angler should start with a smaller Vibrax, Cyclone, Panther Martin, or Mepps.

Access: The best access for Boundary Creek is from the Bechler Ranger Station. Drive 17.1 miles west on Cave Falls Road from its junction with ID 47. Turn left onto the Bechler Ranger Station Road and drive 1.5 miles to the trailheads at the ranger station. Take the Bechler Meadows Trail 1.6 miles to its junction with the Boundary Creek Trail. Stick with the Bechler Meadows trail another 1.9 miles to the point where it crosses the lower end of Boundary Creek. Fish either upstream or down. Alternatively, take the Boundary Creek Trail about the same distance to parallel the creek toward Dunanda Falls. Fish in either direction from any starting point along this route. Dunanda Falls, 8.2 miles from Bechler Ranger Station, is as far upstream as it makes any sense to go. Backcountry campsites are near the junction of Boundary Creek with Bechler River, near the middle of the Bechler Meadows section of the creek, and near Dunanda Falls.

Tributaries: The only tributary that amounts to anything comes off the southwest corner of the escarpment between Ouzel Creek and Boundary Creek. It is fishable up to its canyon, where its steep gradient defeats further penetration by fish.

The Snake River Drainage

The Snake River begins as a series of springs and rivulets that come together under the crest of the Continental Divide, due south of Yellowstone Lake and just barely within the park. A multitude of other creeks, both in and south of the park, start in the same general Two Ocean Plateau area. Flowing west and northwest, these streams gradually come together across the south end of Yellowstone National Park. Upon picking up the Heart River, the Snake takes an abrupt jog and heads southwest. A second major tributary, the Lewis River, joins the Snake just above its exit from Yellowstone at the South Entrance. Now flowing south, the river loses itself in Jackson Lake.

Besides the Heart and Lewis Rivers, this drainage includes three of the four largest lakes in the park and a number of other tributary streams. The name Snake appears to have been derived from the sign-language symbol for the Shoshone Tribe of Native Americans who inhabited the region. At least part of the river had been named Snake by 1812.

Mileage points: The South Entrance Road becomes the John D. Rockefeller Parkway through Grand Teton National Park and reverts to being U.S. Highway 89 as it exits. For the directions in this section, mileage is measured from West Thumb to the north and Moran Junction, just outside the North Entrance to Grand Teton National Park, to the south. Moran Junction is 27.6 miles north of the Wyoming Visitor Center, on the north edge of Jackson, Wyoming. Mileage on Reclamation Road is measured from Flagg Ranch. Mileage on the Grand Loop Road is measured between West Thumb and Old Faithful.

36. Snake River, Headwaters to Heart River

Description: In this roughly 15-mile reach, the Snake River is formed from the joining of many sources along the Continental Divide. Outright waterfalls are rare, but shedding 3,000 feet between snowbank and the Heart River confluence means the river has an average drop of 200 feet per mile. This is steep. The upper ends of many source streams are above timberline. Along most of the stream's course is a mix of meadow and patchy timber. The bottom of the stream is generally medium to large cobble, becoming small to medium cobble in the lower section. To my mind, the most interesting parts of this section are two meadows, Fox Park and the confluence of the Snake and Heart Rivers. Fox Park lies 10 miles above the latter and includes the confluence of the Snake with Plateau Creek. Much of this area was burned over during the fires of 1988.

The annual spring snowmelt keeps these streams in flood well into July. They fish well from mid-July into September, but fishing is poor thereafter. The edges of

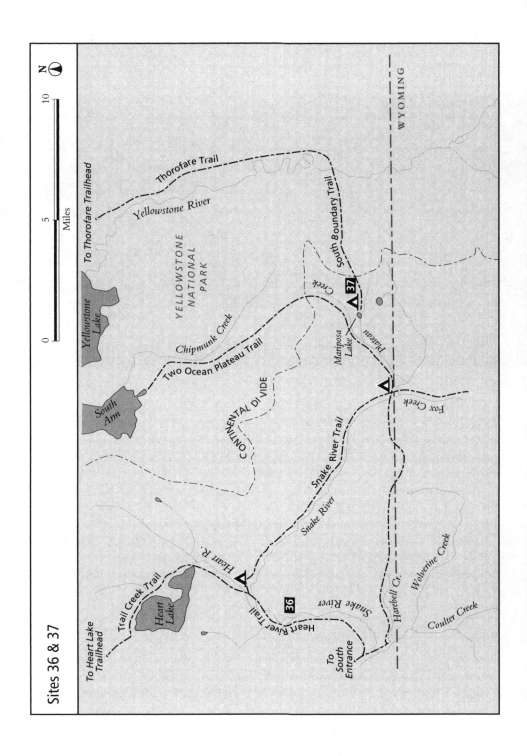

Sites 36 & 37

An angler's path along the bank of the Snake River.

the deeper water at the heads of riffle corners and the pockets around the many boulders are the key waters for the angler to target. The high gradient means the upper ends of the river and most of its tributaries will be either fishless or populated only by tiny fish.

That portion of the river and its tributaries that lies outside Yellowstone National Park closes to fishing on November 1. Be sure to check the Wyoming fishing regulations for Fox Park and nearby waters. The upper, eastern, end of this reach is in the Two Ocean bear-management area. Off-trail travel is prohibited May 15 through July 14 and again after August 22. Between July 15 and August 21, a permit that is obtained from the South Entrance Ranger Station is required for off-trail travel.

The fish: Virtually all of the gamefish in this section are cutthroat. They run 6 to 12 inches. The farther up the river you get, the smaller the fish are.

Flies and lures: Early in the season, Stimulators and Royal Coachman Trudes are your best bet. As high summer kicks in, keep the Trudes and add hoppers, such as a Madam X, to the mix. Use basic nymph patterns such as the bead-head Prince and Hare's Ear. The spin angler should try the smaller sizes of Cyclone and Kamlooper spoons, Mepps, and Panther Martin.

Special equipment: This section of river is 15 to 30 miles away from the road. Serious overnight backpacking equipment is required, as are the appropriate back-country permits.

Access: As a practical matter, the only convenient access to this reach of river is the long overland trek from the South Boundary Trailhead at Yellowstone National Park's South Entrance. The park has not provided much in the way of a trailhead facility. Drive 22 miles south from West Thumb or 28 miles north from Moran Junction and park in the large pullout just outside the South Entrance Station. A trail to the upper ford drops down to the river right behind the station. An alternative ford exists 0.5 mile downstream, near the South Entrance Boat Launch. The South Entrance Picnic Area does not have a designated long-term parking area that I can find, even though it looks like it ought to be the place to start. Alternative points of access, requiring even longer hikes, are the Heart Lake and Thorofare Trails. There is a slightly shorter route from a trailhead on Pacific Creek, outside the area covered by this book.

Tributaries: Named tributaries to the Snake River in this reach include Plateau, Fox, Crooked, and Sickle Creeks. None of them drain a large area, and none provide spectacular fishing. Mariposa Lake (site 37), at one of the heads of Plateau Creek, is another story.

37. Mariposa Lake *(see map on page 103)*

Description: Mariposa Lake is a small and relatively shallow lake. At 9,000 feet, it is also very high, though not quite above timberline. The shore is open, with high timbered slopes all around, except to the southwest, where a fork of Plateau Creek runs through the lake. The bottom is mostly covered by plant growth. Little of the lake is more than 6 feet deep, leading to speculation that freeze-out could be a problem. However, there is no evidence that freeze-out has happened anytime in the last thirty years.

At this altitude the lake is likely to be unapproachable until well into July. Most fishing occurs in July and into August. Colder fall weather puts a skin of ice on the lake by early October. The live stream running through the lake not only provides spawning habitat, it protects against freeze-out. The inlet and outlet areas are the first places to look for fish. Mariposa Lake is in the middle of the Two Ocean bear-management area, so off-trail travel is restricted throughout the season.

The fish: The fish of Mariposa Lake all appear to be cutthroat trout. The average size runs 12 to 14 inches, with some up to 19 inches. The catch-and-release rule appears to have greatly benefited this lake. With its small size and small total population, even one angler killing a couple of large fish would make a real dent in the stock.

Flies and lures: Absent an obvious hatch, my first fly choice here is a Tan Scud in about a #12. Other possibilities are tan and olive Woolly Worms, Woolly Buggers, Skinny Buggers, Hare's Ears, and Prince nymphs. In dries I would want an Adams and orange Stimulator, both in size 12. If fishing with spinning tackle, start with a

Spin-a-Lure. Other good lures here include Mepps and Vibrax spinners and Kamlooper spoons.

Access: The shortest overland route to Mariposa Lake, more than 15 miles, is actually via a trailhead on Pacific Creek far to the south of our discussion area. Consult the Bridger-Teton National Forest trail map. The only route that stays within our area is the South Boundary Trail (see map of Snake River drainage on page 103). Drive north 28 miles from Moran Junction or south 22 miles from West Thumb to the South Entrance. Take the South Boundary Trail east up the Snake River. Follow the South Boundary Trail up Harebell Creek, down to Fox Park, and then up Plateau Creek. The trail runs up along the Mariposa Lake outlet stream and on over the Continental Divide to join the Thorofare Trail up the Yellowstone River.

There are backcountry campsites on Mariposa Lake. This route is about 23 miles long, which beats the 38 miles via the Thorofare Trail. The Two Ocean Plateau Trail running south from the South Arm of Yellowstone Lake is a third alternative. This one only requires 11 or so miles of hiking, but also requires a means to get across Yellowstone Lake.

38. Heart Lake

Description: Sometimes you think you know something, but you're wrong. Thanks to Lee Whittlesey's wonderful book, *Yellowstone Place Names,* I discovered I was wrong to connect the name of Heart Lake to its obvious shape on the map. It turns out that the lake is actually named for Hart Hunney, who hunted the area in the 1840s. The shape of the lake mistakenly inspired the rearranged spelling, and so it remains to this day.

At roughly 3 miles by 2 miles, Heart Lake is the fourth largest lake in Yellowstone National Park. A wilderness lake, the nearest road is more than 7 miles away, as the trail winds. The west shore leads up to Mount Sheridan. The hills flanking the other shores are more moderate. The northern shoreline is mostly open and sometimes marshy, with the timber set back 50 to 100 yards. Timber comes down to the high waterline elsewhere around the lake. The 1988 fires burned the northwest corner of the lake and blew by the southeastern outlet end. A fire in the late 1970s had previously burned much of the drainage to the northeast.

Heart Lake lies at 7,450 feet, a bit lower than the other large lakes of Yellowstone National Park. Yet it still is likely to be covered by ice until early June. Equally important, the access trail tops 8,100 feet and will certainly be snow-gorged in spots until nearly mid-June. In any case, the Bear Management Plan holds the Heart Lake area closed until July 1. The fishing is best in early July. The central part of the summer is likely to be pretty dull, but activity picks up again in October. Key water for the angler is along the western shore and around the inlets and outlet.

The fish: The important game fish in Heart Lake are cutthroat and lake trout. Nongame species include several native suckers and chubs. The 2006 revision of Yellowstone Park's fishing regulations provides for catch-and-release for the

With snow lingering above it, Heart Lake beckons to be fished.
NATIONAL PARK SERVICE PHOTO

cutthroat and unlimited kill for the lake trout. Both the cutthroat and lake trout average around 19 inches in length.

Flies and lures: My first choice is a brown Woolly Bugger. I would be sure to have a few large Adams and some Prince nymphs. Skinny Buggers, Marabou Muddlers (both black and white), Double Renegades, Carey Specials, and plain olive Woolly Worms would also be in my box. Spin fishers should have Spin-a-Lures, Krocodiles, and larger sized Mepps in their gear.

Access: There are only two even remotely practical routes to Heart Lake. Even the shortest route makes for a really tough day trip. Several backcountry campsites are located around the lake.

38a. Heart Lake Trailhead

The Heart Lake Trailhead is located 50 feet off the east side of the South Entrance Road, 7.5 miles south of West Thumb. If coming from the south, drive north 42.5 miles from Moran Junction; the trailhead is on your right and is marked by a sign. The trailhead has a pit toilet. The sign says it is 7.4 miles to Heart Lake. What the sign does not say is that the hike includes a climb of 400 vertical feet up the flank of Factory Hill and a descent of 650 feet back down the other side. The trail approaches Heart Lake

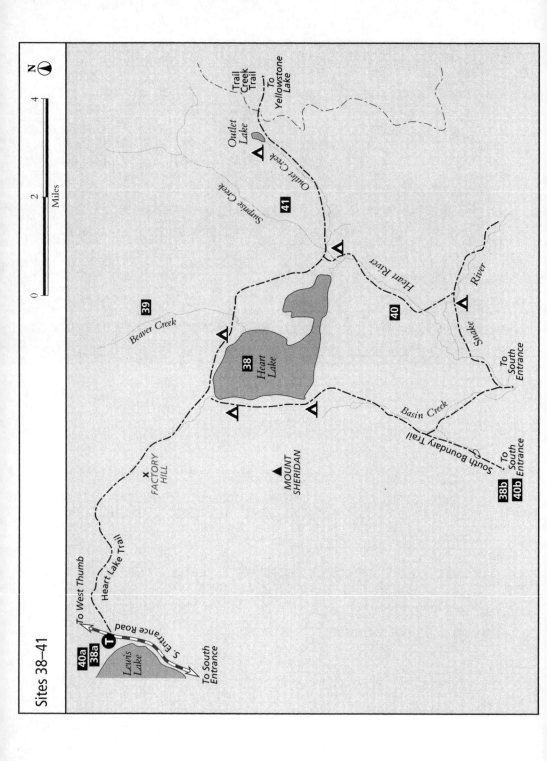

Sites 38–41

via Witch Creek and then splits. One branch goes along the north shore of the lake to connect with the trail up the Heart River and over to Yellowstone Lake. The other branch goes down the west shore of the lake and cuts south to join the South Boundary Trail on the Snake River.

38b. South Boundary Trailhead

Take the South Entrance Road 22 miles from West Thumb to the South Entrance. The South Entrance is 28 miles north of Moran Junction. Take the South Boundary Trail up the Snake River to its junction with the Heart Lake Trail, between Snake Hot Springs and the mouth of Red Creek. Take the Heart Lake Trail north up Red Creek and through the Basin Creek valley to Heart Lake. This route is more than 12 miles long and, since it starts low, involves a lot of climbing. Its only advantage is that it does not get as high, topping out at 7,600 feet, and may therefore be clear of snow a few days earlier than the Heart Lake Trailhead side. Use of this route depends on the Snake River being low enough to ford.

Tributaries: Beaver Creek (site 39) and Witch Creek are the only really large tributaries to Heart Lake. Witch Creek is heavily influenced by thermal activity in the Heart Lake Geyser Basin, which it drains. The other tributaries are either small or very steep or both, rendering them of little interest to the angler.

39. Beaver Creek

Description: Beaver Creek flows somewhat south of southeast, picking up streamlets coming off the Continental Divide between Yellowstone Lake and Heart Lake. The main stem of the stream has a shallow gradient and a fairly fine-grained bottom with a lot of pea gravel. The banks are a mix of large marshy areas, meadows, and timber, most of which was burned during the 1988 fires. The creek joins Heart Lake along its northern shore, 1.5 miles east of the northwest corner of the lake. The Bear Management Plan keeps the area closed until July 1. In any case, snow usually prevents earlier access. Fishing is best in the early summer. Look for specific fish holding around the edges of deeper water.

The fish: I doubt if there are large numbers of resident fish in Beaver Creek. It is certainly used as a spawning stream by the Heart Lake cutthroat, but evidence suggests that they get in and get their business done under the high water in May, before either the season or the trail opens. By summer a few trout are still hanging around, most in the 15- to 20-inch range, plus a lot of suckers and chubs.

Flies and lures: Given that the best way to catch fish in Beaver Creek is by sighting them first, my favorite method is to trail a small attractor nymph, usually a bead-head Prince, behind an attractor dry fly, which in this case would probably be a Turck's Tarantula. Spin anglers should stick to the smaller sizes of Mepps, Spin-a-Lure, Li'l Jake's, or Cyclone spoon.

Access: The best route to Beaver Creek is from the Heart Lake Trailhead. Take the South Entrance Road 7.5 miles south from West Thumb or 42.5 miles north from

Moran Junction to the trailhead. It is located 50 feet off the east side of the highway and is marked by a sign. Take the Heart Lake Trail 7.4 miles to the northwest corner of Heart Lake and then hold to the left fork around the north shore of the lake for an additional 1.5 miles to Beaver Creek. Fish upstream. This is not a practical day hike. Get a permit and plan a stay at one of the campsites on Heart Lake.

40. Heart River (see map on page 108)

Description: The Heart River manages to be three quite different rivers in its mere 4 miles of existence. It exits Heart Lake on a southeasterly course and with a modest gradient. The bottom is mostly small- to medium-size cobble. The banks are fairly open. Not long after being joined by Outlet Creek, the river hooks a right-angle turn to a southwesterly course. The next 2 miles are in a quasi-canyon with timber, burnt in 1988, coming down to the edge of the stream. The gradient is steeper, and the bed is mostly large cobble or boulders here. The last 1.5 miles flatten out again, and the river meanders across a meadow to join with the Snake River. In this section the bed is mostly gravel and small cobble, and the banks are grassy.

By the time you can get over the snowbanks and into the Heart River, the odds are good it will have gotten over its annual spring flood and be fishable. In any case, the Bear Management Plan keeps the area closed until July 1. Fishing is best in July and August. The steep section can be counted upon to produce smaller fish than either of the flatter sections. The structural features in the upper section are the holes around stranded logs and gravel bars. In the lower section, look to the edges of the deeper water against the grass banks and at the heads of the corner riffles.

The fish: For practical purposes, the fish in the Heart River are cutthroat trout and whitefish. Brown trout have been known to make it up as far as the lower part of the river, and a lake trout could slip down from the lake, but both are rare occurrences. The fish typically run in the 10- to 14-inch range.

Flies and lures: Unless I saw something else going on, my first choice would be to start with a Royal Coachman Trude. It is a good idea to have some big orange Stimulators and small yellow Stimulators for the stoneflies that are likely to hatch in July. Hoppers and Turck's Tarantulas are a good idea for the meadow section in August. My nymph box would contain bead-head Princes, Hare's Ears, Bitch Creeks, and olive Woolly Worms. Woolly Buggers and Muddler Minnows are good bets in streamers. If spinning, cast Li'l Jake's, Mepps, Cyclones, and Panther Martins.

Access: Heart Lake Trail, South Boundary Trail.

40a. Heart Lake Trailhead

The shortest route to all but the last mile of Heart River starts at the Heart Lake Trailhead. Driving 7.5 miles south from West Thumb or 42.5 miles north from Moran Junction brings you to the signed trailhead. Take the Heart Lake Trail 7.4 miles to Heart Lake. Take the branch around the north side of the lake to its junction with the

Trail Creek Trail coming down Outlet Creek. Fish downstream. This is a total distance of 11.5 miles, plus however far downriver you get.

40b. South Boundary Trailhead

Take the South Entrance Road 22 miles south from West Thumb to the South Entrance and then take the South Boundary Trail up the Snake River. If coming from the south, go north from Moran Junction 28 miles to the South Entrance. Stay with the South Boundary Trail for 2 miles beyond Snake Hot Springs and then cross the Snake on the Snake River Trail. Stick with the Snake River Trail until it crosses the Snake again above Basin Creek. At this point you are only a few hundred yards below the mouth of the Heart River. Hike up the Snake until you reach the Heart and then fish upriver. This route covers 14 miles, plus however far up the river you fish. The trail will be free of snow by July 1, but the Snake River, which you have to cross twice, may not be fordable until after the middle of July.

Tributaries: The Outlet Creek drainage (site 41) is the only really significant tributary stream to the Heart River.

41. Outlet Creek Drainage (see map on page 108)

Description: The Outlet Creek system consists of Outlet and Surprise Creeks and Outlet Lake. All are in an area that was heavily burned by the 1988 fires. The Surprise Creek drainage is fairly steep. The bed is rocky and debris-laden. Outlet Creek has a much flatter gradient. Its lower 0.5 mile and a second 1-mile-long meadow, a mile upstream, escaped the intense burn of the fires. Outlet Lake is the source of Outlet Creek. It lies under the scarp of Chicken Ridge, which carries the Continental Divide in this area. The name derives from the probable discharge of Yellowstone Lake southward through this gap at some point during the last ice age. July and August are the best times to fish this system.

The fish: Cutthroat trout inhabit the Outlet Creek system. They are generally neither numerous nor large.

Flies and lures: Start with a Royal Coachman Trude. Other useful flies include Prince and Hare's Ear nymphs, hopper patterns, and beetles. Lures to use are Li'l Jake's or Mepps spinners.

Access: Use the Heart Lake Trailhead to reach the Outlet Creek drainage. Drive north from Moran Junction 42.5 miles to find the trailhead 50 feet off the highway on the right. If coming from the north, take the South Entrance Road 7.5 miles from West Thumb; the trailhead is on the left. Take the Heart Lake Trail 7.4 miles to Heart Lake, and follow the branch along the north shore for an additional 4.1 miles to the Trail Creek Trail junction. Fish down Outlet Creek or up either Surprise or Outlet Creeks. The Trail Creek Trail goes on up Outlet Creek and over to Yellowstone Lake's South Arm. There are backcountry campsites near the junction of Surprise with Outlet Creek and at Outlet Lake. The Outlet Creek drainage is out of day-hike range.

Tributaries: Surprise Creek is the only substantial tributary to the Outlet Creek system. The others are all trivial and of no particular interest to the angler.

42. Snake River, Heart River to Lewis River

Description: In this 15-mile stretch of river, the Snake first cuts almost due south from its confluence with the Heart River, through 4 miles of meadow. After dropping through a 2-mile canyon, the river flattens out again in a long narrow meadow valley. It turns northwest between its confluence with Wolverine and Red Creeks. After Red Creek it returns to a southwesterly course to be joined by the Lewis River, 0.75 mile upstream from the South Entrance Station. The Snake only drops 400 feet throughout the length of this section. The bed is mostly medium-size cobble, and numerous gravel bars are the main structural feature. Timber seldom encroaches all the way down to the water's edge, so what is not gravel is grass. The fires of 1988 burned the area around the canyon.

Originating in high country along the Continental Divide, the Snake carries heavy snowmelt in the spring. The water drops into fishable condition sometime in mid-July. The river fishes well from late July into August. September and October are less consistent, though in the latter month, some browns run up out of Jackson Lake to spawn. Riffle corners at the heads of pools and the deeper channels along the outside banks are the best waters.

The fish: The resident fish in this reach are primarily cutthroat and whitefish. There are some browns up as far as Red Creek, and there is an outside chance the angler will encounter a fugitive lake trout from Heart, Lewis, or Jackson Lakes. Typical fish run in the 10- to 14-inch range; a few fish may reach 18 inches. Any lake trout here are likely to be skinny and long. Migrating browns usually run 15 to 20 inches, but most of their spawning activity takes place below this section.

Flies and lures: Start with a Turck's Tarantula or Royal Coachman Trude. Hopper patterns or Stimulators are a good bet during high summer. Gray drakes give way to little Blue-Winged Olives in the fall. Good wet fly choices include the Prince, rubber-legged Hare's Ear, and Golden Stone nymphs. Marabou Muddlers in white and black are the top streamer choices. The spin angler should start with a Cyclone, Kamlooper, Stream-a-Lure, or Mepps.

Access: Take the South Entrance Road south 22 miles from West Thumb to South Entrance Station. Park, walk 0.75 mile up the Lewis River, and ford it. Continue to fish upstream. Alternatively, park and use the South Boundary Trailhead at the South Entrance Station; ford the Snake and work up the south bank. Drive 28 miles north from Moran Junction to reach the South Entrance Station. The best fishing is found upstream in the 2 miles between Red Creek and Snake Hot Springs. Hike 3 miles up the South Boundary Trail and then start fishing upriver. The spring high water lasts into July, so do not push your luck trying to ford a flood. Later in the season the river will be fordable at most bends. There are backcountry campsites at the upper end of this section. Red Creek marks the limit for a practical day trip.

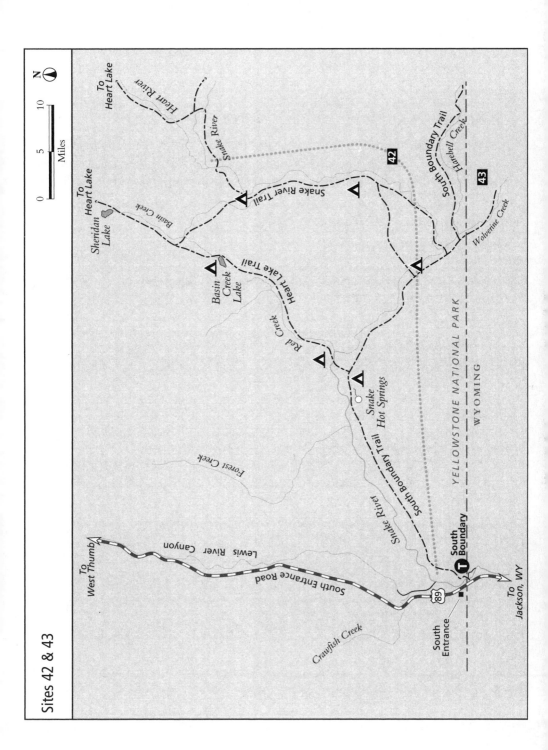

Sites 42 & 43

Take the Snake River Trail northeast from its junction with the South Boundary Trail, about 8 miles upriver. It bypasses the canyon section, which isn't very good fishing anyway, picking up the river again for the remainder of the run to the mouth of the Heart River. There is another campsite near the junction of South Boundary and Snake River Trails. Except for the cutoff, the trail is seldom as much as 0.5 mile from the river. A second trail follows the river through the canyon, starting from the mouth of Wolverine Creek, 10.5 miles up from the South Entrance.

Tributaries: Heart River (site 40) is the major tributary in this reach. Wolverine Creek (site 43), mistakenly thought by some to be the main fork of the Snake, and Basin Creek are the most fishable of the tributaries. Neither Red nor Forest Creeks amount to much for the angler.

43. Wolverine Creek Drainage *(see map on page 113)*

Description: Wolverine Creek was once incorrectly thought to be the main stem of the Snake River. Not clear at first glance was its relatively short, multi branched complex of tributaries, most of them outside Yellowstone National Park. The maps I consulted were unclear as to whether Wolverine Creek or Coulter Creek was the main stream. Most of the fishable water appears to be in Wolverine Creek, and that is what concerns us here. All but about 1,200 yards of the stream are outside the park. The lower 6 miles of Wolverine Creek provide the best fishing. It drops slowly over wide gravel beds contained within a narrow meadow. Most of the surrounding timber was burned in 1988.

Harebell Creek joins Wolverine from the east, 0.5 mile upstream from the Snake River. Most of Harebell Creek has a fairly steep gradient in a narrow valley or canyon. The bottom is mostly cobble. The banks were timbered, but most of it burned in 1988. Coulter Creek joins Wolverine from the south, 1 mile above Harebell Creek. Like Harebell, it flows through a heavily burned, narrow valley. All of these streams run very high and are unfishable until mid-July. They are most productive between then and mid-September.

The fish: Most of the fish in the Wolverine Creek system are cutthroat trout, but it is physically possible for browns, lakers, and whitefish to be found in these streams. The fish range from 6 to 13 inches, most being about 10 inches in length.

Flies and lures: Start with an attractor hopper pattern such as a Turck's Tarantula or Madam X. Other recommended patterns include the Royal Coachman Trude, bead-head Prince, and rubber-legged Hare's Ear. Spin anglers will find the small size of the streams frustrating. Keep lures small; Triple Teazers, Cyclones, and Panther Martins are your best bets.

Access: Drive to the park's South Entrance; it is 22 miles south of West Thumb or 28 miles north of Moran Junction on the South Entrance Road. Take the South Boundary Trail east 10.5 miles to the Snake River Trail junction, only a few yards above the confluence of Wolverine Creek with the Snake River. The junction with

Harebell Creek is 0.5 mile farther; the South Boundary Trail heads east up Harebell Creek, and another trail goes southeast up Wolverine. Fish either creek.

44. Snake River, Lewis River to Jackson Lake
(see map on page 117)

Description: With the addition of the Lewis River, the Snake becomes a major river, winding south to join Jackson Lake right on the Grand Teton National Park boundary. Even in low-water periods, the channel occupies 40 to 60 feet of a bed often twice that wide. The bed is mostly gravel bars between willow-laden banks. Only in the 2 miles of the stream from the South Entrance boat launch through a whitewater section called Flagg Canyon does timber come down to the edge of the river. The lowest 2 miles are a willow-swamp delta with a fine-grained bottom. The best water is the riffle corners at the heads of the bars. The channel may be obstructed by logjams. Fishing in the delta area is poor.

Swollen with immense spring floods, the Snake becomes fishable sometime in July. Late July and August are usually quite steady here, then the fishing tapers off. Fishing slows but does not quite quit in the fall, and in October brown trout move out of Jackson Lake to spawn in this section of the river. This is a small run because browns do not represent a major portion of the lake's fish population. This fact makes the run easy to miss entirely. Lakers and cutthroat also move into the river behind the browns. Most of this reach of river is outside Yellowstone, so it is subject to Wyoming regulations. The river is open from April 1 through October 31.

The fish: Cutthroat and whitefish are the dominant resident fish. A few browns, lake trout, and even a stray brookie are possible but much less likely. Most fish run in the 10- to 14-inch range. Lake trout are commonly in poor condition—long and skinny—as they do not usually fare well in rivers. There is no obvious limit to the maximum size a spawning brown might reach, though most are in the 15- to 20-inch range.

Flies and lures: The Snake has a modest July stonefly hatch, so start with a Stimulator. Stonefly nymphs are always in order. Later in the season use attractors such as a Royal Wulff or Turck's Tarantula and hopper patterns dry and a bead-head Prince wet. For browns, use a Woolly Bugger, Zonker, or Marabou Muddler. Start spin fishing with a Spin-a-Lure. Other good choices are Rooster Tails, Kamloopers, and Mepps.

Special equipment: Hand-propelled craft are allowed on the section of river below the South Entrance boat launch. A nonoperating motor can be carried to use on Jackson Lake. A Grand Teton National Park boat permit is required.

Access: Steamboat Mountain adds to the separation between John D. Rockefeller Parkway and the river as it nears Jackson Lake. This obstruction and the wide willow flats makes a boat potentially useful; however, the lack of a well-located boat ramp on Jackson Lake makes a boat less attractive.

44a. South Entrance

Drive 22 miles south from West Thumb or 28 miles north from Moran Junction to Yellowstone's South Entrance. Park at the picnic area just inside the gate and fish either upstream or downstream. At no point in this entire stretch from the South Entrance to the bridge at Flagg Ranch is the river more than 0.5 mile from the highway.

44b. South Entrance Boat Launch

Take the South Entrance Road 22.5 miles south from West Thumb and turn left into the South Entrance boat launch. Regulations require that craft launched here be propelled by hand. The South Entrance boat launch is 27.5 miles north of Moran Junction. An island complex just upstream from the boat launch provides an alternative ford to cross the river and fish either upstream or down. A Grand Teton National Park boat permit is required.

44c. Grassy Lake (Reclamation) Road

Drive 25.8 miles north from Moran Junction to the Flagg Ranch main entrance. Flagg Ranch is 24.2 miles south of West Thumb. Turn west into Flagg Ranch and then immediately turn right onto Grassy Lake Road, which becomes Reclamation Road. Grassy Lake Road provides excellent access to an additional 2 miles of river beginning at Camp #1 on the left, 1.5 miles west of Flagg Ranch. Camp #4, where Grassy Lake Road turns west away from the river, is 3.1 miles west of Flagg Ranch. Park at any of the several campsites and pullouts along here and fish in either direction. There are no launch ramps at any of these sites, though a boat could be carried to the river. The road is closed to vehicular traffic by Grand Teton National Park's Bear Management Plan between April 1 and May 31.

44d. Snake River Bridge

The highway crosses the Snake River 24.7 miles south of West Thumb. The boat launch is on the north bank and west side of the bridge. Take US 89 north for 25.3 miles from Moran Junction and turn left immediately after crossing the bridge. From the bridge, fish either upstream or down on either side of the river. From this point south to Jackson Lake, the highway is at least a tough mile away from the river. The best water is more easily accessed from Grassy Lake Road.

44e. Lizard Creek Campground

The northernmost access to Jackson Lake is the Lizard Creek Campground. Lizard Creek is open from about mid-June, depending on snow conditions, to the end of the first week of September. Drive north 18 miles from Moran Junction or south 32 miles from West Thumb and turn west onto the Lizard Creek Road. The prospect of floating the upper Snake River is not good: There is no boat ramp or any practical way for trailers to approach the lake. Lizard Creek is 3 miles from the head of the lake, so without a motor it is a really long row or paddle, and a show-stopper for a raft bucking a headwind. Occurring with depressing frequency, headwinds

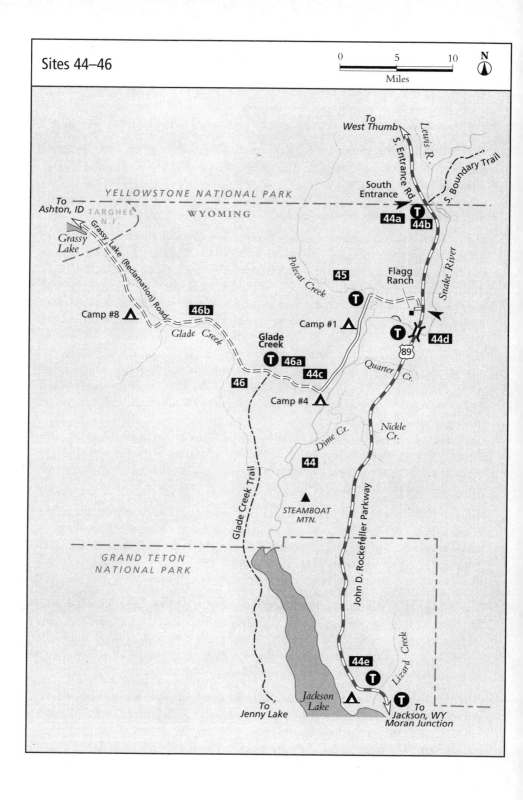

Sites 44–46

0   5   10
Miles

N

To
West Thumb

YELLOWSTONE NATIONAL PARK

To
Ashton, ID   TARGHEE
N.F.

WYOMING

South
Entrance

S. Entrance Rd.

Lewis R.

S. Boundary Trail

44a   T
T   **44b**

Grassy
Lake

Grassy Lake (Reclamation) Road

Snake River

Camp #8

Glade Creek

Polecat Creek

45

T

Flagg
Ranch

Camp #1

46b

T   **46a**
Glade
Creek

44c

T
44d
89

Quarter Cr.

46

Camp #4

Nickle
Cr.

Dime Cr.

44

Glade Creek Trail

STEAMBOAT
MTN.

GRAND TETON
NATIONAL PARK

John D. Rockefeller Parkway

Lizard Creek

44e

T

Jackson
Lake

To
Jenny Lake

T

To
Jackson, WY
Moran Junction

usually kick up at about 1:00 P.M. and can be extremely dangerous to an unwitting boater. The early campground closing date creates another problem for fall floats. Fortunately, the highway meets the lakeshore at a pullout a little less than a mile south of Lizard Creek, 17.2 miles north of Moran Junction. Canoes and other small craft can be manhandled across the beach at this point. The nearest formal boat ramp is another 7 miles, more or less, down the lake at Leeks Marina.

Tributaries: The major tributaries to the Snake River in this section are the Lewis River (site 53), Polecat Creek (site 45), and Glade Creek (site 46). The other tributaries are small change.

45. Polecat Creek (see map on page 117)

Description: Polecat Creek starts along the edge of the bench line defining the Snake River Valley a couple of miles northwest of the South Entrance. It flows more or less south along the lower edge of the bench for 4 miles, joining the Snake 1 mile west of Flagg Ranch. In physical character this stream resembles a spring creek with a very low gradient, clear water, and weed beds. Frequent mud holes can trap an unwary wader. The most fishable part of the creek is the section from the big bend just above the Grassy Lake Road Bridge upstream to about the Yellowstone National Park boundary. Scattered timber along the bank contrasts with what is mostly open meadow. Presentation is critical to successful angling in this sort of water. The channel is fairly wide, 25 to 40 feet, and shallow for the actual volume of water carried, which argues for sight fishing with dry flies and small nymphs rather than spin fishing.

Polecat Creek clears early in the spring runoff season due to its short and low drainage basin. Most of the creek is outside Yellowstone National Park. The Wyoming season opens May 21 and runs through October 31. The stream provides steady, if difficult, fishing opportunities throughout the season.

The fish: The bulk of the fish in Polecat Creek are brown and cutthroat trout. The browns are concentrated in the areas around and upstream from the thermal inflow of the hot springs, which are just upstream from the Grassy Lake Road Bridge. The fish average 10 to 14 inches. The farther upstream you go, the smaller the fish become, and the cutthroat portion of the population increases.

Flies and lures: Pale Morning Duns, Blue-Winged Olives, Pheasant Tails, and Hare's Ear nymphs must be in your box. I also recommend Letort Hoppers, Partridge Caddis, ants, and beetles. With the exception of the hopper, these flies should all be in #18. Only ultralight spin lures are likely to be useful, so try Triple Teazers, #0 Mepps, and #2 Panther Martins on two- or four-pound test line.

Access: Take the Grassy Lake (Reclamation) Road 1.1 miles west from Flagg Ranch to Polecat Creek. There is a parking area on the right immediately across the bridge. Hike upstream on the west side for 100 yards to clear the swamp area at the bridge, and then start fishing upstream. The road is closed by the Bear Management Plan for the months of April and May. Snowpack may limit use of the road well into June.

Beaver ponds are common along Glade Creek.

46. Glade Creek *(see map on page 117)*

Description: Glade Creek has its beginnings in a mountain marsh just east of Grassy Lake. It flows southeast for 6 miles to join the Snake River, 1.5 miles above Jackson Lake. It is more of a swamp than a creek until it passes under a bridge 7.1 miles west of Flagg Ranch on the Reclamation Road. The next 1.4 miles is the most interesting part of the creek as it wanders from beaver pond to beaver pond before tipping over into a swift descent through a short canyon and then across another meadow area, finishing with a final drop to the Snake River Valley. The remaining 0.5 mile joins the willow-crowded floodplain of the Snake. Fishing is best in July and August. Wyoming opens Glade Creek to fishing May 21 and closes it October 31.

The fish: The lower end of Glade Creek can have any of the fish—whitefish, cutthroat, brown, brook, or lake trout—resident in the Snake River. Above the canyon sections the fish are cutthroat. The fish in the steeper sections are generally under 10 inches in length, but the meadow fish reach 14 inches.

Flies and lures: In the steeper sections an attractor such as a Royal Humpy is all that is necessary. The meadow fish are likely to be a lot pickier. Absent a hatch, start with a bead-head Prince. Other productive patterns include the Hare's Ear, Skinny Bugger, Woolly Bugger, Letort Hopper, and Parachute Adams. Cast smaller Panther Martins, Buoyant Spoons, Mepps, or Kamloopers if using spin tackle. Bait may be used in Glade Creek.

Access: The best access to Glade Creek is provided by the Grassy Lake (Reclamation) Road. The Bear Management Plan closes Grassy Lake Road to vehicular traffic during April and May. Access after June 1 depends on the snowpack.

46a. Glade Creek Trailhead

Take Grassy Lake (Reclamation) Road 4.6 miles west from Flagg Ranch to the trailhead. The pullout on the south side of the road is signed. Hike 1 mile down the trail to the lower end of the lower meadow section, then fish upstream. The trail continues down the creek to the edge of the Snake River Valley, which it then follows to tie in with the Grand Teton National Park trail network.

46b. Glade Creek Beaver Ponds

Drive 5.7 miles west on Grassy Lake (Reclamation) Road to the lower end of the beaver pond section. The road runs along the edge of the ponded meadows for the next 1.4 miles before crossing the creek on a one-lane bridge. Three campsites are strung along this reach, ending with Camp #8 0.5 mile past the bridge. Each campsite is provided with a pit toilet and table. Use of this road in the spring is limited by snow conditions and the Bear Management Plan, which keeps it closed to vehicular use until June 1.

The Lewis River Drainage

The Lewis River starts in Shoshone Lake, flows south through Lewis Lake, then splashes over a series of falls and through a grand gorge to merge with the Snake River just inside the south boundary of Yellowstone National Park. Captain Lewis of the Lewis and Clark Expedition never saw any part of the park, much less the river and lake, that now bear his name. Osborne Russell made note of the lake in his 1839 journal. The 1872 Hayden survey named the lake to honor Captain Lewis, and then the name became attached to the river as well.

Mileage points: Mileages for this section are described from Old Faithful, West Thumb, and Moran Junction.

47. Shoshone Lake

Description: Shoshone Lake is the second largest lake in Yellowstone National Park. The name comes from the major Native American tribal group that inhabited the region. Shaped roughly like a hammer, the lake's handle runs along a southwest to northeast line. From ball to claw the lake is 4 miles wide, and from handle to head it is more than 6 miles long. The shoreline bed is mostly cobble except around the inlets of DeLacy, Moose, and Shoshone Creeks. In these areas the flatter gradient of the shoreline helps retain sand and gravel as well. Moving offshore, the depth increases rapidly, as would be expected of a lake more than 200 feet deep. Most of the shoreline is timbered, except around the three inlet streams. The 1988 fires only affected a mile or so of shore on either side of the Lewis River outlet at the southeast corner of the lake.

Certainly one of the largest lakes with no road access in the contiguous 48 states, Shoshone Lake is the park's most popular backcountry destination. In most years the ice goes off the lake in early June. The best fishing here takes place during the three weeks following ice-off and in October. Only hand-propelled craft are allowed on Shoshone Lake, and with no road access this mostly means canoes. This, in turn, limits the angler's ability to get offshore and troll deep, which is about the only tactic that works well throughout most of the summer.

The fish: Fishless before 1890, Shoshone Lake was planted with lake and brown trout. Brook trout were introduced to the tributary streams. The bulk of the fish are lake trout in the 20-inch range. The browns are slightly less common and run slightly smaller, 16 to 19 inches. The few brook trout in the lake are often about 15 inches, though those in the tributary streams are typically much smaller. In 1977 the U.S. Fish and Wildlife Service removed the brook trout from nearby Pocket Lake and its outlet stream to introduce cutthroat from the Heart Lake drainage. At least some recruitment was evident by 1983, but Pocket Lake is biologically poor. Despite that,

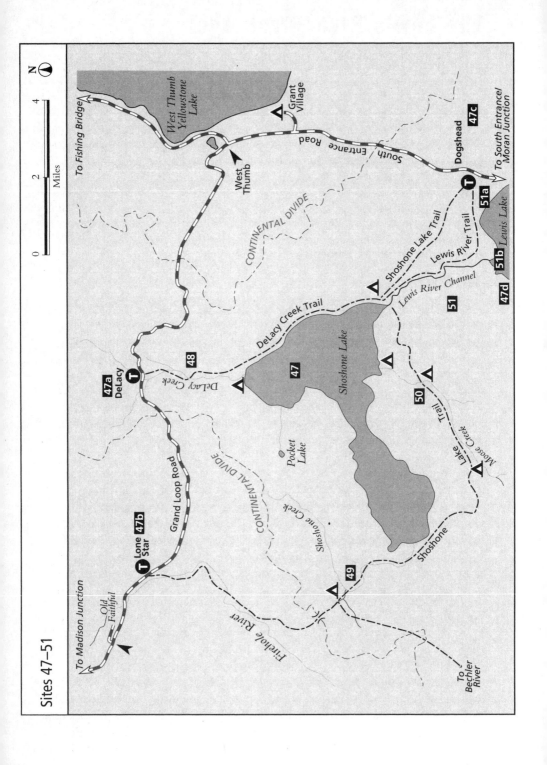

Sites 47–51

the cutthroat have established themselves in good numbers. A remnant population of brookies under 10 inches long hangs on. The Pocket Lake cutts seldom exceed 14 inches.

Flies and lures: Hatches are not particularly common on Shoshone Lake. The best flies are Woolly Buggers, Zonkers, and Kiwi Skunks. If there is surface activity, it is likely to be matched best by Parachute Adams, Gulper Specials, or Flying Ants. For the spinning angler, generally the bigger the better. Try Tor-p-do Spoons, Kamloopers, Spin-a-Lures, Kastmasters, and large Mepps. These fish like flies and lures that are black, white, or both.

Special equipment: Although it is feasible to carry a float tube down the DeLacy Creek Trail, Shoshone Lake is a big lake. Weather can get nasty in a hurry, especially in the afternoon as wind builds. Both Shoshone Lake and the Lewis River between Shoshone and Lewis Lakes are open to hand-propelled craft. As a practical matter, this means canoes. The portage required to get up the Lewis River is only a bit over a mile.

Access: Three main access routes by land and one by water lead to Shoshone Lake. Several backcountry campsites are situated around the lakeshore.

47a. DeLacy Creek Trail

The shortest overland route to Shoshone Lake is the 3-mile-long DeLacy Creek Trail. Drive 8.9 miles west from West Thumb on the Grand Loop Road to DeLacy Creek. It is 8.9 miles east from Old Faithful to DeLacy Creek. The parking area is on the north side of the highway, but the trail runs south down DeLacy Creek. It is 3 fairly easy miles to Shoshone Lake.

47b. Lone Star Trailhead

The best access to the west end of Shoshone Lake is via the Shoshone Lake Trail from the Lone Star Trailhead. Take the Grand Loop Road east from Old Faithful for 2.6 miles to the trailhead. The trailhead is 15.2 miles west from West Thumb. Despite the fact that this trail crosses the Continental Divide at Grants Pass, the vertical climb is less a problem than the fact that it is 8.5 miles to the lake. This is too far to be a practical day-hike approach to the lake.

47c. Dogshead Trailhead/Shoshone Lake Trail

The best walking access to the outlet of Shoshone Lake is via the Shoshone Lake Trail from the Dogshead Trailhead. Drive south from West Thumb 7.7 miles on the South Entrance Road and turn right into the trailhead, which is 50 yards off the highway. The trailhead is on the left 42.3 miles north of Moran Junction. It is 4.7 miles via the Shoshone Lake Trail from the trailhead to the lake. A second trail to the Lewis River uses this same trailhead. The Lewis River Channel Trail intercepts the river and then follows it up to the lake. At 6 miles, it is the long way to the lake.

47d. Lewis River Channel

Canoes and other hand-propelled craft may be taken up the Lewis River Channel into Shoshone Lake. The safest launch point is the boat ramp at the Lewis Lake Campground. Take the South Entrance Road 10.5 miles south from West Thumb and turn right into the campground. The boat ramp is the first facility off the highway. The campground is on the left 39.5 miles north of Moran Junction. Paddle across the south end of Lewis Lake and follow the west shore north to the Lewis River inlet. This is a 3-mile route, but it has the advantage of keeping the angler sheltered by the shore. The channel itself is also 3 miles long, and because the lower 2 miles have a fairly slow and smooth current, that stretch can be paddled. This leaves a 1-mile portage to put your canoe on Shoshone Lake. You can save a mile by crossing the north end of Lewis Lake, but this is the side most exposed to wind-driven surf, so I strongly advise against it. Coming out, the Lewis River is not even class II water, so it is easy to run.

Tributaries: The principle tributaries to Shoshone Lake are DeLacy Creek (site 48), Shoshone Creek (site 49), and Moose Creek (site 50). The other tributaries are mostly trivial and without significant interest to an angler.

48. DeLacy Creek *(see map on page 122)*

Description: DeLacy Creek and its tributary streams flow south from the Continental Divide to unite shortly after crossing the Grand Loop Road between Old Faithful and West Thumb. It is a small stream, seldom exceeding 10 feet in width. The lower 3 miles of its course, before it joins Shoshone Lake, are the most fishable. The banks are generally grass covered, with timber a few yards away. The bed is mostly medium-size cobble, interrupted by the occasional deadfall tree. The structural pockets made by the deadfall and the deeper spots along undercut banks and around rocks are the best places to fish. The creek is usually overlaid with snow until about the middle of June. Fishing is satisfactory through August but poor thereafter.

The fish: Virtually all of the fish in DeLacy Creek are brook trout. The fish run 6 to 10 inches in length. There is an outside chance of catching a brown in the same size range during the summer. In the fall a few larger browns could move into the lower mile of the creek to spawn.

Flies and lures: This stream is so small that it is difficult to fish effectively with lures. I have a hard time picturing myself trying any fly except a Royal Coachman Trude, but in late July or August, I might give a Dave's Hopper a shot.

Access: Take the Grand Loop Road 8.9 miles east from Old Faithful or the same road west for 8.9 miles from West Thumb to the DeLacy Creek Trailhead. Parking and a picnic area are on the north side of the highway. The trail down the stream is across the road to the south. Fish downstream.

49. Shoshone Creek (see map on page 122)

Description: Shoshone Creek rises along the Continental Divide north of Shoshone Lake. Its initial course is southwesterly, then under Grants Pass it hangs an abrupt left, taking a southeasterly course to join Shoshone Lake at its western end. The lower part of the stream runs through the Shoshone Geyser Basin. Except for its final mile and a couple of pocket meadows in its middle reaches, the banks are mostly timbered. The stream runs 15 to 25 feet wide, and most of the bed is medium to large cobble. Holes along cut banks are the best spots to look for fish in the meadows. Work the pockets around the rocks in the rest of the stream.

Winter snowpack prevents access to Shoshone Creek before the middle of June. The section below the geyser basin cannot be expected to produce during July or August. The balance of the stream is productive throughout the summer.

The fish: Most of the fish in Shoshone Creek are brown trout. The remainder are brook trout. None are of any great length, typically 8 to 12 inches.

Flies and lures: Start with an attractor dry fly, say a Royal Wulff, or an attractor nymph such as a bead-head Prince. After the middle of July, a Muddler Minnow is another good choice. In the fall some spawning browns may move into this stream, and for them I would try a Woolly Bugger. Shoshone Creek is barely big enough to use spin tackle. The spinning angler should start with a small Panther Martin or Cyclone.

Access: The principle point of access to Shoshone Creek is via the Shoshone Lake Trail. Drive 2.6 miles east from Old Faithful or 15.2 miles west from West Thumb on the Grand Loop Road to the Lone Star Trailhead. Park at the trailhead and hike up the Firehole River to where the Shoshone Lake Trail splits off to the left. Cross the Continental Divide at Grants Pass and descend to Shoshone Creek. Fish either upstream or down. There is a backcountry campsite near where the trail first meets the creek. This 5.5-mile trek is a brutal day hike.

50. Moose Creek (see map on page 122)

Description: Moose Creek is formed by the conjoining of several small streams that come off the north end of the Pitchstone Plateau. Its first couple of miles are in a large meadow as it flows northeast toward Shoshone Lake. The next mile is timbered along the banks as the creek drops through a steeper canyon section. The final mile crosses a willow flat to enter Shoshone Lake, 2 miles west of the outlet to the Lewis River. The bottom is big cobble in the canyon section; otherwise, it is fairly fine-grained.

Expect the stream to be unfishable until mid-June; thereafter, it is satisfactory until late August. October picks up again in the lower section, with browns moving in from the lake. Key spots to look for are the deeper slots below gravel bars, along cut banks, and the gravel-bottomed pools.

The fish: Moose Creek is inhabited by brook and brown trout. The average size is under 10 inches. The ratio of brooks to browns increases as you go upstream. The fall migrants are more likely to run 16 to 20 inches.

Flies and lures: My first choice of a fly depends on which part of the creek I am fishing. In the steeper canyon section, I will start with a Royal Coachman Trude and probably never stop using it. In the meadow sections I would first look for a hatch, then try to match it with a dry-fly pattern. Absent such evidence, a bead-head Prince or Hare's Ear nymph, and possibly both, would be my starting rig. In high summer a hopper pattern is always in order. A Muddler Minnow is the streamer of choice. Start with a small Panther Martin or Kamlooper if you are using spin tackle.

Access: The shortest overland route to Moose Creek is the Shoshone Lake Trail from the Dogshead Trailhead. Drive the South Entrance Road south from West Thumb for 7.7 miles. The trailhead is off the road 50 yards to the right. Go north 42.3 miles from Moran Junction to find the trailhead on your left. Take the Shoshone Lake Trail 4.5 miles to the lake, ford the outlet, and hike 2 more miles to the west to Moose Creek. Fish either up into the canyon or down into the willow flat. A backcountry campsite is located near the trail crossing of Moose Creek. The trail follows the creek upstream for 2 miles, and another campsite is in the meadow near where the trail cuts west again to return to Shoshone Lake. A canoe campsite is at the mouth of Moose Creek.

51. Lewis River Channel (see map on page 122)

Description: The Lewis River Channel, often referred to as "the Channel," is the 3-mile-long section of the Lewis River connecting Shoshone Lake to Lewis Lake. Snow on the trail and ice on Lewis Lake usually keeps this area inaccessible until sometime in early June. The best fishing is found in the first month and again in October when spawning browns move into the middle section of the river.

The first mile of water below Shoshone Lake is 25 to 40 feet wide and about 2 feet deep. The bottom is mostly medium to large cobble. The banks were heavily timbered before the 1988 fires. There is a steady but moderate current here that is just barely too fast to paddle against. Occasional deadfall and bigger rocks provide some structural cover for the few resident fish.

The next 300 yards flatten out into a 50- to 75-foot-wide channel with a mostly gravel bottom. This area attracts a lot of spawning fish in the fall. The remainder of the channel is much deeper, with a mostly muck bottom. The current is very slow. The principle structural features of interest to anglers are the many deadfall trees lining the banks.

The fish: By far the most common fish in the Channel are brown trout. Lake trout make up the balance, perhaps 15 percent. The browns run 16 to 20 inches. The lake trout are generally slightly larger, running 17 to 22 inches.

Flies and lures: In the spring, fish with a white or black streamer. My first choice is a Marabou Muddler; my second, a Woolly Bugger. In the fall, Glo-Bugs or egg flies are deadly, though the streamers are still a fair bet. Western nymph patterns such as Bitch Creeks and Brown Stones are also effective. If using spin tackle, start with a Kamlooper. Other good choices include Rapalas, Rooster Tails, and Mepps.

Access: The Channel can be reached on foot from the Dogshead Trailhead or by boat across Lewis Lake.

51a. Dogshead Trailhead/Lewis River Trail

Take the South Entrance Road from West Thumb 7.7 miles and turn right into the Dogshead Trailhead. The parking area is 50 yards off the road. The Lewis River Trail is the southern trail out of the trailhead. It is 3 miles to the Channel. Dogshead Trailhead is 42.3 miles north of Moran Junction if you are coming from the south.

51b. Lewis Lake

While only hand-propelled craft are allowed in the Channel itself, motorized craft are allowed on Lewis Lake. Paddle or motor to the inlet, then paddle, row, or walk up the Channel. If hiking, land on the east shore of the Channel to locate the anglers' trail. The safest boat launch is the ramp at the Lewis Lake Campground. Go north 39.5 miles from Moran Junction or south 10.5 miles from West Thumb to find the campground. If your boat cannot be taken up the river, beach or anchor it in sheltered water on the east side of the channel and walk upriver to the fishing zone. This saves a couple of miles of overland hiking. Even a modest breeze can kick up a vicious chop along the exposed northern shore of Lewis Lake, so I do not recommend it even though it is a shorter route.

52. Lewis Lake

Description: Lewis Lake, about 2.5 by 3 miles in area, is shaped roughly like a spinning top. It is the third largest lake in Yellowstone National Park. The Lewis River enters at the lake's northwest corner and exits from the southern point of the lake. The bed is mostly medium to large cobble. The deepest water parallels the eastern shore of the lake, leaving the northwestern quadrant substantially shallower than the rest of the lake. The outlet exits over a shelf of solid lava rock. Much of the timber that formerly lined the shore was burned in 1988. The campground at the southern end of the lake escaped the fires. A series of intermittent tributary channels creates a bog at the northeast corner of the lake.

Lewis Lake is often ice-covered until sometime in early June. The campground may not open until well into June due to snow on the ground. Fishing is best for the first month after the ice goes off and again in October. The inlet and outlet areas are the most consistently productive. Summer fishing pretty much means deep trolling along the southwestern flank of the lake. Find and work the margins of the weed beds that develop along the southwestern shoreline.

The fish: The population of Lewis Lake is dominated by brown trout, roughly three of every four fish caught. The rest are virtually all lake trout, though an occasional

For anglers without a motor, wind can make travel on Lewis Lake a tricky proposition.

brook trout can turn up. The most interesting thing about these fish is that the lake trout are now a critical genetic resource for the effort to return lakers to the Great Lakes, from which Lewis Lake's stock originally came. Most of the fish, brown and lake trout alike, run 14 to 20 inches. On occasion somebody hooks into a monster lake trout weighing upwards of twenty pounds.

Flies and lures: This is streamer country. Use white or black Marabou Muddlers, Zonkers, or Kiwi Skunks. A sporadic gray drake hatch in the outlet area may produce some action on a big Blue Dun or Adams. Watch for midge activity when the lake is calm. Trolling, dead slow, a plain old black Woolly Worm is another good bet. Lure anglers should start with a Rapala. Any big and heavy lure is worth a shot, but try Kastmasters, Tor-p-do spoons, Kamloopers, Spin-a-Lures, and large Mepps.

Special equipment: Lewis Lake is open to motorized craft. The outlet area is a good spot to use a float tube, and powerboat users are cautioned to give such anglers some space. Some of the biggest mosquitoes I have ever seen attack in late June and into July, so repellent and even headnets are useful.

Access: The South Entrance Road closely parallels the east shore of Lewis Lake. Head south from West Thumb 8.5 miles on the South Entrance Road to the first

Sites 52 & 53

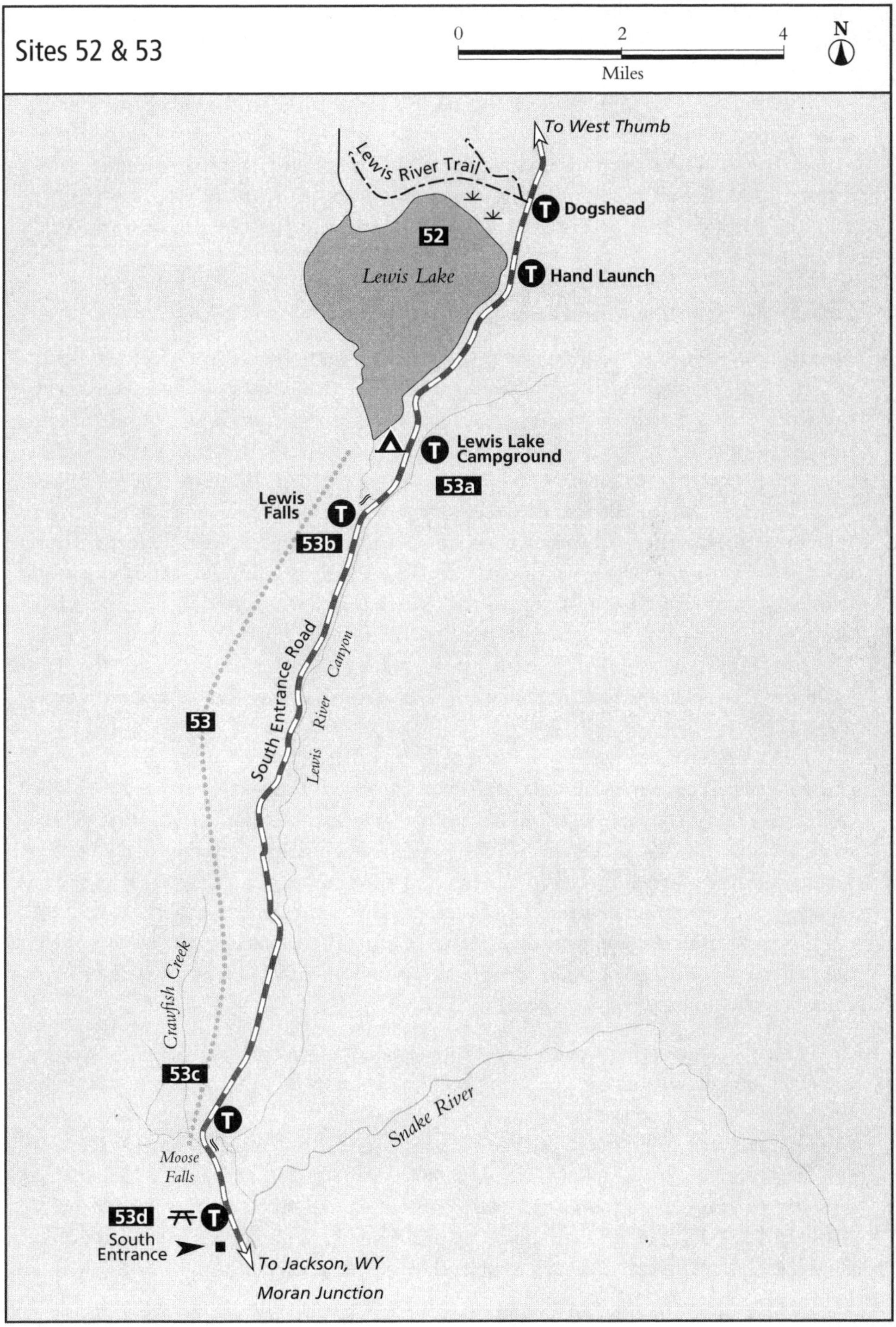

0   2   4

Miles

N

To West Thumb

Lewis River Trail

Dogshead

52

Lewis Lake

Hand Launch

Lewis Lake Campground

53a

Lewis Falls

53b

South Entrance Road

Lewis River Canyon

53

Crawfish Creek

53c

Snake River

Moose Falls

53d
South Entrance

To Jackson, WY
Moran Junction

lakeshore pullout on the right. It is possible to hand-launch a small craft here, though this is a very exposed beach, and high winds, especially in the afternoon, can make paddling dangerous.

The highway continues along the lakeshore for another 2 miles to the Lewis Lake Campground and boat ramp, 10.5 miles south of West Thumb. The campground is 39.5 miles north of Moran Junction. Launch any motorized craft at the campground boat ramp. A hike of less than half a mile down the lakeshore brings you to the outlet. The northern shore is not very accessible by foot in the spring due to a swampy bog.

53. Lewis River *(see map on page 129)*

Description: As the Lewis River leaves Lewis Lake, it is typically 45 feet wide with a fairly flat bottom, much of it lava bedrock. The timber on the west bank was burned in 1988. As the river cuts into the bedrock, big chunks stick up here and there, creating big holes. The river accelerates, and a mile down from the lake it takes an abrupt turn to the east and drops over Lewis Falls. Finding a new equilibrium, the next couple of miles of water below the highway bridge are much flatter. In some places the pace of the river becomes almost lakelike. Often 70 feet wide, it now has a bottom of gravel and small cobble. Again speeding up, the river vaults another pair of waterfalls as it digs its way down into a 600-feet-deep canyon. Here the bottom is a mix of bedrock and large cobble, and the width of the stream is back into the 50-foot-wide range. The final mile, before joining with the Snake River, is again less steep. The bottom, in the last mile, is a mix of gravel and medium and large cobble.

I cannot recall ever seeing the Lewis River really muddy, but the heavy spring snowmelt brings the river up to an unfishable level and stains it the color of tea. The outlet area can be fished as soon as the ice is off the lake. The remainder of the stream does not really kick in until July. A serious hatch is required to make the flat section between Lewis Falls and the head of the canyon anything but frustration city during the summer and fall. The faster sections produce fish until the end of the season. Browns coming up out of Jackson Lake in the fall may be found up to the base of the first serious cascade section, about halfway up the canyon. The browns are catch-and-release below Lewis Falls.

The fish: The upper part of this reach hosts brown, brook, and lake trout. The brookies are numerous, tiny, and spooky. The browns are fewer, bigger, and make the brookies look like idiots. The flat section holds a few really big fish. One occasionally gets over 4 pounds, like the one my friend Paul Brunn took and released one July on a #16 dry Mormon Girl. Below the midcanyon cascades, cutthroat start to show up in increasing numbers, as do whitefish. Fish in this reach typically range between 10 and 14 inches, with some up to 18 inches. The few lake trout look like they could use a month of square meals; they are long and skinny.

Flies and lures: Scattered emergences of green and gray drakes and golden stones provide some of the best action for the dry-fly angler. Absent a hatch, use an attractor pattern like a Coachman Trude in the pockets of the faster water. Stonefly nymphs and Woolly Buggers are good fall bets. If spinning, use Buoyant, Kamlooper, and Cyclone spoons along with Mepps and Panther Martin spinners.

Access: Even in the canyon, none of this stretch of river is as much as a mile from the South Entrance Road. There are numerous pullouts that provide access to or at least overlook the river.

53a. Lewis Lake Campground

Drive north 39.5 miles from Moran Junction or south 10.5 miles from West Thumb to park at the Lewis Lake Campground. Walk 0.5 mile south along the lakeshore to reach the top of the outlet reach. Fish downstream.

53b. Lewis Falls

Take the South Entrance Road 11.8 miles south from West Thumb. There are pullouts on both ends of the bridge that spans the Lewis River just below the falls. Drive north 38.2 miles from Moran Junction to the Lewis Falls parking area. If going up the river toward Lewis Lake, it is best to start on the south side of the bridge and head west upriver.

53c. Crawfish Creek

Just 1.2 miles north of the South Entrance Station, Crawfish Creek provides a route into the lower end of the Lewis Canyon. Drive south 20.8 miles from West Thumb or north 29.2 miles from Moran Junction and park in the Moose Falls pullout, located on the east side of the South Entrance Road. Bushwhack down the north bank of Crawfish Creek to the Lewis River. This gets you to the river at a point where the canyon is only a couple of hundred feet deep. Work upstream.

53d. South Entrance Picnic Area

Immediately inside the South Entrance is a picnic area on the east side of the highway. Park here and hike approximately 1 mile north up the Snake to the mouth of the Lewis River. Fish up the Lewis toward Crawfish Creek.

Tributaries: Aster and Crawfish Creeks are the only significant tributaries to the Lewis River in this section. Neither is any great shakes as a fishery. Aster Creek has some small brookies, and Crawfish Creek is, as the name implies, home to crayfish. Crawfish Creek is heavily impacted by thermal flows that can run its summer temperature up to 100 degrees. A tributary stream, Spirea Creek, does hold some tiny cutthroat.

Lake Corner, the Upper Yellowstone and Shoshone Drainages

Most of this section deals with the headwaters of the Yellowstone River and Yellowstone Lake. Much of the eastern boundary of Yellowstone National Park was determined in an exchange many years ago of USDA Forest Service and National Park Service lands to conform to drainage boundaries in the area. The southeast corner of the park was left in its original rectangular state. The other major exception is the East Entrance corridor. From the crest of Sylvan Pass 6.5 miles east to the East Entrance, the park retained part of the Shoshone River drainage. This stream, Middle Creek, joins the North Fork of the Shoshone just outside the park at Pahaska Tepee. The Shoshone, in turn, collects much of the drainage from the east flank of Yellowstone National Park while heading east to join the Bighorn River in northcentral Wyoming.

Mileage points: Mileage points for this section are at the stop light at the Buffalo Bill Historical Center at the west edge of Cody, Wyoming, on U.S. Highway 20 and Fishing Bridge Junction in the park, where the East Entrance Road joins the Grand Loop Road. The internal reference point is at Pahaska Tepee, where Middle Creek joins the North Fork. On the Grand Loop Road, mileage reference points for this section are found at Canyon, Fishing Bridge, and West Thumb Junctions. Mileage on the South Entrance Road is measured between the West Thumb and Moran Junctions.

North Fork Shoshone River Drainage

54. Middle Creek

Description: Middle Creek rises on the east sides of Top Notch Peak, Mount Doane, and Mount Langford, along the spine of the Absaroka Range, which generally defines the east flank of Yellowstone National Park. It flows northeast for 7 miles to join the North Fork. The lower 6 miles, which contain all the really fishable water, drop about 100 feet per mile, which makes the creek steep and fast. The bed is medium to large cobble interspersed with big boulders and logjams. For the most part, the banks are timbered. A few clumps of alder brush and occasional pocket-sized meadows make up the rest of the banks.

The 2 miles of creek outside Yellowstone National Park are subject to Wyoming regulations. Middle Creek is usually too high and muddy to fish for most of May

Trees that have floated down or fallen into Middle Creek provide fish-holding structure.

132

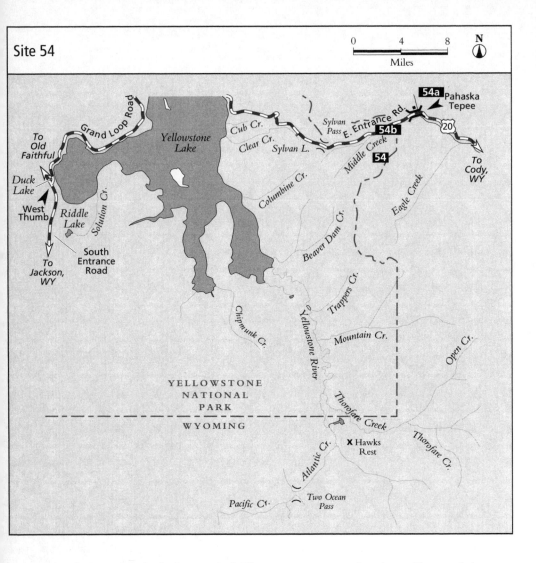

and early June. July is the best period. The structures around rocks and logs and the occasional deeper hole provide the best opportunities to find fish.

The fish: Cutthroat trout are the most common fish in Middle Creek. There are a few whitefish in the lower section, and the upper parts of the creek contain small brook trout. The cutthroat are typically in the 8- to 12-inch range. The brookies seldom exceed 9 inches. Cutts and cutbows move up into the lower parts of the creek during spring to spawn, and a fair number of them are still there when the water drops into fishable range. These fish are commonly 13 to 16 inches long.

Flies and lures: Start with an attractor pattern dry fly such as a Royal Coachman Trude or Royal Wulff. Other flies to have along include Prince nymphs,

Stimulators, and Elk Hair Caddis. If spin fishing, start with a small Cyclone Spoon or Panther Martin.

Access: Pahaska Tepee, reputed to have been Buffalo Bill Cody's hunting camp, is 50.7 miles west of Cody on US 20. It is 29.2 miles east of Fishing Bridge Junction in the park on the East Entrance Road. The East Entrance Road stays quite close to the creek for several miles, until it begins its climb up to Sylvan Pass.

54a. Pahaska Tepee

Drive west from Cody 50.7 miles or east from Fishing Bridge Junction 29.2 miles to Pahaska Tepee. The confluence of Middle Creek with the North Fork of the Shoshone is less than 100 yards to the south and in plain sight. Fish up the creek. This section is in Wyoming. There are a couple of pullouts on the south side of the East Entrance Road between Pahaska Tepee and the east boundary of Yellowstone National Park. Use any pullout that isn't already occupied by an angler's vehicle. The East Entrance Station is 2.4 miles west of Pahaska Tepee and 26.8 miles east of Fishing Bridge.

54b. Top Pullout

The last pullout providing convenient access to Middle Creek is found by driving 4.3 miles west from Pahaska Tepee or 24.9 miles east from Fishing Bridge. It is on the south side of the highway. From here the East Entrance Road starts to climb up the mountain toward Sylvan Pass. The largest of the Middle Creek meadows is 0.7 mile upstream from this point. The meadow itself is about 0.5 mile long. There is little point in fishing above this meadow as the brookies are tiny—and the bears are not. Use other pullouts between the East Entrance and the last pullout to obtain access to intermediate sections of the creek located 100 to 300 yards south of the highway.

Upper Yellowstone Drainage, Headwaters to Chittenden Bridge

The upper Yellowstone country is truly remote. Some parts are more than 25 miles in a straight line from any road, more isolated, it is said, than any other location in the contiguous 48 states. Rising along the ridgelines of the Absaroka Range and the Continental Divide, the Yellowstone River gathers tributary waters during its 30-mile journey north to Yellowstone Lake. The lake receives this river and a number of other tributaries. With more than 100 miles of shoreline, Yellowstone is not only the biggest lake in the park, it's a big lake by any standard. As the river leaves Yellowstone Lake, it is full-blown. An additional northward run of 15 miles carries the river to the brink of the Grand Canyon at Chittenden Bridge, the end point of our discussion here.

Those portions of the Yellowstone and its tributaries south and east of the park boundary are, of course, subject to Wyoming regulations. The practical effect of that is a creel limit of two fish, only one of which may exceed 20 inches. The seasons are more effectively set here by the weather than by any rule. The park regulations are discussed with the site descriptions that follow.

55. The Thorofare

Description: Trickles from snowbanks along the crests of the Absaroka Range and the Continental Divide collect themselves as they tumble northward toward Yellowstone Lake. The river, which is the dominating and namesake watershed of Yellowstone National Park, is at first no more than a mountain freshet miles south of Yellowstone's southeast corner. By the time Atlantic and Thorofare Creeks have been gathered about 11 miles downstream of the river's area of origin south of Yellowstone Lake, the Yellowstone has earned the title of River.

The upper reaches of the Yellowstone River and its tributaries are so steep that they hold few fish larger than 6 inches, and often none at all. As these creeks come together, though, as far as 20 miles south of the lake, they have reached a flat-floored valley. The river drops fewer than 300 feet in the entire remaining distance to the lake. This makes for a meandering stream. Most of the shoreline is either grass or short alpine willows that are used to spending six months buried in snow. The creeks coming off the mountains run over beds of cobble. In the upper, southern, end of the valley, the cobble grades to gravel. By the time the river reaches the lake, much of the gravel has been replaced by silty sand. At the head of each meandering bend, a riffle leads into the subsequent pool. The edges of that riffle and the water along the higher cut bank along the outside of the bend are the places to look for fish.

The spring snowmelt will barely have gotten under way by late May when the ripe fish in Yellowstone Lake start to look for places to spawn. During June they work their way up the river and into the lower ends of its tributaries. Those reaches of stream in the park open July 15. Just getting to the river south of the Yellowstone National Park boundary depends on the weather. The passes leading into this area may not be cleared of snow much earlier than the onset of the fishing season. Mosquitoes and other biting insects dictate that waiting until August to fish here may be the better part of valor. By mid-July the fish have spawned and are starting to drift back down toward the lake. About the only thing left in any of these streams by Labor Day is a population of tiny fish.

The fish: The fish in the upper Yellowstone are cutthroat trout. The resident fish are mostly concentrated in the tributary streams and that section of the river above the mouth of Atlantic Creek. These fish are generally 6- to 10-inchers. The spawners out of the lake average about 16 inches but range 14 to 22 inches.

Flies and lures: These fish are not particularly selective in their choice of pattern and sometimes will forgive presentational errors as well. Start with a Letort Hopper in a dry fly or a Woolly Bugger in a wet. Royal Wulffs, Humpies, Elk Hair Caddis, bead-head Prince, and Hare's Ear are other patterns worth having along. The spin angler should start with a Li'l Jake's. Other good bets include Mepps, Panther

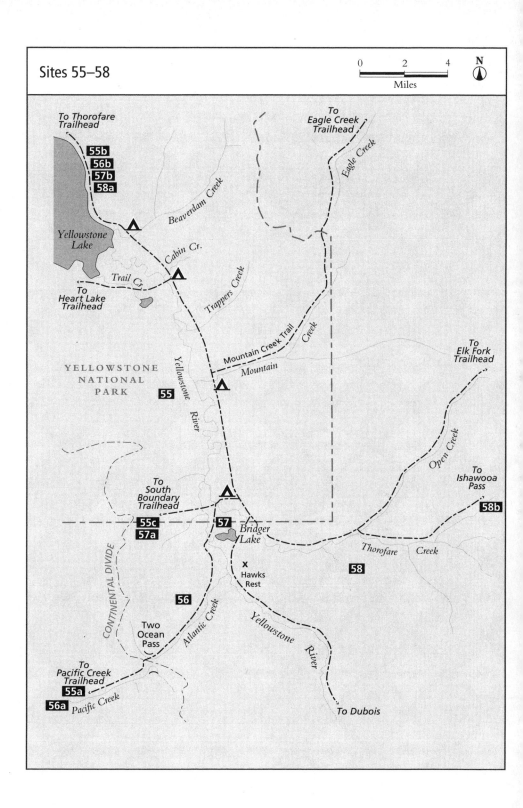

Sites 55–58

0   2   4
Miles

N

To Thorofare
Trailhead

55b
56b
57b
58a

To
Eagle Creek
Trailhead

Eagle Creek

Beaverdam Creek

Yellowstone
Lake

Cabin Cr.

Trail Cr.

Trappers Creek

To
Heart Lake
Trailhead

Mountain Creek Trail

Creek

To
Elk Fork
Trailhead

YELLOWSTONE
NATIONAL
PARK

55

Yellowstone River

Mountain

Open Creek

To
Ishawooa
Pass

To
South
Boundary
Trailhead

55c
57a

57

Bridger
Lake

58b

58

Thorofare   Creek

CONTINENTAL DIVIDE

x
Hawks
Rest

56

Two
Ocean
Pass

Atlantic Creek

Yellowstone   River

To
Pacific Creek
Trailhead

55a

56a   Pacific Creek

To Dubois

Martins, and Kamlooper spoons. Wyoming allows the use of bait, but I cannot imagine a need to use it here.

Special equipment: This is serious backcountry. Do not even think about visiting it unless you are prepared for long hikes or horseback rides and several days away from TV, telephones, and the convenience store. Insect repellent is highly recommended, as is pepper spray to ward off an aggressive bear in the unlikely event of an encounter.

Access: There are a number of access routes to this area, all of them involving lengthy hikes. The issue is complicated by travel restrictions imposed by the Bear Management Plan. Useful backcountry campsites are located on the Thorofare Trail at the junction of Trail Creek Trail, on Mountain Creek, and at the ford across Thorofare Creek.

55a. Pacific Creek

Probably the shortest route is via Pacific and Atlantic Creeks. The trailhead is far outside our area of discussion, on Pacific Creek northeast of Moran Junction. Check a Bridger-Teton National Forest trail map for particulars.

55b. Thorofare Trail

The Thorofare Trail starts at the East Entrance Road and goes south up the east shore of Yellowstone Lake and then up the river. Drive 9.2 miles east from Fishing Bridge Junction or 20 miles west from Pahaska Tepee to the trailhead on the south side of the highway. Take the Thorofare Trail south along the lake and up the river.

It is 18 miles to the Cabin Creek Patrol Cabin and the junction with the Trail Creek Trail. This is the first point at which it makes any sense at all to fish the river. It is another 12.5 miles to the junction with the South Boundary Trail near the confluence of Thorofare Creek with the Yellowstone River. If boat transportation across Yellowstone Lake is available, you can save a lot of walking. It is still 16.5 miles from the landing at Beaverdam Creek to the South Boundary Trail ford across Thorofare Creek.

The Bear Management Plan controls travel on the east shore of Yellowstone Lake. Prior to August 11 travel on this route is restricted to the trail itself between the trailhead and Park Point on the lake. Your first leg must cover at least this 6 miles to the backcountry campsites near the patrol cabin.

55c. South Boundary Trail

The South Boundary Trail starts at Yellowstone's South Entrance Station on the Snake River. It ascends along the Snake and Harebell Creek, crosses Big Game Ridge, drops down again to the Snake, goes up Plateau Creek past Mariposa Lake, and finally descends along Lynx Creek to the Yellowstone River. You are then in camp at the Thorofare Creek ford, 34 miles from your start. Drive south 22 miles from West Thumb on the South Entrance Road or 28 miles north from Moran Junction to the trailhead. This route crosses the Two Ocean bear management zone. Between July 15 and August 21, a permit is required for off-trail travel. This permit is available at the South Entrance Ranger Station. After August 22 off-trail travel is prohibited.

Other Routes

Taking the Heart Lake Trail to its junction with the Trail Creek Trail and the latter around the south end of Yellowstone Lake, connects you with the Thorofare Trail near Cabin Creek. A trail ascends Eagle Creek on the North Fork of the Shoshone east of Pahaska Tepee. It crests the Absaroka Range via Eagle Pass at 9,628 feet and drops down Mountain Creek to the Yellowstone River. An even longer trail ascends the Elk Fork of the North Fork and descends Open Creek to Thorofare Creek.

Tributaries: There are a lot of tributaries, many never officially named. Descriptions of Atlantic Creek (site 56) and Bridger Lake (site 57) follow immediately. In general, the other streams, to the extent that they are in the Yellowstone's valley, are fishable. Their upper reaches will host only tiny fish, if any.

56. Atlantic Creek *(see map on page 137)*

Description: Two centuries after the hunt for the Northwest Passage killed Henry Hudson, Captains Lewis and Clark had that same search assigned to them. They missed it. A bit over 6 miles south of Yellowstone National Park's south boundary, North Two Ocean Creek divides around a rock in its slide down the flank of a saddle astride the Continental Divide. Half turns west and becomes Pacific Creek, flowing to the Snake. Half turns east and becomes Atlantic Creek, flowing to the Yellowstone. In mid- to late June, the saddle is awash with snowmelt, and a fish moving up one stream could easily find itself across the great divide going down the other side. South Two Ocean Creek does not divide as obviously, most of it turning east into Atlantic Creek.

At its upper end in Two Ocean Pass, Atlantic Creek is a braided series of channels in a willow meadow. In the next 2 miles, it drops 100 feet from the pass to the floor of the Yellowstone's valley. For 2 miles more, it slowly meanders its way across the valley to join the river. This is the most fishable section, the streambed mostly small gravel and the banks either grass or short willow. The south side of the creek from Two Ocean Pass to the river was heavily burned in 1988. The creek valley itself is mostly open grass and scrub willow.

Atlantic Creek is outside the park so it is subject to Wyoming regulations. As a practical matter, it is difficult to gain access to the creek before mid-July. The best time to fish, then, is through mid-August. Thereafter, most of the fish will have returned to Yellowstone Lake. The earlier you arrive here, the worse the mosquitoes and biting flies will be.

The fish: Atlantic Creek resident fish are cutthroat trout that seldom reach, much less exceed, 6 inches in length. In the lower end, spawners from Yellowstone Lake run between 16 and 20 inches during spawning season.

Flies and lures: Absent a hatch to provide a clear strategy, my first choice is a bead-head Prince. Other flies I would be sure I had in my kit include Royal Wulff, Elk Hair Caddis, a yellow Stimulator, Black Gnat, and Adams in dries; Hare's Ear nymph, olive Woolly Worm, Woolly Bugger, and Muddler Minnow would be my choice in wets. The angler's best bet in a lure would be a Li'l Jake's, followed by a Mepps or Kamlooper.

Access: Access to Atlantic Creek is similar to access for the upper Yellowstone River. This area is remote.

56a. Pacific Creek

The main route to Two Ocean Pass is outside the scope of this guide. General directions are to take the Pacific Creek Road east from its junction with U.S. Highway 89 about a mile north of Moran Junction. The trailhead is a dozen or so miles up the creek. Consult the Bridger-Teton National Forest trail map. Once at Two Ocean Pass, the trail follows the creek down to the Yellowstone's valley and then cuts north to join the Thorofare Trail.

56b. Thorofare Trail

The Thorofare Trailhead is located 9.2 miles east of Fishing Bridge Junction or 20 miles west of Pahaska Tepee on the East Entrance Road. Take the Thorofare Trail south along the lakeshore and up the Yellowstone River to Thorofare Creek, and then take the Two Ocean Pass Trail to Atlantic Creek. It is 34 miles to Atlantic Creek from the trailhead. A heap of walking can be saved by getting a ride across Yellowstone Lake to Beaverdam Creek. This cuts the hike to 19.5 miles.

Tributaries: North and South Two Ocean Creeks are too small and hold too few fish to be of much interest to anglers.

57. Bridger Lake *(see map on page 137)*

Description: Bridger Lake is on hummocky ground between the confluence of Thorofare Creek with the Yellowstone River. Hard under Hawks Rest, it discharges through a short channel to the Yellowstone from its western end. Much of the timber surrounding the lake was burned in 1988. The bottom is fairly solid sand, gravel, and rock in most places. It is 1 mile long and over 0.5 mile across at its widest point.

The ice is usually off of Bridger Lake before July 1. In Wyoming the lake is open all year, but access is restricted by snow and water conditions until summer. In any case, the biting bug problem makes it unattractive until mid-July. Fishing is best before mid-August.

The fish: Bridger Lake fish are cutthroat trout ranging from 10 to 16 inches.

Flies and lures: My first choice for Bridger Lake is a small Woolly Bugger. Other good bets include bead-head Hare's Ear nymphs, olive Scuds, Skinny Buggers, and

Hawks Rest is reflected in the still water of Bridger Lake.
NATIONAL PARK SERVICE PHOTO

Adams. If spinning, start with a Spin-a-Lure. Also take along Mepps, Panther Martins, Kamloopers, and Kastmasters.

Access: Bridger Lake shares access routes with the rest of the Thorofare country.

57a. South Boundary Trail

The South Boundary Trail starts at Yellowstone National Park's South Entrance, 22 miles south of West Thumb or 28 miles north of Moran Junction. Take the South Boundary Trail to the junction with the Two Ocean Pass Trail, and the latter south to the west end of Bridger Lake. This is a total distance of 35 miles.

57b. Thorofare Trail

Take the East Entrance Road to the Thorofare Trailhead 9.2 miles east of Fishing Bridge Junction or 20 miles west of Pahaska Tepee. Hike south on the Thorofare Trail to its junction with the South Boundary Trail and continue up Thorofare

Creek to the Yellowstone River Trail junction. Cross Thorofare Creek and hike another mile to the east end of Bridger Lake. This is a total distance of 33 miles, though getting a boat ride across Yellowstone Lake to Beaverdam Creek cuts the distance to 18 miles. A trail skirts the south shore of the lake, connecting the Yellowstone River Trail with the Two Ocean Pass Trail.

Tributaries: A small stream joins the lake at its southeastern corner, but it is too small to be of much interest. The outlet stream is very short, and your attention should focus on Thorofare Creek (site 58) or the Yellowstone River (site 67).

58. Thorofare Creek (see map on page 137)

Description: In the early days, everybody and everything in the Yellowstone area moved on foot or by horseback. The stream valleys crisscrossing the area in and surrounding the southeast corner of Yellowstone National Park provided so many routes, it was considered a "thorofare"; hence, the name. Thorofare Creek itself is by far the largest tributary drainage to the Yellowstone River above Yellowstone Lake.

Rising on the west flank of the Absaroka Range, the streams that come together as Thorofare Creek flow west to the Yellowstone River. The most fishable sections are the lower few miles of Thorofare and Open Creeks. The stream meanders across open grass or scrub-willow flats. The streambed is generally gravel or silty gravel, sometimes broken up by beaver dams. Look for fish in the riffle corners at the heads of pools or lower down in the pools along the outsides of bends. High water in Thorofare Creek subsides by the middle of July. The stream will fish best from then until late August.

The fish: The fish in Thorofare Creek are cutthroat trout. As is usual with small streams, near the tops of these drainages the fish will either be absent or available only in two sizes, small and extra small. The best fish are migrants from Yellowstone Lake, and they are gone by the end of August.

Flies and lures: Thorofare Creek fish are seldom selective. My first-choice dry fly in the flat water that abounds is a Dave's Hopper. My box also would include bead-head Prince and Hare's Ear nymphs, Letort Hopper, Hair-Wing Variant, Pale Morning Dun, Blue-Winged Olive, Muddler Minnow, and Woolly Bugger. The angler using spinning tackle should start with a Stream-a-Lure. Other good bets include the Kamlooper, Cyclone spoon, Panther Martin, and Mepps.

Access: Once a thorofare, this is now one of the most remote parts of the country. The passes from the Shoshone River drainage into the upper parts of Thorofare Creek are all at or near 10,000 feet. They simply will not open before July. Most of these routes are far outside the scope of this guide.

58a. Thorofare Trail

The best access from within our scope is via the Thorofare Trail. Drive east 9.2 miles from Fishing Bridge Junction or west 20 miles from Pahaska Tepee on the East

Entrance Road to the Thorofare Trailhead. The 31.5-mile hike from the trailhead to Thorofare Creek can be shortened if a boat takes you across Yellowstone Lake to Beaverdam Creek. It is still 16.5 miles to either of the trail crossings on Thorofare Creek. It is a bad idea to try to bushwhack across the meadow to the confluence of Thorofare Creek with the Yellowstone River; the angler will encounter willow swamp and very tough going. It's better to stay along the stream, even if it means a couple of extra miles of walking. The trail ascends alongside Thorofare Creek for several miles and eventually hooks into the network of trails coming out of the Shoshone.

58b. Ishawooa Pass

Driving southwest from Cody on Wyoming Highway 291 brings you to the South Fork of the Shoshone. The Ishawooa Pass Trailhead is approximately 32 miles southwest of Cody. Consult the Shoshone National Forest trail map for details, as this is well outside the scope of this guide. It is still over 15 miles up Ishawooa Creek to the pass, and nearly 10 more miles down Pass Creek to Thorofare Creek. An alternative route, about the same length, ascends the Elk Fork of the Shoshone and follows Open Creek down to Thorofare Creek.

Tributaries: Thorofare Creek has a number of tributaries. The largest of the lot is Open Creek. In general, these streams are either going to follow the same pattern as Thorofare Creek or be too small and steep to be of interest to an angler.

59. Yellowstone Lake

Description: Yellowstone Lake occupies part of the great Yellowstone Caldera, the surface manifestation of the magma convection plume that drives the region's thermal activity. A big lake by any measure, Yellowstone is said to be the largest lake at its altitude—7,733 feet—on the planet. It has over 100 miles of shoreline. Yellowstone Lake has a unique underwater geyser basin. It is more than 250 feet deep over much of its area, and extends for 20 miles from north to south and 15 miles from east to west.

The shoreline is generally composed of medium- to large-size cobble, with some gravel and sand beaches. In most cases, except around the southern end, timber comes to the high-water line. Islands vary from the nearly 2-mile-long Frank Island to the sometimes submerged Carrington Island, a pile of rocks no more than a few yards across. The prevailing winds track across from southwest to northeast. In their long sweep across the lake, they often raise a substantial surf, particularly along the exposed northeastern shore.

The ice usually goes off Yellowstone Lake around Memorial Day. The fishing season, however, opens June 15. The first month presents the best fishing because fish are close to shore feeding on the tiny critters growing in the sun-warmed shallow water. The best places to look for fish are in the sheltered bays, around points, near the inlet streams, and at the outlet to the Yellowstone River.

A view of Yellowstone Lake from Lake Butte. MICHAEL SAMPLE PHOTO

The fish: Until recently the fish in Yellowstone Lake were thought to be all cutthroat trout plus some sucker and minnow species of no interest to anglers. It has now been discovered that some years ago, probably about 1970, lake trout were clandestinely introduced to the lake. The cutthroat run 10 to 22 inches, with most being in the 14- to 17-inch range. Lake trout taken by anglers are mostly in the 15- to 20-inch range, but researchers turned up one that exceeded twenty pounds.

Flies and lures: One of the best flies for Yellowstone Lake is the plain olive Woolly Worm. A hatch of large gray mayflies takes place sporadically, making an Adams another good bet. Other flies that I would be sure were in my box are Prince and Hare's Ear nymphs, Woolly Buggers, Muddler Minnows, olive Scuds, and Elk Hair Caddis. Without question the leading lure on Yellowstone Lake is the Spin-a-Lure. Larger Kamlooper spoons, Kastmasters, Krocodiles, and Mepps also have a good record. If trying for a lake trout, bigger is generally better.

Special equipment: A float tube can be used on the lake, but please be cautious. It is a big lake subject to severe winds and weather. If you get blown offshore at Rock Point, it will be a *looong* time before you wash up in Sedge Bay. Yellowstone National Park requires a boat permit for all floating craft, including float tubes. Small craft are required to stay within 400 yards of the lakeshore. The southern arms of the lake have speed-limit and hand-propelled-craft-only zones.

Access: I am not going to discuss every point of access since roads closely follow more than 25 miles of shoreline. I will start at the northeast quadrant and move counterclockwise around the lake to the southwest. There are a number of back-country campsites along the shore that are reached either by trail or as boat camps. The site on Peale Island is strictly a canoe camp, as it is in a hand-propelled-craft-only zone.

Tributaries: Most of the tributary streams do not open until July 15; Clear and Cub Creeks remain closed until August 11. Please note, however, that for 100 yards on either side of these inlet and outlet areas, the lake is closed to fishing until the streams open. The other major tributary to the lake, Pelican Creek, has been heavily impacted by whirling disease. This stream has been closed to fishing for the foreseeable future.

The marina, harbor, and channel areas at Bridge Bay and Grant Village are closed to fishing. Fishing from shore is prohibited in the West Thumb Geyser Basin. There, careless anglers have boiled themselves and their fish, and risk damaging some of the thermal features. Yellowstone Lake regulations require the killing of any lake trout caught in the lake.

59a. Thorofare Trail

Drive east 9.2 miles from Fishing Bridge on the East Entrance Road and turn right into the Thorofare Trailhead. If coming from Cody, take the East Entrance Road 20 miles west from Pahaska Tepee to the trailhead. Park and hike south on the Thorofare Trail. The trail closely parallels the shoreline, from the mouth of Clear Creek on. Clear Creek is 2 miles from the trailhead. This is bear management zone J-1, closed to off-trail travel and shore fishing until August 11 between the trailhead and Park Point. The entire east shore of Yellowstone Lake north of Beaverdam Creek is available from this trail. It is 14.5 miles to Beaverdam Creek.

59b. Sedge Bay

The south end of Sedge Bay is the most southerly point on the shore before the East Entrance Road cuts east, away from the lake. Take the East Entrance Road for 8.1 miles east from Fishing Bridge or 21.7 miles west from Pahaska Tepee to Sedge Bay. There are a couple of parking areas where the road runs right along the beach. Small craft not requiring a boat ramp can be launched here. This is a very exposed beach that has a substantial surf anytime there is much of a breeze. Winds tend to be stronger in the afternoons, so what was an easy launch in the morning may be a wet landing later in the day.

59c. Storm Point

Drive 3.3 miles east from Fishing Bridge on the East Entrance Road to the Storm Point Trailhead. This is on the south side of the road near the fishless Indian Pond, 25.9 miles west of Pahaska Tepee. Hike 1 mile out to Storm Point and work the

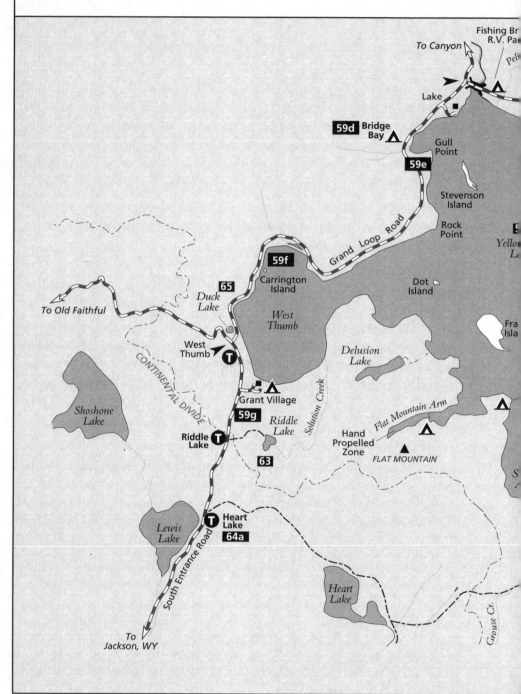

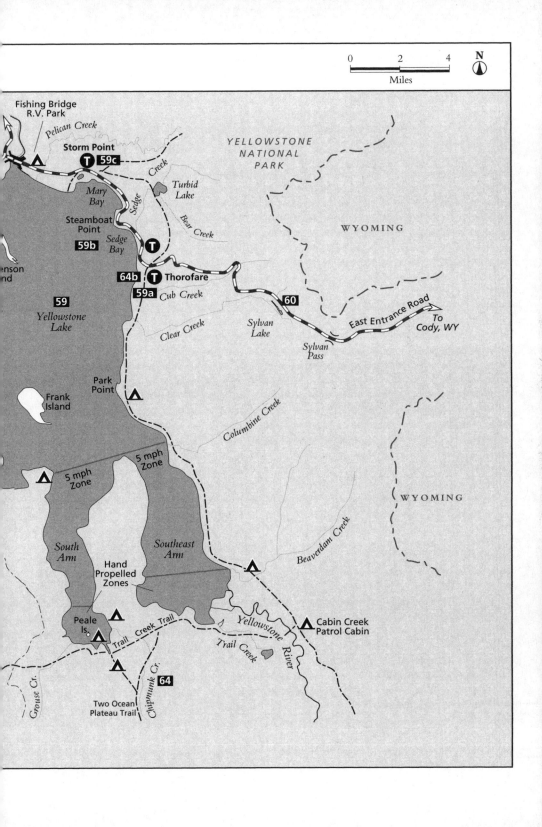

shoreline either to the east or west. This area is likely to be best in the morning before the surf kicks up, but the east side may have a little shelter, depending on the bearing of the wind.

59d. Bridge Bay

Go south 3.5 miles from Fishing Bridge Junction or north 17.7 miles from West Thumb on the Grand Loop Road to the entrance to the Bridge Bay complex. There is a major campground and a full-service marina at Bridge Bay. A concessionaire provides party and rental boats, as well as launch and fuel services.

59e. Gull Point Drive

The north end of Gull Point Drive is 3.8 miles south of Fishing Bridge Junction. The south end is 15.7 miles north of West Thumb. Take Gull Point Drive to access 2 miles of shore bypassed on the Grand Loop Road.

59f. Carrington Island

Driving north 4.4 miles from West Thumb or south 16.8 miles from Fishing Bridge on the Grand Loop Road brings you to a parking area on the east side of the road, 200 yards north of Carrington Island. The island itself sits 200 yards offshore. It looks for all the world like a couple of dump-truck loads of rocks, with a single scraggly pine tree sticking up from the middle. This island appears to be the principle spawning area used by the lake trout. Most of the lakers taken by anglers and researchers have been in West Thumb, many of them in the vicinity of Carrington Island. A second lake trout spawning area has been identified across the thumb at the west end of Breeze Channel, which connects West Thumb to the rest of the lake. It is in 60 feet of water on a submerged reef parallel to the shoreline. Fishing is best here during the first month of the season and again in October.

59g. Grant Village

The entrance road to the Grant Village area is found on the South Entrance Road 1.9 miles south of West Thumb or 48.1 miles north of Moran Junction. Grant Village has a major campground, lodging, service station, and marina facilities. It is the last, or first, auto access to Yellowstone Lake. Opening dates for the campground depend on bear usage of the nearby spawning creeks.

Tributaries: Many streams run into Yellowstone Lake. Most are small and of little interest to anglers because they have few, if any, resident fish. We will discuss Cub Creek (site 61), Clear Creek (site 61), Sedge Creek (site 62), Bear Creek (site 62), and Chipmunk Creek (site 64), Sylvan Lake (site 60), Riddle Lake (site 63), and Duck Lake (site 65). Turbid Lake acts as a chemical and thermal barrier to fish. Indian Pond and Delusion Lake are without fish.

Whitecaps and waves are a common occurrence, especially during the afternoon, on Yellowstone Lake.

60. Sylvan Lake *(see map on pp. 146–147)*

Description: Sylvan Lake is a narrow lake a little less than a mile long that is adjacent to the East Entrance Road just west of Sylvan Pass and between two forks of Clear Creek. Its inlets and outlets are intermittent or subsurface. Surrounded by tall timber, Sylvan Lake hosts a popular picnic area and attracts casual anglers because of its ease of access. The bottom is rocky.

The lake lies at 8,414 feet. While the ice is usually off by early June, the lake does not open to fishing until July 15. Despite the catch-and-release regulation, angling success is often poor. While the lake is deep enough to avoid freeze-out, there is every reason to suspect that reproductive success here is as intermittent as the lake's tributaries.

The fish: Sylvan Lake is populated by cutthroat trout and suckers. The latter may have found their way up from Yellowstone Lake, but it is also possible somebody dumped a bait bucket. Trout in the lake range up to 14 inches, but most are smaller, about 10 inches.

Flies and lures: Absent rising fish to suggest a particular dry fly, my first choice would be an olive Woolly Worm. Also in my box would be Woolly Buggers, Prince nymphs, and a few Adams. The lure angler might as well start with a Li'l Jake's. Other potentially effective lures include Little Cleo, Mepps, and Stream-a-Lure.

Access: Sylvan Lake is right on East Entrance Road 11.5 miles west of Pahaska Tepee. If coming from the west, it is 17.7 miles from Fishing Bridge Junction.

61. Clear and Cub Creeks

Description: Both Clear and Cub Creeks rise on the flank of the Absaroka Range and flow west to Yellowstone Lake. Clear Creek runs about 15 feet wide, Cub Creek about half of that. While each has some small meadow areas, they more typically chuckle over rock and deadfall as they flow through heavy timber. The frequent small pools often have bottoms of small gravel.

Because both streams are important cutthroat spawning streams, they attract bears during the spawning run. As a consequence, the Bear Management Plan restricts use of the area to passage on the Thorofare Trail until August 11. Fishing on the streams is closed until August 11, and by then most of the spawners have run back to the lake.

The fish: The resident fish in these two streams are small cutthroat trout, usually under 7 inches in length. The running spawners typically are 16- to 18-inch cutts.

Flies and lures: If I were forced to fish either of these creeks, I would start with a Royal Coachman Trude. If that did not work, I would try the deepest water I could find with a bead-head Prince. If neither worked, I would go home. Because of the small size of the streams, lures are not easy to use. Try really small Mepps, Panther Martins, or Cyclone spoons.

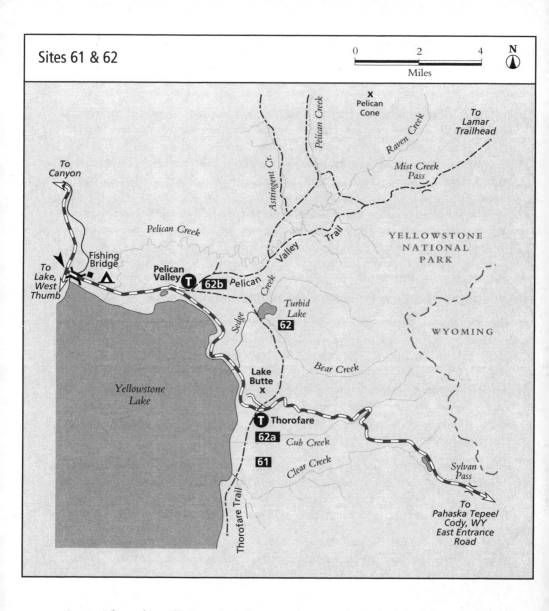

Access: The only really practical access to these creeks is the Thorofare Trail. Take the East Entrance Road 9.2 miles east from Fishing Bridge Junction or 20 miles west from Pahaska Tepee to the Thorofare Trailhead. Park and hike south on the Thorofare Trail. It is 1.25 miles to Cub Creek, about twice that to Clear Creek. Launching a small boat or canoe at Sedge Bay on Yellowstone Lake is an alternative that allows you to fish your way to these creeks.

Tributaries: There are no tributaries to these streams worth mentioning other than Sylvan Lake (site 60).

62. Bear and Sedge Creeks (see map on p. 151)

Description: Bear Creek and Sedge Creek rise along the spine of the Absaroka Range on Yellowstone National Park's eastern border. They flow west, meeting at Turbid Lake; then Sedge flows south to join Yellowstone Lake. Turbid Lake is a geothermal feature that represents a chemical and thermal barrier in the stream beyond which fish cannot pass. The upper ends of both streams are steep and without fish; the streambeds consist of rubble. The lower 2 miles, more or less, of each stream have a more moderate gradient over a gravel bed. These stream segments meander through meadows; the upland timber surrounding them was burned by the 1988 fires.

The streams are about 10 to 15 feet wide and are fairly shallow, except where deeper areas have been scooped out by currents around bends or obstructions. These provide the most productive spots to find fish. The worst of the spring flood is over by the time these streams open for fishing on July 15. Since Turbid Lake separates them from Yellowstone Lake, any fish are resident fish and will be available to the angler throughout the summer and into September.

The fish: Since Yellowstone Lake was at one time much higher than at present, a remnant population of cutthroat trout was left isolated above Turbid Lake. Some additional cutthroat from Yellowstone Lake were introduced to Bear Creek beginning in the 1920s and ending in 1941. The result is a separate strain of cutthroat trout that is not genetically programmed to run to Yellowstone Lake. Because of that trait, these fish are an important biological resource, supporting introductions elsewhere in the region. The fish available to the angler are generally under 11 inches, averaging around 7 inches.

Flies and lures: My first and probably only choice here is a Royal Coachman Trude. If that does not work, I would try a bead-head Prince. If neither works, it is time to go home. The angler using spin tackle needs to keep lures small. Start with a Triple Teazer, and if that fails, try a small Mepps, Panther Martin, or Li'l Jake's.

Access: During the fishing season, which opens July 15, the Bear Management Plan restricts this area to day use between the hours of 9:00 A.M. and 7:00 P.M.

62a. Bear Creek

The short route to Bear Creek is to take the Turbid Lake Trail from the Thorofare Trailhead. Drive east 9.2 miles from Fishing Bridge Junction or west 20 miles from Pahaska Tepee on the East Entrance Road to the trailhead. The Turbid Lake Trail crosses the highway and heads north up and around Lake Butte. Take the Turbid Lake Trail 1.75 miles to where an unnamed tributary of Bear Creek makes a close approach to the trail. Either follow the creek down to Bear Creek, about 500 yards, and fish downstream or stick with the Turbid Lake Trail, stopping at any point that strikes your fancy, and fish back to this stream.

62b. Sedge Creek

The best route to Sedge Creek is the Turbid Lake Trail, but from the Pelican Valley Trailhead. To find this trailhead take the East Entrance Road 3.5 miles east from Fishing Bridge Junction or 25.7 miles west from Pahaska Tepee. The trailhead is on a stub road to the north of the highway. Hike east and then hold to the right on the Turbid Lake Trail when the trail splits about a third of a mile in from the trailhead. When the trail reaches Turbid Lake, a little shy of 3 miles, bushwhack another 0.5 mile north around the west side of the lake to the inlet of Sedge Creek. Fish upstream.

63. Riddle Lake *(see map on pp. 146–147)*

Description: Riddle Lake is a medium-size lake surrounded by a fringe of grass and rushes. The name comes from the fact that for a time it was not known if it had an outlet or to whence it drained. The discovery of Solution Creek solved that problem. The bottom is mostly muck. Timber, mostly burned in 1988, surrounds the lake some yards back from the shore. The western shore has an extensive lily pad fringe. The ice is off the lake long before the season opens on July 15, and the fishing, such as it is, is best right out of the box, declining thereafter. The north shore is the most solid place from which to fish.

The fish: The Riddle Lake fish are cutthroat trout. They will run 10 to 14 inches. With no substantive inlet and a shaky outlet, reproductive opportunities rate low. This certainly contributes to the low population numbers here.

Flies and lures: Absent a clear hatch bringing fish to the surface, my first choice is a Woolly Bugger. I am also sure to carry Skinny Buggers, olive Scuds, bead-head Princes, olive Woolly Worms, and an Adams or two. A Spin-a-Lure is the first choice for the spinning angler. Kastmasters, Kamloopers, Krocodiles, and Mepps are other good choices.

Special equipment: There is no great difficulty in carrying a float tube into Riddle Lake, and it could prove useful to get offshore. The relatively poor fishing here, however, suggests that even the little work involved may be too much.

Access: The Riddle Lake Trailhead is 4.3 miles south of West Thumb on the South Entrance Road. This puts it 45.7 miles north of Moran Junction. The trailhead is only marked by the hiker symbol on the sign. The parking area is on the east side of the road. You actually cross the Continental Divide while driving south from West Thumb. Do not panic; Riddle Lake is a short, flat, 2-mile hike.

64. Chipmunk Creek *(see map on pp. 146–147)*

Description: Chipmunk Creek is the second largest of the southern tributaries to Yellowstone Lake. It is similar, in most ways, to its smaller cousins, Grouse and Trail Creeks. The creek rises south of Yellowstone Lake and flows generally northward to its outlet on the South Arm of Yellowstone Lake. The upper end of the stream is small, steep, and rocky; it is of little interest either to fish or anglers. The lower section, with a flatter gradient and a sand or gravel bottom, is heavily used by spawning cutthroat. The banks are a mix of meadow, marsh, and willow. Much of the Chipmunk Creek basin was burned during 1988. The season opens on July 15, and the stream is most productive during the first couple of weeks. Few fish larger than fry remain beyond the end of August.

The fish: The fish in Chipmunk Creek are cutthroat trout. Resident fish are likely to be pretty small, under 10 inches. The spawners that run upstream every spring range between 14 and 22 inches, with most measuring in at around 16 inches.

Flies and lures: These fish are not all that selective. Start with a Turck's Tarantula. If that does not work, try a bead-head Prince. The small size of the stream argues against using lures, but if you must, keep them small. Cast Li'l Jake's, Panther Martins, or Kamloopers.

Access: The best way to get to Chipmunk Creek is by boat across Yellowstone Lake. Take note of and obey the hand-propelled-craft-only zone that begins 1.5 miles north of the outlet of Chipmunk Creek. There is a backcountry campsite on the lakeshore just north of the mouth of the creek.

Overland access is via Trail Creek Trail, which serves this section of the park.

64a. Trail Creek Trail/West

The west end of the trail is reached by driving to the Heart Lake Trailhead. The trailhead is on the east side of the South Entrance Road, 7.5 miles south of West Thumb and 42.5 miles north of Moran Junction. Take the Heart Lake Trail and the branch around the north side of Heart Lake to Outlet Creek. Hike up Outlet Creek on the Trail Creek Trail, over the divide, and down Grouse Creek to Yellowstone Lake. Continue east on the Trail Creek Trail until reaching the Two Ocean Plateau Trail. The junction is 19.5 miles from the trailhead. Either take the Two Ocean Plateau Trail to go up Chipmunk Creek or stay with the Trail Creek Trail an additional 1.5 miles to lower Chipmunk Creek. A backcountry campsite at the junction of the Trail Creek and Two Ocean Plateau Trails serves this area.

64b. Trail Creek Trail/East

The east end of the trail is reached from the Thorofare Trailhead, which is on the East Entrance Road 9.2 miles east of Fishing Bridge Junction or 20 miles west of Pahaska Tepee. Take the Thorofare Trail 18 miles south to the junction with the Trail Creek Trail at Cabin Creek. Hike east 6 miles, crossing the Yellowstone River and descending Trail Creek, until you come to a junction with the Two Ocean Plateau Trail. An additional mile brings you to Chipmunk Creek on either branch of the trail.

65. Duck Lake *(see map on pp. 146–147)*

Description: Duck Lake is a round lake in what looks like a crater, less than a mile northwest of West Thumb. The timber around the shore was burned in 1988. The bottom is mostly rubble and drops off fairly quickly from shore. The ice is usually off the lake by Memorial Day, and since the lake has no surface connection to Yellowstone Lake, it opens with the regular season. It will fish best during June and poorly thereafter. A couple of small, somewhat intermittent tributary streams flow into the lake. The discharge must be through groundwater flow, as the rim of the crater lies at least 30 feet above the lake's highest level in all directions.

The fish: At one time planted with brown trout, Duck Lake was poisoned in 1967 to remove the nonnative fishes. A survey in 1990 found that the lake now supports a small population of cutthroat trout. These fish appear to be the result of clandestine stocking by amateurs. Since the tributaries only provide about 30 yards of potential spawning habitat, it is not clear whether the lake will sustain fish over the long haul. The fish surveyed in 1990 were all about five years old and 18 to 20 inches long.

Flies and lures: Try an olive Woolly Worm first. Stripping a Woolly Bugger is a good second move. If there is a hatch, five minutes of observation beats hours of random fly changing. If fishing with spin tackle, start with a Spin-a-Lure.

Special equipment: The only difficulty in using a float tube on Duck Lake is getting it back up the rim.

Access: The access road for the West Thumb Geyser Basin and general store is 0.1 mile north of West Thumb Junction, which puts it 21.1 miles south of Fishing Bridge Junction on the Grand Loop Road. The trailhead for Duck Lake is at the West Thumb parking area. Take the trail northwest back across the highway. It is less than 0.5 mile to the lake.

Tributaries: The only even remotely fishable part of the tributary trickles are their outlet areas.

66. Yellowstone River, Fishing Bridge to Chittenden Bridge

Description: In this 13.5-mile reach, the Yellowstone River takes on several different characters. Its course is generally northwesterly. The first 3 miles below the lake is placid but with a definite current running over a gravel bottom. The banks are mostly grass-covered. The river then tips over in a rush down Le Hardy Rapids, which in some respects is the real outlet to Yellowstone Lake. A half-mile later the river starts to slow as it rounds a bend, taking a more westerly course. The bottom in this section is medium- to large-size cobble. Approaching the Nez Perce Ford area, between 3.5 and 6.2 miles north of the lake, the river slows again and the bottom returns to gravel. In the upper area of this section, timber hugs the river closely but fades back in the lower end. There is another short rapids section at the Sulphur Caldron. From this point on, the river is back to a gravel bottom with some weed beds poking up here and there, right up until the cobble returns under the Chittenden Bridge.

The outlet of Yellowstone Lake turns into the Yellowstone River at Fishing Bridge.
MICHAEL SAMPLE PHOTO

The Yellowstone is 150 or more feet wide in this reach. The middle of the channel is generally too deep to ford, even late in the season. The exception is Nez Perce Ford, where a complex of gravel bars and islands makes wading across the river a practical proposition earlier than anywhere else. Caution: The Yellowstone is a big, hard-running river; use a wading staff and be prepared to back out if the going is too difficult.

The season opens here on July 15. The best fishing takes place during the first month, and then there are fewer and fewer fish as the summer population returns to the lake. Virtually every structural feature in the river will have fish stacked up around it. The best strategy is to locate fish by sight and then cast to them.

There are a number of closed zones in this section. The river is closed from the outlet buoy above Fishing Bridge downstream for 1 mile. A section about 400 yards long at Le Hardy Rapids is closed. The channel around an island next to the highway just above Nez Perce Ford is closed. All of these sections are closed to protect spawners, and each has a fish interpretive site. From the Sulphur Caldron downstream to the mouth of Alum Creek, a run of 6 miles, the river is again closed. The rationale here is that the closure reduces disturbances to nesting waterfowl, as the area is thick with geese, ducks, swans, and pelicans.

The fish: While few in number, cutthroat trout are the resident fish here. In years past, thousands of fish moved out of Yellowstone Lake into this reach of river to spawn in June. They got their business done and then started to work their way back up into the lake. By Labor Day they were mostly back in the lake, leaving the river populated only by fry. The fish were typically 14 to 20 inches in length. Unfortunately, these runs have been significantly reduced in recent years by the triple whammy of drought, whirling disease, and the invasion of lake trout.

Flies and lures: The cobble-bottom sections generate a stonefly hatch just about the time the river opens to fishing. Otherwise, routine patterns here are Pale Morning Duns, Blue-Winged Olives, and various caddis patterns in dry flies. In nymphs the necessary patterns are Pheasant Tails, Hare's Ears, and Princes. The angler using spin tackle should start with a Stream-a-Lure. When I fished with spinning tackle, I thought very well of the Little Cleo for this water. Other good bets include the Kamlooper, Cyclone, Mepps, and Spin-a-Lure.

Access: The Grand Loop Road closely parallels this entire reach of river. There are numerous parking spots.

A satisfying moment on the Yellowstone River.
MICHAEL SAMPLE PHOTO

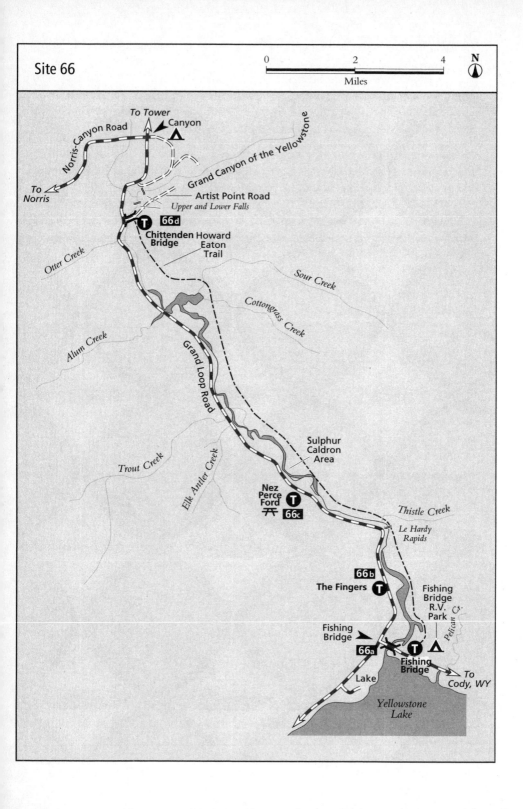

Site 66

0   2   4

Miles

N

To Tower

Canyon

Norris-Canyon Road

To
Norris

Grand Canyon of the Yellowstone

Artist Point Road
Upper and Lower Falls

66d

Chittenden
Bridge

Howard
Eaton
Trail

Otter Creek

Sour Creek

Cottongrass Creek

Alum Creek

Grand Loop Road

Sulphur
Caldron
Area

Trout Creek

Elk Antler Creek

Nez
Perce
Ford

66c

Thistle Creek

Le Hardy
Rapids

66b

The Fingers

Fishing
Bridge
R.V.
Park

Pelican Cr.

Fishing
Bridge

66a

Fishing
Bridge

Lake

To
Cody, WY

Yellowstone
Lake

Mist rises from the Yellowstone River at Nez Perce Ford.
MICHAEL SAMPLE PHOTO

66a. Fishing Bridge

The Howard Eaton Trail runs through on the east side of the river from Fishing Bridge to Canyon. Take the East Entrance Road from Fishing Bridge Junction 0.4 mile and cross the bridge to the Fishing Bridge Store. The Fishing Bridge Trailhead is officially by the East Entrance Road. A more practical access point is to drive in behind the store and garage buildings to the north end of the old cabin area. Park out of the way where the service road and trail start north along the river. Hike in at least a mile to clear the closed area before beginning to fish. It is 3 miles to the head of Le Hardy Rapids and a 13.5-mile hike if you push all the way through to Canyon. Nowhere in this first reach is the river wadeable from the west bank, so this helps get you away from those unwilling to walk.

66b. The Fingers

At only one point is the west side of the river far enough from the road to be hidden. Just north of Fishing Bridge Junction, the road is in the timber and almost a mile from the river. Drive 1.6 miles north from the junction or 14.2 miles south from Canyon to an unmarked pullout just big enough for one or two cars on the east side of the Grand Loop Road. Park here and take the anglers' track through the trees toward the river. Instead of getting tangled up in the swamp at the foot of the hill, hold along the edge of the high ground to the right and head out onto the far bend of the river. The bottom here is a series of gravel bars running out across the current. Depending on the river level, these bars can be anywhere from a few inches to 3 feet beneath the surface, and the holes behind them are usually another foot or so deeper. The fish lie in the slots between the bars.

66c. Nez Perce (Buffalo) Ford

Taking the Grand Loop Road 5.2 miles north from Fishing Bridge or 10.6 miles south from Canyon brings you to the access road to the Nez Perce Ford Picnic Area. This just may be the single most famous fishing spot in the whole park. The reason is that the river is spread out over several acres of ideal spawning gravel. When the season opens, there are usually hundreds of pairs of fish still hanging around their redds. The river is broken up here by several islands that, in combination with the gravel bars, provide a couple of routes to ford the river. This cannot usually be done safely until about August 1. The exact timing depends on water level, which, in turn, depends on the previous winter's snowpack. The official name for the ford itself is Nez Perce Ford. Because the picnic area was named Buffalo Ford until recently, at least three generations of anglers know no other name. Once across the river, fish in either direction.

66d. Chittenden Bridge

Chittenden Bridge crosses the effective head of the Grand Canyon of the Yellowstone. The river is closed to fishing from the bridge downstream, but that will be discussed later. Drive south 2.3 miles on the Grand Loop Road from Canyon to the Artist Point Road and, taking the Artist Point Road, cross the Yellowstone on Chittenden Bridge. Immediately across the bridge, turn right into a large parking and trailhead area. The Artist Point Road is 13.5 miles north of Fishing Bridge Junction. An anglers' track goes south up the riverbank. The Howard Eaton Trail heads south from the far end of the parking area. Walk south up the trail for 1 mile to a spot where a gap in the trees leads toward the river. The gap is closed by trees in a couple of places but does lead you to the riverbank, 0.5 mile or so below the mouth of Alum Creek. This area does not get a lot of pressure, compared to Nez Perce Ford. On the other hand, it is the area first vacated by fish moving back to the lake.

Tributaries: All but one of the tributaries in this section that are large enough to hold fish are also closed for one reason or another. Otter Creek, the exception, does not support a fish population, though there may be a few fish in its outlet area early in the season.

The Yellowstone River Drainage from Chittenden Bridge to the Lamar Confluence

The Yellowstone River flows northward 15 miles through its spectacular Grand Canyon, downstream from Chittenden Bridge. People often mistakenly assume that the river and the park take their name from the predominant yellow rock of the canyon walls. It is more likely that the aboriginal name of the stream was the Elk River. It comes to us as the Yellowstone because Le Roche Juene, "yellow stone" in French, is the name that Lewis and Clark had for the river. They got this name from French-Canadian explorers who had ascended the Missouri as far as the Mandan villages in what is now central North Dakota. The Mandan, in turn, almost certainly were referring to the yellowish rimrocks of the lower river near present-day Billings, Montana. The junction of the Yellowstone with the Lamar marks the end of the Grand Canyon and this section of the river.

The Lamar is the largest tributary drainage of the Yellowstone River within the park. It and its tributaries comprise a major portion of this section of the guide. Tower and Broad Creeks, plus several other less substantial tributaries, also join the Yellowstone in this reach.

Mileage points: Grand Loop Road mileage points for this section are located at Tower, Canyon, Norris, and Fishing Bridge junctions. Mileage on the Northeast Entrance Road is measured between Tower Junction and Cooke City, Montana. The Northeast Entrance Road becomes U.S. Highway 212 upon leaving the park, but since there is no risk of confusion, the whole section is referred to as the Northeast Entrance Road.

67. Seven Mile Hole

Description: From the moment the Yellowstone passes beneath the Chittenden Bridge, it is cutting its way into the Grand Canyon. The 108-foot Upper Falls is just around the bend, soon followed by the 308-foot leap over Lower Falls. The river digs its way down through more than 1,000 feet of the plateau by the time it reaches Silver Cord Cascade some 3 miles downstream. This entire upper section of the river is permanently closed to fishing, primarily for the safety of anglers.

The only practical and legal spot to fish in this reach is Seven Mile Hole. The bank is mostly without vegetation here. The bed of the river is formed of large rocks and boulders. The fish are concentrated around the rocks, particularly just above and below the mouth of Sulphur Creek. When the season opens, the water will not yet be extraordinarily high, but snow melting off the canyon walls makes the river unfishable here due to mud. The river crests here in late June and will not reach a

Seven Mile Hole is the only place in the canyon section of the Yellowstone River where fishing is permitted. MICHAEL SAMPLE PHOTO

fishable level or clarity until after the middle of July. The first big event is the salmonfly hatch that takes place in late July. Seven Mile Hole produces from then until the end of September.

The fish: The fish in this section are cutthroat trout. They range from 8 to 18 inches. The average is typically 13 to 16 inches.

Flies and lures: These fish are relatively unsophisticated. If the salmonfly hatch is on, my first choice is a Parks' Salmonfly. Other productive patterns include orange Stimulators and Matt's Stones. Later in the season, start with a Royal Coachman Trude. Other flies to have in your gear are bead-head Brooks' Stone, olive Woolly Worm, Bitch Creek nymph, bead-head Prince, yellow Stimulator, and Letort Hopper. Start with a Rooster Tail or Stream-a-Lure if using spin tackle. Other good bets are Spin-a-Lures, Cyclone spoons, and Panther Martins.

Access: The short story about Seven Mile Hole is "7 miles in, 77 out." It actually is only 5 miles. The trail begins at the Glacial Boulder Trailhead on the Inspiration

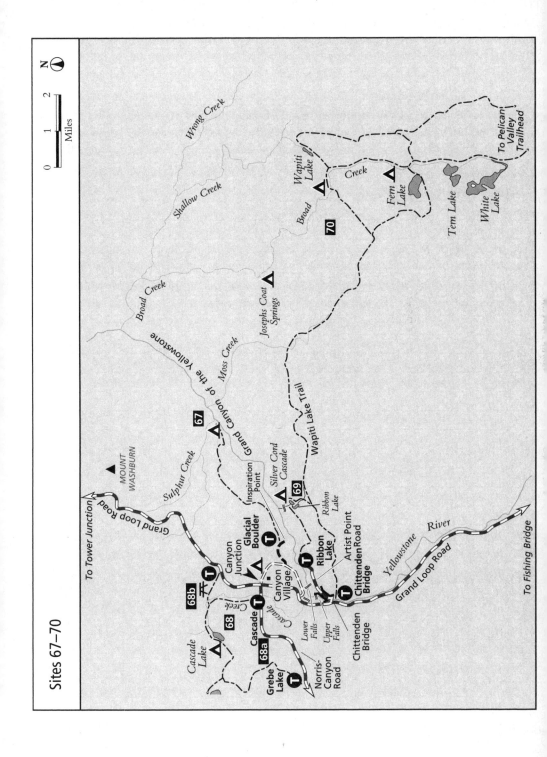

Sites 67–70

Point Road in the Canyon complex. Take the Canyon Rim Drive east from Canyon Junction 0.9 mile to the Inspiration Point Road and the latter 0.5 mile to the trailhead. The trail follows the canyon rim northeast for most of the distance. It is the last 1.5-mile section that is the killer—1,280 vertical feet down. The good news is there are backcountry campsites at the bottom of the hill.

Tributaries: There are two tributary drainages of note in this section. Cascade Lake (site 68) feeds Cascade Creek, which joins the Yellowstone between the Upper and Lower Falls. Surface Creek flows through Ribbon Lake (site 69) before rippling off the canyon rim in Silver Cord Cascade.

68. Cascade Lake

Description: Cascade Lake is shaped like a kidney bean. It lies up against the south base of the Washburn Range just a little west of Canyon, in the central part of the park. Its outlet, Cascade Creek, is about 4 feet wide and hooks first east, then south, and then back to the east, entering the Yellowstone River between Upper Falls and Lower Falls. The northwest flank of the lake is open and rocky, and the southeast flank's timber burned in 1988. The lake is small enough that most of it can be covered from shore, but there is enough muck on the bottom to make wading difficult.

The lake is free of ice early in the season, as it sits at only 8,000 feet. The best fishing takes place between mid-June and mid-July. Start with the area around the outlet and then work southwest around the shore, because the main trail, which continues on to Grebe Lake, is on the other bank.

The fish: Originally without fish, Cascade Lake now holds cutthroat trout and grayling. The fish run between 8 and 16 inches, with most coming in at about 12 inches.

Flies and lures: Unless there is some obvious hatch, start with an olive Scud. A small Woolly Bugger or Egg Sucking Leech would also be a good choice. Flies to have in the box include bead-head Hare's Ear, Prince, A. P. Black, and Pheasant Tail nymphs. Plan on carrying a few Pale Morning Duns, Blue-Winged Olives, and Elk Hair Caddis as well. If using spin tackle, start with a Spin-a-Lure. Other lures to have include Krocodiles, Little Cleos, Mepps, Stream-a-Lures, and Panther Martins.

Special equipment: Cascade Lake is a straightforward hike with minimal changes in altitude, making the lake a reasonable off-road float-tube destination.

Access: Either of two routes, both essentially the same length, 2.5 miles, will take you to Cascade Lake. They actually converge after the first 1.5 miles.

68a. Cascade Trailhead

Take the Norris-Canyon Road 0.6 mile west from Canyon or 11.4 miles east from Norris Junction to the Cascade Trailhead. The trailhead is on the north side of the road and within sight of Canyon Village. Park and hike to Cascade Lake. This trail parallels Cascade Creek.

68b. Cascade Picnic Area

Taking the Grand Loop Road north from Canyon 1.3 miles brings you to the Cascade Picnic Area and trailhead. This is 17.5 miles south of Tower Junction on the Grand Loop Road. The picnic area is on the west side of the highway. The Cascade Trail strikes west from the picnic area and joins the other trail 1 mile before Cascade Lake. There are backcountry campsites on the lake, contributing to its popularity.

69. Ribbon Lake *(see map on page 163)*

Description: Ribbon Lake is oddly shaped. The major portion of the lake has an oval shape, but there is a stringy, shallow bay off the western end. Excluding the bay, the lake is roughly 120 yards wide and 220 yards long. Surface Creek flows through the lake from south to north on its way over Silver Cord Cascade into the Grand Canyon of the Yellowstone. The shore of the major, fishable section drops off quickly, making wading of little use. The bottom is mostly muck or peatlike. At 7,800 feet, the ice goes off the lake at about the same time the season opens. Ribbon Lake fishing is best before mid-July. Surface Creek is just big enough to support the

When you've fished enough for one day, take in the majestic scenery of the Grand Canyon of the Yellowstone.

MICHAEL SAMPLE PHOTO

reproduction of fish but not really big enough to be a fishery in its own right. Its inlet and outlet areas are good places to start fishing.

The fish: Ribbon Lake holds rainbow trout. They are not particularly big, ranging from 6 to 14 inches. Most are under 10 inches.

Flies and lures: Start with a brown Leech or Woolly Bugger. Olive Scuds and Hare's Ear, bead-head Prince, and A.P. Black nymphs should also be in your box, along with some Adams. The spin angler should start with a Stream-a-Lure. Some other good bets are Kastmasters, Spin-a-Lures, Mepps, and Cyclone spoons.

Special equipment: The short, level hike makes this a reasonable float-tube target— or at least it would if the fish justified the labor, which probably is not the case.

Access: Drive south 2.3 miles on the Grand Loop Road from Canyon to the Artist Point Road. This is 13.5 miles north of Fishing Bridge Junction. Take the Artist Point Road 1.5 miles to its end. The Ribbon Lake Trailhead is at the Artist Point parking area. Hike the 2 miles of the Ribbon Lake Trail to the lake. Bypass the west bay and fish in the main body of the lake. There is a backcountry campsite on Ribbon Lake. An alternative route, much longer, is to take the Wapiti Lake Trail from the Chittenden Bridge Trailhead to its junction with the Ribbon Lake Trail, and the latter to the east end of the lake. This route is 3 miles long.

Tributaries: The only substantive tributary to Ribbon Lake is the already described Surface Creek.

70. Broad Creek (see map on page 163)

Description: Broad Creek begins in White Lake on the flank of the Mirror Plateau. It flows north and west to join the Yellowstone in the middle of the Grand Canyon. Overall, Broad Creek's course is about 15 miles long, divided into two unequal sections. The upper 10 miles, from White Lake to Josephs Coat Springs, is on the plateau and only drops 200 feet. The lower 5 miles cut into the canyon and drop 1,700 feet. The fires of 1988 burned most of the upper part of the upper section from just west of the Wapiti Lake Trail crossing to south of Tern Lake. This water fishes best between late June and mid-August.

The relatively small population of fish is concentrated in the section between Josephs Coat Springs and Fern Lake. This reach is characterized by a broad, shallow channel with a small-cobble and rubble bottom. The banks are fairly open, with a mix of meadow grass and timber. The best spots to look for fish are at the heads of the pools formed by the many meander corners and along the deeper undercut banks. Extremely high spring runoff in 1996 and 1997 has churned the bottom and engorged many of the holes. The stream will restructure itself if given a couple of years of more average snowpacks.

The fish: The extremely steep lower canyon of Broad Creek is an insurmountable barrier for fish in the Yellowstone River. There is no record of any official introduction of fish to the stream above Josephs Coat Springs, but cutthroat trout were planted by somebody prior to 1975. They range from 6 to 16 inches, with most being between 12 and 14 inches. I have never heard that there were large numbers of fish in this section, but they are generally considered to be less discriminating than the average park fish. Wapiti Lake and the entire tributary system to Broad Creek remains without fish.

Flies and lures: Odds are a Royal Wulff or Royal Coachman Trude will get the job done. A hopper in high summer, or a bead-head Prince if they will not come to the surface, are other good choices. The stream is pretty small, so good lure choices include Li'l Jake's, Panther Martins, Cyclones, and Kamloopers.

Access: The best access to Broad Creek is the Wapiti Lake Trail. Starting at Canyon, drive 2.3 miles south on the Grand Loop Road to the Artist Point Road. This junction is 13.5 miles north of Fishing Bridge Junction. Cross the Yellowstone on Chittenden Bridge and immediately turn right into the trailhead parking area. The Wapiti Lake Trail is on the east side of the parking lot. Hike 14 miles east on the Wapiti Lake Trail to the Broad Creek ford. Fish either upstream or down.

There are a number of backcountry campsites along the creek between Josephs Coat Springs and Fern Lake. The area south of Fern Lake, including all of the upper Pelican Creek drainage, is in a day-use-only bear management area. This makes access on the trails up Pelican Creek virtually impossible without a horse and no picnic with one.

71. Yellowstone River Drainage, Broad Creek to Lamar River

Description: Isolated by high and impassable canyon walls, the middle section of the Grand Canyon of the Yellowstone is unavailable to the angler. The lower, northern end of the canyon opens up with several accessible stretches. The sheer rock walls of the upper canyon give way to more gently sloped walls interspersed with mineral-stained, nearly vertical sections capped by basalt. Several islands create classic gravel-bar riffle corners. More common is a steep bank, often dropping from a timbered bench within the canyon, terminating in scattered boulder fields. The river is impossible to wade, even in low water, but access is available to both banks. The fish are concentrated in the riffle corners and the boulder fields.

The Yellowstone is often too dirty to fish on opening day and rises steadily until well into June. The first real chance to make anything happen is after the river crests and starts to clear. The salmonfly hatch occurs here around the middle of July. Fishing is best between mid-July and Labor Day, though there will be some activity right up until the end of the season. Note that Agate Creek and the area around its mouth are closed until July 15 to protect spawning fish.

The fish: The vast majority of the fish in this reach are cutthroat trout. There are a few cutbows up as far as Tower Creek and an occasional rainbow around the mouth of the Lamar. I have even caught a brook trout or two just above Tower Creek, the stream from which they obviously had strayed. The fish range from 6 to 19 inches, with most falling between 11 and 14 inches.

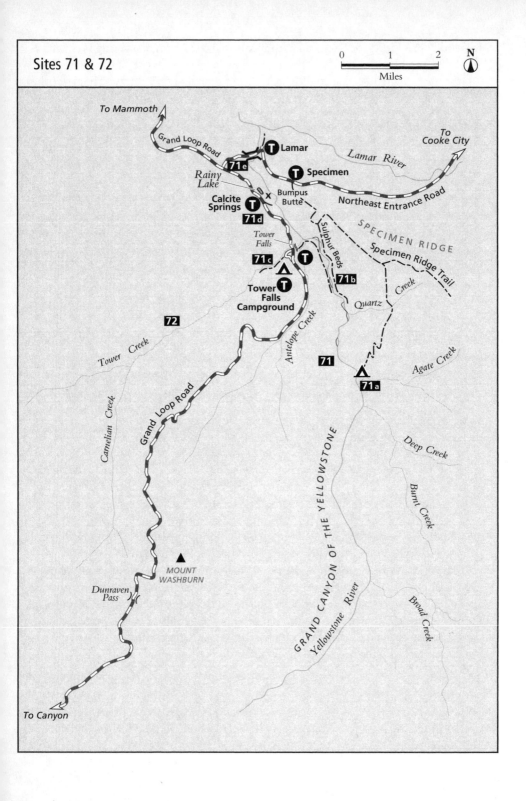

Sites 71 & 72

0   1   2
Miles

N

To Mammoth

Grand Loop Road

T Lamar

Lamar River

To Cooke City

71e

Rainy Lake

T Specimen

Bumpus Butte

Northeast Entrance Road

Calcite Springs **T**

71d

SPECIMEN RIDGE

Specimen Ridge Trail

Tower Falls

71c

T

Sulphur Beds

71b

Tower Falls Campground **T**

Quartz Creek

72

Antelope Creek

71

Agate Creek

Tower Creek

71a

Carnelian Creek

Grand Loop Road

Deep Creek

Burnt Creek

MOUNT WASHBURN

Dunraven Pass

GRAND CANYON OF THE YELLOWSTONE

Yellowstone River

Broad Creek

To Canyon

Flies and lures: Start with a double bead-head Bitch Creek or bead-head Brooks' Stone nymph as the water drops and clears. Once the salmonfly hatch gets under way, switch to an Elk Salmonfly or orange Stimulator. During the rest of the season, use Royal Coachman Trudes, Letort Hoppers, or bead-head Princes. Late in the season, Blue-Winged Olives match the hatch; at this time the fish may become more selective. The lure angler should start with a Cyclone spoon. Other good choices include the Kamlooper, Mepps, and Panther Martin.

Access: The Bear Management Plan closes most of the Antelope Creek drainage, and in the process prevents access to the west side of the river, starting 2 miles above Tower Falls. This closure zone has a lobe extending across the river to the east bank between Quartz and Agate Creeks.

71a. Agate Creek

Agate Creek joins the Yellowstone from the east some 6 miles above the Lamar confluence. Take the Northeast Entrance Road for 2 miles east from Tower Junction, or 31.1 miles west from Cooke City, to the Specimen Trailhead. The parking area is on the north side of the road. Several large boulders backed by pines rim the parking area. The trail heads south from across the road. Take the Specimen Trail 3 miles to the Agate Creek Trail junction and follow the latter another 3 miles to the mouth of Agate Creek. Agate Creek itself has very little fishable water, but a mile of the east bank of the Yellowstone, mostly below Agate Creek, is available. A backcountry campsite makes this a nice overnight trip, but it is really out of range for a day trip. A horse is nice here: The trail first climbs 1,240 feet and then drops back 1,140 feet.

71b. Sulphur Beds

The better part of 3 miles of the east bank of the Yellowstone is accessible via the anglers' track generally called the Sulphur Beds Trail. This is not a formally maintained trail. Take the Northeast Entrance Road to the Specimen Trailhead. This is 2 miles east of Tower Junction or 31.1 miles west of Cooke City. Take the Specimen Trail 1.25 miles to the ridge top. The Yellowstone River is clearly visible to the south up the canyon, and the Specimen Trail obviously goes on east up the face of the ridgeline.

The anglers' track drops straight down a ridge to the river in an area where thermal activity has prevented any plant growth. The stench makes it obvious why this is called the Sulphur Beds. The track continues 2 miles upriver to a point above Quartz Creek, and you can also go downstream 0.5 mile to just below and across from the mouth of Tower Creek. Going another 100 feet east up the Specimen Trail cuts another anglers' track heading up the canyon. This one makes better use of the contour to cut the river 0.5 mile above the corner where the first trail comes down. It will often work to go in on the first trail but out on the second, because a day's fishing usually gets you at least that far upriver. The vertical component of this trail is up 350 feet from the trailhead and down 400 feet to the river, the latter having a very steep gradient as well.

71c. Tower Falls

Tower Falls is the highest point to access the west side of the river. Drive south on the Grand Loop Road 2.4 miles from Tower Junction or north 16.4 miles from Canyon Junction. The Tower Falls parking area is on the east side of the highway. The Tower Falls store helps keep the parking area full. You may have to circle it a couple of times to find a parking spot during the height of the summer season. The access road to the Tower Falls Campground is directly across the highway to the west. Take the paved trail to the Tower Falls Overlook, which goes north from the store. A short hike of 0.25 mile gets you down to the confluence of Tower Creek with the Yellowstone River. Fish upstream. An anglers' track crosses the mouth of Antelope Creek and heads upriver. It is often best to bypass the first 400 yards of river until you are around the bend and out of sight of the casual visitor. You have 2 miles of river upstream before you get cut off by impassable terrain. The drop to the river from the parking area is only 277 feet, making this one of the easier routes to the water.

71d. Calcite Springs

Taking the Grand Loop Road 1 mile south from Tower Junction past Rainy Lake brings you to an unmarked pullout on the left side of the road. This pullout is on the right, 17.8 miles north of Canyon Junction. The pullout is just big enough for one or two cars. A poorly defined anglers' track drops through a heavily timbered break in the canyon wall to the riverbank just upstream from the Calcite Springs vents. The vertical on this tough route is 350 feet. No more than 500 yards of riverbank is accessible from this point before being cut off by canyon walls both up and downstream. There is just enough room here for one party of no more than three people for about half a day, so if somebody has beat you to the spot, forget it.

71e. Tower Junction Bridge

The Northeast Entrance Road crosses the Yellowstone 0.6 mile east of Tower Junction or 32.5 miles west of Cooke City. Limited access, both upstream and down on both sides of the river, is available at the bridge. It is a steep 50 feet down to the river. As the highway winds its way back up out of the canyon on the east side, a stub road goes north to a parking area on the canyon rim. A 0.5-mile hike to the north brings you to the confluence of the Lamar with the Yellowstone. Unless the water is too high, you can get upstream for some distance back toward the Tower Junction Bridge from the confluence. It has to be pretty low before you can get all the way along the base of the cliff.

Tributaries: The tributaries of interest to the angler in this section are Broad Creek (site 70) and Tower Creek (site 72), and the Lamar River (sites 73 and 79). The Lamar and its tributaries make up a major portion of this section. Antelope Creek has only a few small fish, and its upper section is closed by the Bear Management Plan. Deep, Agate, and Quartz Creeks are not of much use to the angler.

72. Tower Creek *(see map on page 168)*

Description: Tower Creek lives in a canyon. Its sources drop off the north flank of the Washburn Range 1,000 feet or more in their first mile or two. Thereafter, the gradient is only moderate in comparison to the first headlong rush. The 132-foot Tower Falls spills between two of the stone pillars that prompted the name for the stream, just 100 yards upstream from its confluence with the Yellowstone River. The lower 4 miles was burned in 1988. The bed, 20 to 30 feet wide, is steep and consists of pools between big boulders. There is a fair amount of deadfall, particularly in the lower section. Runoff makes the stream unfishable until late June or early July. Fishing is concentrated in the pools.

The fish: Tower Creek is two entirely different streams when it comes to fish. Below Tower Falls the stream is dominated by cutthroat trout up out of the Yellowstone. Above Tower Falls the population is a mix of midget brook trout and smallish rainbows. The July cutthroat below the falls are typically 13 to 16 inches long. The brookies above the falls, and the few that get over the falls into the lower creek, range from 4 to 11 inches, with the average between 7 and 9 inches.

Flies and lures: Above the falls start and finish with a Royal Coachman Trude. Below the falls, during the salmonfly hatch on the adjacent river, start with an Elk Salmonfly. Later in the season, it is back to the Trude. Because of the small size of the stream, keep spinning lures small. Begin with a Cyclone spoon. If that does not get results, try Panther Martins, Rooster Tails, or Kamloopers.

Access: All access to Tower Creek is from the Tower Falls area. Take the Grand Loop Road 2.4 miles south from Tower Junction or 16.4 miles north from Canyon to Tower Falls. Upstream access is to the west off the Tower Falls Campground loop. The trailhead is at the top of the hill on the north edge of the campground. Fish upstream. The lower 100 yards of stream is reached by taking the Tower Falls Overlook Trail from the parking area at the store to the viewing platform, and then the trail that switchbacks down to the mouth of the creek. Fish up the creek from the mouth.

Tributaries: Carnelian Creek is the largest tributary to Tower Creek. It is of little interest to the angler because it provides nothing that cannot be found more easily in Tower Creek itself.

The Lamar River Drainage

The Lamar River rises on the west flank of the Absaroka Range, which defines Yellowstone National Park's eastern border. We are fortunate not to have to use the full moniker, Lucius Quintus Cincinnatus Lamar, of the Secretary of the Interior for whom the river is named. The river is more than 43 miles long, making it the largest single tributary basin to the Yellowstone River within the park. From the angler's perspective, the defining characteristic of the Lamar is its tendency to get quite muddy from the lightest of rains.

Mileage points: Mileages in this section are described driving east from Tower Junction or west from Cooke City.

73. Lamar River, Hoodoo Basin to Soda Butte Creek

Description: The Lamar River tumbles north off Lamar Mountain and hooks west through the jumbled country of the Hoodoo Basin. Gathering in the Little Lamar and Cold Creek, its course bends to the northwest to pick up successively Miller, Calfee, and Cache Creeks. These drainages are all steep. The streambeds are generally rubble and boulders with frequent logjams. The area was burned extensively in 1988. After Cold Creek, the tributaries coming from Specimen Ridge to the west are short, steep, small, and generally without fish. All told, it is 30 miles from Lamar Mountain to Soda Butte Creek. Each tributary adds some water, and the Lamar's gradient gets flatter below Miller Creek. The gradient does not flatten enough to support larger fish until the last 3 miles below the river's confluence with Cache Creek.

   The Lamar is roaring on opening day. One year it was discharging 20,000 cubic feet per second on June 5, but by October of that year it was doubtful that it was flowing at a rate much above 200 cubic feet per second. The river reaches a fishable level sometime around mid-July most years. In the upper section the best water is found in the pools formed around the logjams. Between Miller and Cache Creeks the fishable water is formed by pools created by cobble and gravel bars, but the fishable segments are relatively short. Below Cache Creek the river flattens, widens over large bars formed of gravel and cobble, and slows. In this water the riffle corners and following pools are the key waters to search for fish.

   Historically, the Lamar has been subject to extreme seasonal water-flow fluctuations. Because its upper sections cut through old glacial lake beds, and tributaries cut barren slopes of soft materials, even small amounts of rain flush massive amounts of mud downstream. This has been characteristic of the Lamar throughout my experience.

Sites 73 & 74

0   2   4
Miles

N

Northeast Entrance

Silver Gate

Cooke City

REPUBLIC MTN.

▲ 4WD only

212

MONTANA

WYOMING

Pebble Creek

▲ *ABIATHAR PEAK*

74c

Republic Pass

To **Red Lodge, MT**
Cody, WY

▲

Thunderer Ⓣ **74b**

▲ *The Thunderer*

YELLOWSTONE NATIONAL PARK

To Tower

Northeast Entrance Road

Soda Butte Creek

Cache Creek

74

ABSAROKA RANGE

Lamar River Ⓣ
74a

Lamar

MOUNT NORRIS ▲

Lamar River Trail

Calfee Creek

Boot Jack Gap

To Crandall Creek

Miller ▲ *Creek*

73

Hoodoo Basin

▲ *LAMAR MTN.*

Little Lamar

Mist Creek

Cold Creek

To Pelican Creek Trailhead

The fish: The upper segment of the Lamar River holds cutthroat trout. There is an outside chance the angler will encounter a cutbow as far upstream as the short canyon section below Cache Creek. At the lower end of this reach, the fish range from 8 to 20 inches, with most between 13 and 16 inches. As you go upstream the average size shrinks, though in the small waters above Calfee Creek, the cutthroat tend to hold their size better than brookies.

Flies and lures: Except for the lower couple of miles, basic attractor patterns such as a Royal Coachman Trude or Prince nymph is all that is required. During high summer a Dave's Hopper is also usually a good bet. In the lower section of the river, fish are much more selective. This part of the river also has a hatch that can really turn fish on in August and September, a hatch best matched by a large Blue Dun. The spinning angler should start with a Kamlooper or Stream-a-Lure. Get down to ultralight Mepps in the upper reaches.

Access: This segment of the Lamar can only be reached by road at its lower end. Drive east 15.2 miles from Tower Junction on the Northeast Entrance Road or west 17.9 miles from Cooke City to the Lamar Trailhead. It is on the east side of the highway on a bluff overlooking Soda Butte Creek 1 mile upstream from where the two come together. Take the trail southeast across the flat to meet the Lamar about 1 mile upstream from the confluence. Alternatively, wade across Soda Butte Creek just upstream from its mouth and fish up the Lamar. The Lamar River Trail ascends the river for several miles. Trails go up Cache and Miller Creeks as well, hooking up to the south with the Pelican Creek Trail via Mist Pass. The Miller Creek Trail follows that stream to its head, then climbs over the divide to Crandall Creek through Boot Jack Gap. All of these are long trails, generally exceeding 15 miles. There are many backcountry campsites along the upper Lamar and Miller Creek.

Tributaries: The most fishable tributaries to the Lamar in this reach are the Little Lamar River, Miller Creek, Calfee Creek, Cache Creek, and Soda Butte Creek. Of these, only Cache Creek (site 74) and Soda Butte Creek (sites 75 and 77) rate their own descriptions.

74. Cache Creek (see map on page 173)

Description: Cache Creek has its beginnings on the back side of Republic Peak south of Cooke City. It flows southwesterly to join the Lamar. In general, it parallels the course of Soda Butte Creek, but on the east side of the mountain ridge defined by Abiathar Peak, The Thunderer, and Mount Norris. If Soda Butte is muddy, assume that Cache Creek is as well, and vice versa. Like the other upper tributaries to the Lamar, Cache Creek is steep and runs on a bed of rubble. The fish are not evenly distributed. The steeper sections, even though they have pockets that appear capable of holding fish, really do not produce much. Then you get to a bigger pool behind a boulder or deadfall dam and find it holding several fish. On balance, the stream runs 10 to 15 feet wide. The drainage was subjected to intense fire activity during 1988.

The fish: The fish in Cache Creek are all cutthroat trout ranging between 6 and 13 inches, with most being in the 9-inch class.

Flies and lures: Start with a Royal Coachman Trude or Royal Wulff. In August a Dave's Hopper or yellow Stimulator should be effective. If these do not produce results, changing flies probably will not help. The stream is so small that the spin angler will find it tough going. Keep lures small—Mepps, Panther Martins, or Triple Teazers.

Access: There are three main routes into Cache Creek. Only the first is really useful as a day trip.

74a. Lamar River Trail

Take the Northeast Entrance Road west 17.9 miles from Cooke City or east 15.2 miles from Tower Junction to the Lamar River Trailhead on Soda Butte Creek. The parking area is on a bluff overlooking the creek to the east. Take the Lamar River Trail 3.1 miles to Cache Creek. Fish up the creek. There is a backcountry campsite near the junction of the Cache Creek and Lamar River Trails. The Cache Creek Trail closely parallels the creek as far as it is useful to the angler.

74b. Thunderer Trailhead

Drive west from Cooke City 12.5 miles on the Northeast Entrance Road to Thunderer Trailhead. The trailhead is 20.6 miles east of Tower Junction. Take the Thunderer Cutoff Trail 5.3 miles to its junction with the Cache Creek Trail. Fish downstream. It is 10.6 miles back down to the Lamar River. There are some intermediate backcountry campsites. High water prevents fording Soda Butte Creek until late June or early July, but that is no problem since the pass crests at 8,800 feet and is blocked by snow until then anyway. This is not for the casual hiker. It is 1,900 vertical feet up from Soda Butte and 1,120 feet back down to Cache Creek. The Cache Creek Trail continues up over Republic Pass to Cooke City.

74c. Republic Pass Trailhead

At the west end of Cooke City, between the first buildings and the woods, take Republic Street heading south toward Soda Butte Creek. Unless you have a serious four-wheel-drive vehicle, use the space near the solid waste transfer station to park. From this point cross Soda Butte Creek. The road initially turns right down Soda Butte, and then, within 100 feet, there is another track heading left up the hill. This track goes to the defunct Irma Mine. It only saves about a mile of walking, but there are 400 vertical feet in that mile. It is 11 miles from the transfer station to the junction with the Thunderer Cutoff Trail. The trail crests at 10,000 feet in Republic Pass before starting back down again. In my estimation, this is not even for the stout of heart.

75. Soda Butte Creek, Headwaters to Pebble Creek

Description: Soda Butte Creek really begins in springs alongside U.S. Highway 212 just east of Cooke City. It generally flows west and southwest to its confluence with the Lamar River. Miller and Republic Creeks, both of which join Soda Butte Creek in Cooke City, help make it a stream that runs 15 to 20 feet wide. These tributaries are too steep to hold fish. Republic Creek, for instance, drops over 1,500 feet in its 4-mile existence. The short section of Soda Butte above Cooke City has also been degraded by old mine tailings dumped in its bed.

Soda Butte Creek sheds 700 feet of altitude in 14 stream miles from the mouth of Republic Creek to its junction with Pebble Creek. This relatively moderate gradient provides for a stream that meanders through a mix of timber and meadow over a bed of gravel and cobble. The pools formed by the gravel bars and frequent deadfall are the best spots to look for fish. While theoretically open on the third Saturday of May, that section outside the park remains unfishable at that time due to spring snowmelt. I do not expect anything of Soda Butte until after the Fourth of July. Most years this section will provide fishing through early September but not much thereafter.

The fish: Until recently it was thought that all the fish in this section of the Soda Butte drainage were cutthroat trout. In the last couple of years, though, a few brook trout have turned up above Silver Gate. The good holding water and moderate gradient have given the stream an opportunity to grow fish larger than one might expect from a small mountain drainage. They range from 6 to 18 inches, with good numbers of fish in the 11- to 14-inch range.

Flies and lures: Absent any evidence to the contrary, start with an attractor such as a Royal Coachman Trude or bead-head Prince. In late summer a hopper pattern is always in order. The thing to watch for, especially later in the season, is the big gray drake hatch. This bug gets the fish cranking even when there are only a few of them on the water at any one time. The nymph for this is an olive Hare's Ear, or, if you'd rather use a dry fly, try a big Blue Dun. The size of the stream suggests that the spin angler should keep it small. Try Mepps, Panther Martins, Cyclones, and Li'l Jake's.

Access: At no point is Soda Butte Creek as much as a mile from the road throughout this whole reach. The top 4 miles, however, have restricted access due to private property, mostly homesites, between the highway and the stream. You will not miss much. Icebox Canyon can only be entered from its lower end. Use the Thunderer Trailhead, located 12.5 miles west of Cooke City or 20.6 miles east of Tower Junction on the Northeast Entrance Road, to access Icebox Canyon. Sometimes a stream that is out of sight behind some trees is also out of mind. The Northeast Entrance Road crosses the stream twice, providing obvious access, and there are numerous other pullouts. Find a section that somebody else is not already using.

Tributaries: Many intermittent channels drop off the flanking peaks. They can carry immense quantities of water and debris but are more often dry. Miller, Republic, Warm, and Amphitheater Creeks flow all year but are all too steep, too small, or both to be viable fisheries. Pebble Creek (site 76) is the only tributary of interest to the angler.

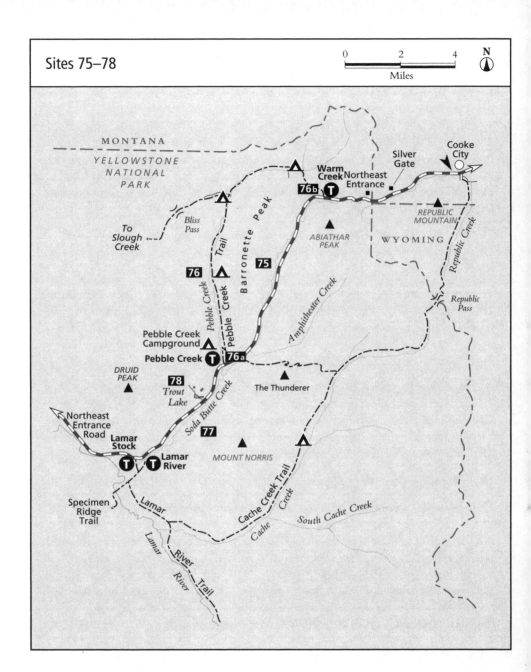

0   2   4   Miles

N

MONTANA

YELLOWSTONE
NATIONAL
PARK

To
Slough
Creek

Bliss
Pass

Barronette Peak

Warm
Creek

Silver
Gate

Cooke
City

Northeast
Entrance

76b

REPUBLIC
MOUNTAIN

WYOMING

ABIATHAR
PEAK

75

Republic Creek

Republic
Pass

Pebble Creek Trail

Pebble Creek

76

Amphitheater Creek

Pebble Creek
Campground

Pebble Creek

76a

DRUID
PEAK

78

Trout
Lake

The Thunderer

Soda Butte Creek

Northeast
Entrance
Road

Lamar
Stock

Lamar
River

77

MOUNT NORRIS

Cache Creek Trail

Specimen
Ridge
Trail

Lamar

Cache Creek

South Cache Creek

Lamar River Trail

River

76. Pebble Creek

Description: Pebble Creek begins in the extreme northeast corner of Yellowstone
National Park and flows generally south for 10 miles to its confluence with Soda
Butte Creek. The uppermost 2 miles are very steep and too small to interest anglers,
as the streamlets hold either small fish or no fish at all. The fishable section of the

creek is divided into two sections. The upper 5 miles is a series of meadows, across which the stream wanders with a moderate gradient. The creek is generally about 15 feet wide in a channel 20 to 25 feet wide. The pools at the heads of the corners and next to undercut banks are the places to look for fish. This upper part of the drainage was burned during 1988.

The lower 3 miles of Pebble Creek are in a steeper canyon section. Here the best water is the pools formed by the big cobble and boulders that characterize the bed. There are also frequent deadfall trees that make miniature dams. The creek drops and clears enough to become fishable in early July. It is not unusual for it to be clear when the Lamar River and Soda Butte Creek are not. The best time to fish Pebble Creek is in July and August.

The fish: Pebble Creek holds cutthroat trout. The fish range from 6 to 15 inches. In the canyon section the average is under 10 inches, but in the meadow area the average is a little larger.

Flies and lures: This is another place where I would start with a Royal Coachman Trude and probably never switch. A bead-head Prince is the wet equivalent. In the meadow section, particularly in August, a Dave's Hopper is a good idea. Anglers using spin tackle need to keep the lures small. Try Panther Martins, Cyclones, Mepps, Kamloopers, or Triple Teazers.

Access: The only vehicular access is the Northeast Entrance Road, which crosses Pebble Creek just above its junction with Soda Butte Creek. The Pebble Creek Campground is a small facility on the creek with a much nicer character than the large, industrial-scale campgrounds found in much of the park. The Pebble Creek Trail provides access to the rest of the creek.

76a. Pebble Creek Trailhead

The best access point for the canyon section and the lower part of the meadow section is the Pebble Creek Trailhead. Drive west on the Northeast Entrance Road 13.3 miles from Cooke City. The trailhead is located on the north side of the highway. If coming from the Tower Junction side, drive east 19.8 miles. Find the trailhead on the left just after crossing Pebble Creek. Take the trail north along the creek. The trail parallels the creek for 11 miles. Even when the creek is out of sight at the bottom of the hill behind trees, it is seldom more than 200 yards away. If using horses the stock trailhead is 0.2 mile to the west at the campground.

76b. Warm Creek Trailhead

The best route providing access to the upper section of Pebble Creek, or if you are planning to take the Bliss Pass Trail into upper Slough Creek, is the Warm Creek Trail. Take the Northeast Entrance Road west 5.1 miles from Cooke City or east 28 miles from Tower Junction to the trailhead. A 0.1-mile stub road on the north side of the highway brings you to the new trailhead facility. The trail heads north and then west over the saddle between Barronette Peak and Meridian Peak. It is 1.5

miles to the upper end of the meadow section of the creek. The bad news is that the trail climbs up 1,000 feet and drops down 250 feet in that mile and a half.

77. Soda Butte Creek, Pebble Creek to Lamar River
(see map on page 177)

Description: Pebble Creek joins Soda Butte Creek in Round Prairie, a 1-mile-diameter meadow. The lower 6 miles of Soda Butte only drops 200 feet, a big chunk of it in the 0.5-mile-long section where the creek tips out of Round Prairie. Pebble Creek adds a substantial amount of water, making Soda Butte run 20 to 30 feet wide. The stream flattens out again in Soda Butte Meadow. Large gravel bars, with their associated riffles and pools, dominate the streambed. Most of this section meanders across open grass meadows. Braided channels around the gravel bars are common. The one little canyon section is dominated by small pools around large boulders.

Soda Butte Creek is unfishable until sometime in July. The angler should target the edges of the riffle corners and pools along the grass banks. The Soda Butte often carries a touch of sediment, so, absent a serious hatch, fish the structure. The fishing holds up remarkably well into the fall. The fish become increasingly wary, so one should not expect to catch a lot of them. Typically, the fish in the canyon section are more numerous, smaller, and less critical of the angler's offering. Do not expect to find solitude on Soda Butte Creek. Its quality, notoriety, and accessibility all make for heavy pressure from large numbers of anglers.

The fish: Cutthroat trout dominate this section of Soda Butte Creek. A rainbow or cutbow is not impossible in the lower couple of miles of this section. In Round Prairie the fish range from 10 to 16 inches, with most at the small end of the scale. In the canyon section the fish run 5 to 12 inches, most under 9 inches. In Soda Butte Meadow the range is 8 to 22 inches, with substantial numbers between 14 and 18 inches.

Flies and lures: Morning fishing tends to be very slow in Soda Butte Creek. Start with a Royal Coachman Trude or bead-head Prince. In the afternoon look to a yellow Stimulator or hopper pattern. Watch for the gray drake emergence, as that will excite the fish; a big Blue Dun is the best bet for this hatch. The spin angler should keep lures small. Start with a Cyclone spoon, and if that does not produce, try Panther Martins, Stream-a-Lures, or Triple Teazers.

Access: There is no mystery about access to this section of Soda Butte Creek. For practical purposes, it is all within sight of the Northeast Entrance Road, with numerous useful pullouts. The section begins at the junction of Pebble Creek with Soda Butte Creek and ends at the Soda Butte's confluence with the Lamar River. If coming from Tower Junction, this stretch is between 13.8 and 19.6 miles east along the Northeast Entrance Road. If coming from Montana, you will cross Pebble Creek 13.5 miles west of Cooke City; follow the creek closely to the confluence 19.3 miles west of Cooke City.

Tributaries: The only significant tributary to Soda Butte Creek in this reach is Trout Lake (site 78).

78. Trout Lake *(see map on page 177)*

Description: Trout Lake is a small lake, roughly 250 yards across. It lies in a fold on the side of the Soda Butte valley and is largely surrounded by timber. The western end has a more open grass-and-sagebrush bank. A small stream runs through the lake, entering on the north and exiting to the southeast. The bottom is fairly solid and can be waded to some extent, but offshore weed beds limit an angler's ability to cover the lake from shore.

Ice is not generally a factor on Trout Lake. The stream running through the lake has a short and low drainage, so the spring mud, very much a factor elsewhere, is not an issue here. The lake opens for fishing on June 15, but be aware that the inlet stream stays closed until July 15, the end of the spawning season. Fishing is usually best during this first month. Weed growth makes for difficult fishing in high summer, and by fall the fish are deeper and spookier.

The fish: Trout Lake carries a mix of rainbow, cutthroat, and cutbow trout. The average size is 14 to 18 inches. Some of the fish, rainbows in particular, attain extraordinary size. I have seen fish to 29 inches and weighing more than ten pounds. Trout Lake fish have experience with anglers and are seldom easy to catch.

Flies and lures: First choice on Trout Lake should be a damselfly nymph pattern such as a Skinny Bugger. Other good bets include the Woolly Bugger, tan Woolly Worm, Otter nymph, tan Scud, and Hare's Ear nymph. If a hatch and rise are on, do the obvious thing. Pale Morning Duns, Blue-Winged Olives, midges, and large caddis imitate the more common hatches. Spin anglers should try Rapalas, Mepps, Cyclones, and Kamloopers.

Special equipment: Trout Lake is a good location to use a float tube. The hike is short, and the tube provides position, particularly in relation to the timber around much of the shoreline. I have even seen people carrying canoes up here, and in truth, I am sure there are far worse portages.

Access: There is no sign announcing Trout Lake nor is there any reason to suspect its presence. Take the Northeast Entrance Road 14.8 miles west from Cooke City or 18.3 miles east from Tower Junction to the parking area. The pullout is a large one on the north side of the road. There are usually at least one or two vehicles ahead of you. If coming from the Tower side, the Soda Butte, a hot-spring cone on the side of the road that is signed, is 2.1 miles before the Trout Lake Trailhead. The trailhead is 1.3 miles past Pebble Creek if coming from the Cooke City side. Take the trail that goes up the hill from the west end of the parking area. A short hike of about 400 yards brings you to the east end of the lake between the inlet and outlet.

Tributaries: The stream running through Trout Lake is closed during the only time any part of it would be of interest to anglers. Leave it alone.

79. Lamar River, Soda Butte Creek to the Yellowstone Confluence

Description: The Lamar takes on two different characters in the lower 14-mile stretch of river. Most of it is in the Lamar Valley, described by Osbourn Russell in his 1836 journal as "this beautiful Vale" of "wild romantic scenery." The valley runs a bit more than 1 mile wide and 7 miles long. The river meanders from side to side across the valley, its streambed characterized by broad gravel bars and its bank covered with tall grass. A herd of bison munches its way up and down the valley, while in the hills the howl of the wolf again reverberates as it must have in Russell's day. Specimen Ridge, a layer cake of petrified trees, agate, and volcanic ash, forms the south rim. Rounded hills covered by short bunch grass, sage, and scattered aspen patches flank the north side.

Next is a short canyon section where the riverbed is formed of big rocks, the smaller ones the size of Volkswagens, the bigger ones the size of buses. The Northeast Entrance Road crosses the river at the bottom of the canyon. The remaining 5 miles of the river are characterized by scattered big boulders in a bed of medium-size cobble. There are big pools separated by short steep sections. The fish-holding water is in the pools and around the boulders.

In most years this reach of the Lamar, unfishable due to flood and mud on opening day, starts to kick in about mid-July. The complex of stonefly emergences we call the salmonfly hatch reaches the Lamar around the third week of July. This gets the season going. By mid-September activity is much slower and depends on the angler's ability to find fish working the remnants of some particular scattered mayfly or caddis hatch. Ready access by road contributes to the Lamar fish being hit hard by experienced anglers. The fish quickly become leader-shy, selective, and downright quirky.

The fish: The dominant fish in this section is the cutthroat trout. There are also a fair number of rainbows and cutbows, particularly in the section below the bridge carrying the Northeast Entrance Road across the river. The fish range from 6 to 22 inches, but most will run 10 to 16 inches.

Flies and lures: Leading up to and during the salmonfly hatch, use double bead-head Bitch Creeks, bead-head Brooks' Stone, or Yuk Bugs for nymphs; Parks' Salmonflies, Matt's Stones, or Stimulators in dries. The remainder of the season various hopper, ant, and beetle patterns are meat and potatoes. The gravy comes from the scattered green drake and gray drake hatches. Use a Green Drake or big Blue Dun. A Woolly Bugger or Muddler Minnow is usually a good choice in a streamer. The lure angler should start with a Spin-a-Lure or Stream-a-Lure. Other good choices include Panther Martins, Mepps, Cyclones, and Kamloopers.

Access: The Northeast Entrance Road parallels the river, in some spots very closely, for this entire 14-mile segment. Try to find a spot (not always easy to do) that some other angler is not already working. Use any of the numerous pullouts and fish either upstream or down.

Site 79

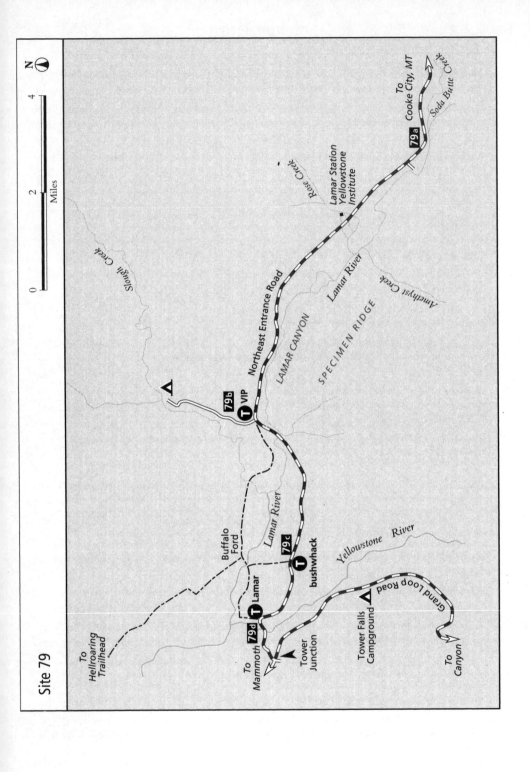

79a. Soda Butte Confluence

Soda Butte Creek joins the Lamar 13.8 miles east of Tower Junction on the Northeast Entrance Road. There are two pullouts 200 yards apart at the confluence on the north side of the highway 19.3 miles west of Cooke City. There is a period early in the season when Soda Butte Creek and the Lamar River above their junction are individually wadeable, but the Lamar below is not. Park here to ford Soda Butte Creek and then the Lamar River to hike down and fish the water below the confluence.

79b. VIP Pullout

At one time a two-track road went west along the bank of the Lamar from the entrance to the Slough Creek Road to the lower end of Slough Creek and its VIP Pool. While the road has been closed, its route continues to provide a trail along the north side of the Lamar in the stretch where the highway is on the south side. Drive east 6.2 miles on the Northeast Entrance Road from Tower Junction and turn left on the Slough Creek Road. The parking area is on the left, exactly at the junction of the Slough Creek Road. Hike downstream to fish back toward your car. Take the Northeast Entrance Road 26.9 miles west from Cooke City to the VIP Pullout.

79c. Lamar Bushwhack

Take the Northeast Entrance Road 2.6 miles east from Tower Junction to an unmarked pullout on the north side of the highway. This pullout is on the outside of a bend overlooking some remnant glacial ponds in the slope down to the Lamar River. It is 30.5 miles west of Cooke City. Follow the game trail 1 mile down over the sage and bunch grass–covered slopes to the Lamar River and fish either up or downstream. By midsummer it is possible to wade the Lamar here at a natural ford shown on some maps as "Buffalo Ford." Do not confuse this with the Buffalo Ford Picnic Area on the Yellowstone River between the lake and Canyon.

79d. Lamar Outlet

Just 0.9 mile east of Tower Junction, and right after crossing the Yellowstone River on the Northeast Entrance Road, turn left into a large parking area on the canyon rim. Drive 32.2 miles west from Cooke City on the Northeast Entrance Road and turn right into the parking area. Take the trail north from the parking area 0.5 mile to the confluence of the Lamar with the Yellowstone. Fish up the Lamar. It is difficult , even in low water, to wade across the mouth of the Lamar, but by late July it is usually possible to ford the Lamar about 300 yards upstream.

Tributaries: Most of the tributaries in this section are trivial and of no interest to anglers. Rose Creek has a few fish, but the really small streams like Crystal and Amethyst Creeks do not. The principle tributary system is the Slough Creek drainage.

The Slough Creek Drainage

Slough Creek is the Lamar's most famous tributary, in some minds overshadowing the main stem stream. It rises outside the north boundary of Yellowstone National Park in the Absaroka-Beartooth Wilderness and flows generally south to its confluence with the Lamar.

Mileage points: Mileages are given from Cooke City to the east and Tower Junction to the west.

80. Lake Abundance

Description: Lake Abundance lies at the head of Lake Abundance Creek, which flows for 6 miles to the west before joining Slough Creek. Larger than many alpine lakes at a little over 17 acres and deeper than most at 37 feet, it is the best of the headwaters lakes in the Slough Creek drainage. Most of the rest are without fish, and none of the others produce anything bigger than 10 inches. The bottom is rocky. Except for the eastern end, the lake is surrounded with timber that burned in 1988. Grass and marsh banks circle the eastern end of the lake.

Lake Abundance is subject to Montana regulations, but the weather really sets the calendar. At 8,400 feet, the ice is usually off before anybody can get in through the higher passes providing most access routes. The lake can be expected to fish well through the summer. For a backcountry lake it gets a lot of traffic, so do not expect to have it to yourself.

The fish: Lake Abundance was poisoned in 1969 to clean out a large crop of chubs that probably were brought in as angler's bait and was restocked with cutthroat trout from McBride Lake. These fish have thrived. They now range from 12 to 22 inches, with most falling between 14 and 17 inches.

Flies and lures: Start with a Woolly Bugger. The lake is loaded with enough crustaceans to redden the meat, so a good second choice is a tan Scud. Other good choices include bead-head Prince and Hare's Ear nymphs, tan Woolly Worm, Skinny Bugger, and an Adams just in case fish come to the surface. The spin angler should start with a Spin-a-Lure. Kastmasters, Kamloopers, Stream-a-Lures, Mepps, Panther Martins, and Rapalas are other good bets.

Special equipment: If you have a suitable vehicle, getting a float tube onto Lake Abundance is not impossible.

Access: The nearest approach to Lake Abundance is from Cooke City. Take the Daisy Pass Road, which heads north up the flank of Henderson Mountain, at the east end of Cooke City. The first 3.5 miles of this road are steep, rough, and impassable due to snow until sometime in July. That is the good part. Once through Daisy

Sites 80–84

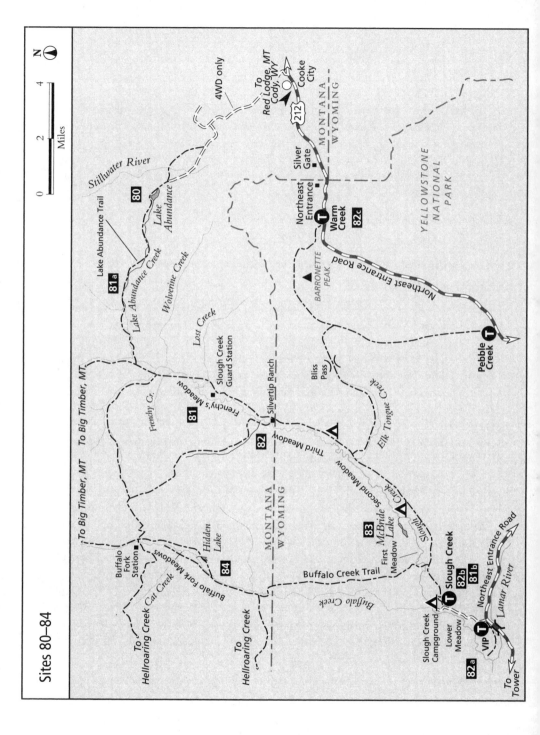

Pass the road continues north along the flank of Fisher Mountain toward Lulu Pass. The Lake Abundance track (I cannot in good conscience call it a road) is only passable with serious four-wheel-drive vehicles. It cuts left downhill to cross the upper end of the Stillwater River and then climbs up to the wilderness boundary in Abundance Pass.

If you can get to the wilderness boundary, it is less than a mile up and over a low pass to Lake Abundance. If you have to hike from Cooke City, it is 7.5 miles and a lot of work. A climb of 1,900 feet to Daisy Pass is followed by a drop of 1,200 feet to the Stillwater, another climb of 200 feet through Abundance Pass, and a drop of 300 feet to the lake. The pack trail continues down Lake Abundance Creek to tie into the network of trails through the Slough Creek drainage.

Tributaries: There are no tributaries of significance to Lake Abundance. The outlet stream holds fish, which are smaller than the lake fish.

81. Slough Creek, Headwaters to Silvertip Ranch
(see map on page 185)

Description: On a map, the many branches of upper Slough Creek look like a winter cottonwood. The upper segments of Slough Creek and its tributaries are small, steep, and of little interest to the angler. They have mostly been gathered together into the main trunk 4 miles north of the Yellowstone National Park boundary at Frenchy's Meadow. Here, Slough Creek takes on the character famous around the world. The stream is 10 to 15 feet wide, running from riffle pool to riffle pool between grass banks in a wide-open meadow. The bottom is mostly small- to medium-size gravel. The mountains flanking the valley were burned in 1988, but little evidence shows on the valley floor. Places to look for fish are along the outsides of the bends and up into the riffle corners leading into pools.

Several hundred acres of Frenchy's Meadow are actually privately held as part of the Silvertip Ranch. The last mile of Slough Creek north of the park boundary line is more closely bordered with timber. The gradient of the stream is steeper, even sporting a 10-foot-high waterfall. The main Silvertip Ranch buildings are just outside the park. The ranch is run seasonally as a guest ranch, not a cattle operation. The only other permanent structure around is the USDA Forest Service's Slough Creek Guard Station.

These waters are subject to Montana regulations. The season runs from the third Saturday of May through the end of November. As a practical matter, the area is unfishable due to the spring runoff until early July. The stream fishes best from mid-July through Labor Day. The other notable feature of Slough Creek is that July is bug month; mosquitoes, deerflies, and buffalo flies are a major pain.

The fish: Slough Creek is home to native cutthroat trout. The upper ends of Slough and its tributaries hold only small fish or none at all, the exception being Lake Abundance. Starting in lower Frenchy's Meadow, the average size goes up dramatically. The range is from 9 to 16 inches, most being about 12 inches.

Flies and lures: I expect to spot most of the fish feeding in the pools. Choice fly patterns are the Royal Wulff, Gray Wulff, Dave's Hopper, and Blue Dun. The fish that will not take one of these may be looking for ants or beetles. A bead-head Prince and a Woolly Bugger should take care of the wet end of the fly box. Anglers using spin tackle should start with a small Mepps or Cyclone spoon. It is a good idea to have Panther Martins and Li'l Jake's along as well. These fish are not as sophisticated as the ones in lower Slough Creek, so you will be able to get away with a heavier leader and sloppier presentations.

Access: Upper Slough Creek is a long way from anywhere. Trails lead in here from the north up the Boulder River from Big Timber, Montana; from the east down Lake Abundance Creek from Cooke City; from the west through the Absaroka-Beartooth Wilderness north of the park; and up Slough Creek itself from within Yellowstone National Park. Consult a trail guide for more complete information.

81a. Lake Abundance Trail

The Lake Abundance route is not less than 10 miles from the end of the road to Frenchy's Meadow. Even that assumes that you have the high-profile four-wheel-drive vehicle necessary to make use of the really rotten track. Take the Daisy Pass Road north from the east end of Cooke City 4 miles to the junction of the Lake Abundance Trail. Head west on the Lake Abundance Trail, cross the upper Stillwater, and park as near to the wilderness boundary as you can get. That will save 7.5 miles of really grueling hiking. Cross Abundance Pass and follow Lake Abundance Creek downstream to its confluence with Slough Creek.

81b. Slough Creek Trail

Slough Creek Trail is the water-level route. Take the Northeast Entrance Road 6.2 miles east from Tower Junction to the Slough Creek Road. If coming from Cooke City, it is 26.9 miles west to the Slough Creek turnoff. Turn north on the Slough Creek Road and drive 1.9 miles to the trailhead. During July and August a day with fewer than twenty-five vehicles at the trailhead is a light day. Check to make sure the creek is not muddy! The trail is a wagon road heading out of the east end of the parking area up the hill. It is 11 miles to the park boundary and another 1.5 miles to get into Frenchy's Meadow.

Tributaries: Numerous small streams join Slough Creek in this section. Most have some fish. None are worth profiling.

82. Slough Creek, Silvertip Ranch to Lamar River
(see map on page 185)

Description: Slough Creek got its name when a party of would-be miners, on their way to strikes around what is now Cooke City, got their daily scouting report of the trail ahead. "T'was but a slough," was the report. By the way, it is pronounced as if it were spelled slew. It is only a little over 11 miles in a straight line from where

Slough Creek enters Yellowstone National Park to its confluence with the Lamar. The course runs to the southwest, overseen by Cutoff Mountain, with the characteristic notch in its west end.

Slough Creek meanders across four great meadows. Only a short section of faster water and timber near the mouth of Elk Tongue Creek separate the Third Meadow above from the Second Meadow below. A mile-long cut through encroaching hills draped in timber divides the Second Meadow from the First Meadow. Another 1.5 miles of much steeper canyon, with a floor of boulders and downed timber, divides First Meadow from the Lower Meadow. A final 150-yard pitch through big cobble and boulders tips Slough Creek into the Lamar River.

In all of the meadows, the stream flows over a bed of gravel between 3- to 4-foot-high grass banks. The spring floods widen the channel in each bend. The creek itself is usually 25 to 30 feet wide; the gravel bars spread another 10 to 20 feet. The pools are usually 2 to 4 feet deep, but in some of the bigger bends, depths may exceed 10 feet. These dimensions are a bit more modest in the Third Meadow and a little more pronounced in the Lower Meadow. Sight fishing is the rule here. Look for fish in the pools and along the edges of the riffles heading into them. The fish in Slough Creek get hammered day after day by anglers of all skill levels. If you can avoid hooking another angler on your back cast, you may get a good chance to have large trout laugh at your best effort at presenting a fly. The farther up the creek you get, the less sophisticated are the fish. These days you never really get away from other people.

Slough Creek is usually unfishable on opening day. The meadows can look remarkably like lakes, and muddy ones at that. The water level drops through June, reaching a fishable flow in early July. After the spring flood passes, the creek rarely gets as muddy as do the Lamar River and Soda Butte Creek. Buffalo flies, mosquitoes, and deerflies make life miserable for most of July. Bring bug juice and headnets.

The fish: Once populated exclusively by cutthroat, upper Slough Creek has been invaded by a few rainbows that Yellowstone Park requests you kill. The Lower Meadow, particularly its last big pool, also holds some cutbows and rainbows. The fish in the rapids sections range from 6 to 14 inches, with most around 10 inches. The meadow fish run 11 to 22 inches and average between 14 and 18 inches. The meadow fish tend to be very deliberate about everything they do, including taking your fly. Many times I have seen an overeager angler take a fly right away from a rising fish.

Flies and lures: Mornings are slow. The day-in, day-out producers are hopper patterns such as Dave's or Letort hoppers. The fish that will not take a hopper can often be persuaded by a small beetle or black ant. The sporadic hatches can be matched by tiny Pale Morning Duns, Cream Midges, big Blue Duns, and micro Partridge Caddis. Toward evening a Woolly Bugger may get some play. I always carry, but seldom use, Prince, Hare's Ear, and Pheasant Tail nymphs. Midge Pupae and Brassies are also sometimes the ticket. Often, trailing a small nymph or terrestrial behind a hopper will get you into a fish that has refused either alone. The clarity and

Soda Butte Creek joins the muddy Lamar River. MICHAEL SAMPLE PHOTO

smoothness of the meadow water necessitates fine tippets. This is the place to break out the 6X and 7X. Think ultralight if using spin gear. Try tiny Mepps, Panther Martins, or Triple Teazers.

Access: The principle access to Slough Creek is from the Slough Creek Road. Drive east 6.2 miles on the Northeast Entrance Road to the Slough Creek Road. It is 26.9 miles west from Cooke City. There are several pullouts providing ready access to the lower meadow in the 2.4 miles between the highway and the Slough Creek Campground.

The Slough Creek Drainage

82a. VIP Pool

A trail following a long-closed two-track to the lower end of the Lower Meadow starts right at the junction of the Slough Creek Road with the Northeast Entrance Road. Park on the left and follow the trail to the last pool in the Lower Meadow. This pool, the VIP Pool, holds what may be both the biggest and most difficult fish in the entire stream. Fish weighing more than four pounds have been taken here. The first pullout on the left, 0.5 mile in on the Slough Creek Road, also provides the head of an anglers' track that goes to this pool.

82b. Slough Creek Trailhead

Take the Slough Creek Road 1.9 miles to the trailhead, which is equipped with a handy toilet. The road makes a sharp left turn, and parking is strung out around the bend. Parking for the horse packers is an additional 200 yards off to the left. A typical summer day may see fifty to seventy-five vehicles and a dozen or more horse trailers parked here. The trail is a wagon road that takes off from the north end of the parking area. Silvertip Ranch brings their guests and supplies in with buckboards, a surrey with a fringe on top, and even a tank wagon for diesel oil that runs their generator. Nobody envies the mules hauling that one up the hill.

The first mile of the trail is the toughest part. It climbs 420 feet before dropping back down 160 feet to the First Meadow. It is just under 2 miles to the First Meadow, a bit over 4 miles to the Second Meadow, and 8 miles to the Third Meadow. This puts much of the Second and all of the Third Meadow out of reach for a day trip. There are several backcountry campsites in the Second and Third Meadows. Inexperience and a quick look at the map may trick you into thinking it is easier to just go up the creek from the campground; that way there would only be 230 feet to climb. Big mistake. It starts out okay but then you get into a canyon that is a perfect jumble of boulders overlain with deadfall, as if God had decided to play pick-up-sticks with tree trunks.

82c. Bliss Pass Trail

A fairly popular multiday backpack route comes into Slough Creek at Elk Tongue Creek. Start at the Warm Creek Trailhead on Soda Butte Creek. Drive west 5.1 miles from Cooke City or east 28 miles from Tower Junction on the Northeast Entrance Road to the trailhead. A 0.1-mile stub road on the north side of the highway brings you to the new trailhead facility. Take the Pebble Creek Trail over the back end of Barronette Peak to upper Pebble Creek and descend Pebble Creek 5.5 miles to the base of the Bliss Pass Trail. A backcountry campsite at the trail junction is the usual first-night stop. It is 6 miles up over the divide between Pebble and Slough Creeks. You will need the backcountry campsite at the mouth of Elk Tongue Creek. An 8-mile hike takes you back down to the Slough Creek Trailhead. With two mountain ridges to climb, this is a trek only for the prepared and conditioned hiker.

Tributaries: Slough Creek has two major tributaries in this section, McBride Lake (site 83) and Buffalo Creek (site 84). Elk Tongue Creek and the other tributaries are too small to be of interest to anglers.

83. McBride Lake *(see map on page 185)*

Description: James McBride served with the army administration of Yellowstone National Park and transferred to the fledgling National Park Service when it was created. He became Yellowstone's chief ranger and knew the Slough Creek area well before retiring in 1929. The lake bearing his name is long, narrow, and hidden in a fold in the ridge that divides the First Meadow from the Second.

Glaciers advancing down the Slough Creek valley polished the rocks of the ridge. Scattered trees, most of them burned in 1988, and patches of grass separated by granite outcrops rim the lake. The tiny outlet stream flows north and hooks east to join Slough Creek in the Second Meadow. A thin layer of sediment supports a ring of rushes around much of the lake, giving way to small rubble in the outlet area. The lake is considered to be one of the most fertile lakes in the park, supporting a large and diverse population of critters to feed the fish. The narrowness of the lake caters to the angler. Look for cruising fish and intercept them.

McBride Lake is open long before an angler can get there. It is on the north side of Slough Creek, with the trail on the south side. Only a fool would attempt to wade Slough Creek during the spring runoff in June. Wait until mid-July. The lake produces until well into September.

The fish: The McBride Lake cutthroat is considered a distinct strain of fish. Montana's Department of Fish, Wildlife & Parks maintains this stock in its hatchery system to supply high mountain lakes that cannot sustain reproduction. The rainbow and grayling once introduced to the lake have long since disappeared. The unofficial chubs discovered in the 1970s are still there but not, fortunately, in any great numbers. I think the cutts are happy to eat little chubs.

Flies and lures: Scuds are the name of the game here. Start with a tan Scud or tan Woolly Worm. Other flies that should be in your kit include Hare's Ear, olive Hare's Ear, and Prince nymphs, Skinny and Woolly Buggers, Midge Pupae, Adams, and Letort Hoppers. For spinning lures take Mepps, Spin-a-Lures, Kastmasters, Krocodiles, and Kamloopers.

Special equipment: This is a long way to carry a float tube, almost 4 miles, and up that hill to boot. It has been done, though the narrow configuration of the lake makes it not very important.

Access: Take the Northeast Entrance Road 6.2 miles east from Tower Junction or 26.9 miles west from Cooke City to the Slough Creek Road. Turn north onto the Slough Creek Road and drive 1.9 miles to the Slough Creek Trailhead. Hike 3 miles north on the Slough Creek Trail to the upper end of the First Meadow. At this point an unmarked but obvious anglers' track peels off to the left around the upper end of the meadow, while the wagon road continues up the divide. The anglers' track hits Slough Creek just below its exit from the timber. The stream can be forded here. Early in the season there is not much indication of where to go from this point. Cut a diagonal up the hill to the north away from the creek. The saddle containing McBride Lake is more obvious when looking up the meadow from near the patrol

Shoreline rocks on McBride Lake invite the angler to sit and fish.
NATIONAL PARK SERVICE PHOTO

cabins than it is when you are on the ground. The lake is less than 0.5 mile from the ford. The only real way to miss it is to stay too low down on the hill and pass under it, at which point you will find yourself in timber and then the Second Meadow. Getting above the lake will at least put you in sight of it. Later in the season this is not much of a problem, as enough feet will have beaten a path to follow.

84. Buffalo Creek (see map on page 185)

Description: Outside Yellowstone National Park the maps call this Buffalo Fork. Buffalo Creek drops off the south flank of the divide, separating it from the upper Boulder River, and flows almost due south. It joins Slough Creek directly opposite the Slough Creek Campground.

The first couple of miles are very steep and of little interest to anglers. Beginning 5 miles north, at the park boundary, it flattens out into a meadow much like those of Slough Creek. The stream is typically 15 to 20 feet wide on a bed of gravel. Grassy or marshy banks border the creek; there are burnt-timber ridgelines 0.5 mile off on either flank. As always in this kind of water, the structures to fish are the riffle corners and along the deep edges of the pools.

Just east of Buffalo Creek, behind a screen of trees, lies Hidden Lake. This is a small lake with a muck bottom set in marsh. The trees that hide it from the creek also mark the division between the upper and lower meadows.

The character of Buffalo Creek changes radically just where it enters the park. The remaining 5 miles of its course drop rapidly through an isolated canyon. It sheds 1,300 feet, which means an average drop of 260 feet each mile. The bed is now mostly boulders, and frequent deadfall clutters the channel. The targets are the many little pocket pools around the boulders and deadfall.

The meadows are outside the park, so technically they are open for fishing the third Saturday of May. As a practical matter this water is not fishable until July because of the spring runoff. Anglers can expect some success until well into October. The Montana season closes at the end of November, but by then the weather will have pretty well chased everybody, even the elk hunters, out of the high country.

The fish: The fish in Buffalo Creek are rainbows. In the Buffalo Fork Meadows, they run 10 to 18 inches, most averaging 14 to 16 inches. An occasional fish in the 22-inch range turns up. The same is true of Hidden Lake. The fish are much smaller in the canyon section, ranging from 6 to 12 inches, with most running around 10 inches.

Flies and lures: In the canyon section start with a Royal Coachman Trude and quit if it does not produce. The meadow fish are much more selective. Try Dave's Hoppers, black ants, beetles, and, if an appropriate hatch is on, Pale Morning Duns or Blue Duns. Bead-head Prince, Hare's Ear, and Pheasant Tail nymphs should be in your box. For streamers, try the Woolly Bugger or Muddler Minnow. For Hidden Lake add the Skinny Bugger and a tan Scud. The spin angler should simply stay out of the canyon section. Begin with Panther Martins or Cyclone spoons. In Hidden Lake start with a Spin-a-Lure.

Access: Buffalo Creek is a wilderness stream. Starting up from its confluence with Slough Creek boxes you into really tough going for small fish. The trail network outside Yellowstone National Park leads in here from the west, north, and east. In each case the hike is a major project. Consult the Gallatin National Forest trail map.

The route within the purview of this guide starts at Slough Creek. Go east 6.2 miles from Tower Junction or west 26.9 miles from Cooke City on the Northeast Entrance Road to the Slough Creek Road. Drive north 1.9 miles on the Slough Creek Road to the Slough Creek Trailhead. Hike in 2 miles to the junction with the Buffalo Creek Trail, sometimes called the Buffalo Plateau Trail. Take the Buffalo Creek Trail 6 more miles to the start of the meadow on the park border. Fish upstream. Hidden Lake is 12.5 miles from the trailhead. The ranger station at the upper end of the meadow section is 15 miles from the trailhead. There are no backcountry campsites within the park along this route. A cautionary note: This trail requires fording Slough Creek, which may not be possible until sometime in July.

Tributaries: Only Hidden Lake, discussed above, is of any great interest to anglers. The others, such as Cat and Grassy Creeks, are too small to be of much value to the angler.

The Yellowstone River Drainage from the Lamar Confluence to Yankee Jim Canyon

From its confluence with the Lamar River and 35 miles downstream to the head of Yankee Jim Canyon, the Yellowstone River flows in a northwesterly direction through canyon and narrow valley country. The upper segment from the Lamar River to Gardiner is in Yellowstone National Park. The lower segment from Gardiner to Yankee Jim is in Montana; hence, Montana fishing regulations apply. The key features of Montana's regulations are the year-round season and catch-and-release for cutthroat. Montana's tributary streams are open from the third Saturday in May through November. With few exceptions these waters are high and unfishable during the spring runoff period in May and June. Several tributaries, the most significant of which is the Gardner River, join the Yellowstone in this section.

Mileage points: There are several mileage points for this section. On the Grand Loop Road within Yellowstone National Park, they are at Tower Junction and Mammoth, where the North Entrance Road joins the Grand Loop Road. On the North Entrance Road, they are at this same junction in Mammoth and the North Entrance Station at Gardiner, Montana.

Mileage on the Jardine/Bear Creek Road is measured from its junction with U.S. Highway 89 in Gardiner. Mileage on Old Yellowstone Trail South is measured from the Teddy Roosevelt Arch in Gardiner and the junction with the Cinnabar Road near the Corwin Springs Bridge. Mileage on the Cinnabar Road is measured from its diversion from Old Yellowstone Trail South north of Corwin Springs. Mileage on US 89 is measured between the rodeo grounds on the west end of Gardiner and the intersection with Interstate 90 at Livingston.

85. Black Canyon of the Yellowstone

Description: The Black Canyon proper extends from the Yellowstone River's confluence with the Lamar River 19 miles downstream to Bear Creek. This section is characterized by a narrow canyon with steep walls. In many places sheer rock faces preclude walking along the stream bank. There are several extreme rapids and the 15-foot-high Knowles Falls. The fish are concentrated in the numerous big eddy pools and a few more-open riffle sections. The canyon walls are composed of the very old, dark volcanic metamorphic rocks that give this section its name. The south side of the river is often heavily timbered. The north side is more open, with isolated trees or timber patches interspersed with occasional sage or willow bushes.

The Yellowstone exits the Black Canyon a couple of miles east of Gardiner at the mouth of Bear Creek. The section between Bear Creek and Gardiner is fast, with the fishing primarily in the shoreline pockets, though there are a couple of big eddy pools. The banks here are typically composed of big boulders with intermittent brush patches.

The fish: Overall, this reach sustains a good population of only moderately sophisticated, medium-size fish. At the upper end of the Black Canyon, the population is almost exclusively cutthroat. As you go downstream you gradually pick up a few cutbows and rainbows. Knowles Falls, 7 miles above Gardiner, is a fish barrier. Below this point there are also brown trout and large numbers of whitefish. There are a few whitefish above Knowles Falls, but I have never caught one as high as the Hellroaring area. Isolated brook trout turn up, particularly around the mouths of Blacktail Deer and Elk Creeks. The river fish usually run in the 11- to 14-inch range, with some upwards of 17 inches. The brook trout are in the 6-inch class, and the whitefish average 13 inches.

Flies and lures: Big stonefly nymphs such as the Brooks' Stone or olive Woolly Worm and modest-size streamers, say a Muddler Minnow or Woolly Bugger in size 8 or 10, are always in order here. The salmonfly hatch kicks off the dry-fly season, usually coming up through the Black Canyon sometime in mid-July. Start with a Parks' Salmonfly or Matt's Stone. Trudes, Stimulators, Wulffs, or other attractors and, in high summer, hoppers, are the usual dry patterns the rest of the year. In the big eddy pools use heavier spin lures such as the Spin-a-Lure or Kastmaster.

Access: The Black Canyon is a 19-mile reach of river without 1 inch of adjacent road. Because the Yellowstone River Trail goes all the way through the canyon, and Yellowstone National Park has provided backcountry campsites in the canyon, it is a popular overnight destination as well as day-use area.

Beginning at Tower Junction and moving downstream, four trailheads and two informal access points provide the best means of getting to the river.

85a. Yellowstone River Trail, near Tower Junction

To fish the upper end of the Black Canyon, take the Northeast Entrance Road 0.3-mile east from Tower Junction to the Yellowstone River Trailhead. The first mile is a dry hike over a sagebrush-laden bench and low ridge. From there on the trail parallels the river all the way through to Gardiner, 21 miles downstream. In this first segment the trail is generally about 100 yards above the river along the south bank. Game tracks cut down to the river at numerous points, and an anglers' track runs along a few feet above the high-water line in most places. Take whichever track gives you the length of bank you want. Work upstream or down. To return, get back on the main trail, as it is easier walking than anywhere else.

85b. Hellroaring Trail

At a little less than a mile down to the river, the Hellroaring Trail is the shortest day-trip access to the Black Canyon. The Hellroaring Trailhead is 0.3 mile north of the Grand Loop Road at the end of a dirt access road. The entry is 15 miles east of

Sites 85 & 86

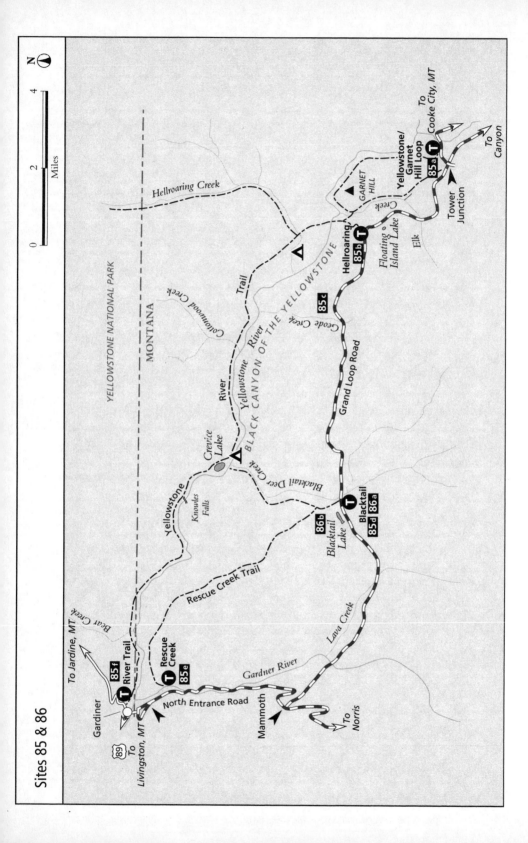

Mammoth or 3.8 miles west of Tower Junction. The access is 0.4 mile west of Floating Island Lake. If you're coming from Mammoth, it's too easy to miss because it is behind a tree and joins the highway at an acute angle.

A caution is in order for those not used to the high altitude here or those with health problems: At the end of the day, there are about 600 vertical feet to climb between the river and the trail. Even though it is a switchbacked and maintained pack trail, this is still a lot of vertical to pack into less than a mile.

Near the bottom of the hill, the Garnet Hill/Yellowstone River Trail from Tower Junction joins the Hellroaring Trail. There are several options for the angler at this point:

1) Just after the trails join, you may take the 300-yard-long anglers' track to the right. This goes to the big eddy known as Yancey's Hole at the mouth of Elk Creek. Continuing upstream on the south side of the river works just like coming downstream from Tower.

2) The main trail crosses the Yellowstone on a suspension bridge over an inaccessible gorge. To fish upstream from the gorge on the north side of the river, cross the bridge. About 100 yards after crossing the bridge, take the volunteer track splitting off the main trail to the right that cuts back upstream, hitting the river above the sheer rock canyon walls.

3) The vertical canyon walls persist for a mile downstream from the bridge on both sides of the river. To bypass them, stay with the Yellowstone River Trail for another mile to Hellroaring Creek. Take the anglers' track to the left down Hellroaring Creek to access the Yellowstone at the Hellroaring confluence.

The segment of river between Hellroaring and Blacktail Deer Creeks is generally out of range for a day trip, but intermediate campsites make it a good overnight trip. The trail from here west toward Gardiner remains on the north side of the river.

85c. Geode Creek Bushwhack

To fish the Yellowstone near the mouth of Geode Creek, take the Grand Loop Road 12.6 miles east from Mammoth or 6.2 miles west from Tower Junction to an unmarked pullout at the bottom of a hill on the north side of the road just east of Geode Creek. Find the game track slanting off downhill from the west end of the pullout. Sandwiched between impassable canyon sections, nearly a mile of the south side of the river is fishable. If a parked vehicle suggests anglers have beaten you to it, the hike—about 2 miles of bushwhacking and 800 vertical feet to climb out—is probably not worth your time and energy. On the other hand, if you are there by yourself during the salmonfly hatch, Katie-bar the door.

85d. Blacktail Trail

To find the Blacktail Trailhead, go 6.9 miles east from Mammoth or 11.7 miles west from Tower Junction on the Grand Loop Road. The trailhead parking area is behind a screen of trees on the north side of the road. Take the trail 4 miles down Blacktail

Deer Creek to the Yellowstone River. This is a very long day hike. Backcountry campsites at the mouth of Blacktail Deer Creek and along the river make an overnight trip to this segment of the canyon a good idea. A bridge connects with the Yellowstone River Trail on the north bank of the Yellowstone. Cross the bridge and fish either up or downriver. Canyon walls limit passage along the south bank.

85e. Rescue Creek Trail

The Rescue Creek Trail is on the east side of the road 0.75 mile south of the North Entrance Station at Gardiner. Take the trail about 1.25 miles across the open flat. An obvious anglers' track splits off left toward the Yellowstone River before the trail starts to climb up the mountain. Take this trail to reach the south bank at a big eddy pool in a bend of the river. Fish upstream because downstream access is limited by a cliff. Canyon walls opposite the mouth of Bear Creek prevent further upstream access on this side of the river.

85f. Yellowstone River Trail, Gardiner End

The trailhead for the Gardiner end of the Yellowstone River trail has very limited space. Take the Jardine Road 1 block from its junction with US 89 in Gardiner to White Lane. Turn right on White Lane and drive 150 feet to the trailhead sign. There is very limited parking and no stock-loading facility. The trail follows an easement between the Rocky Mountain Campground and the Mormon Church, then drops down the hill to the top of a stone wall along a pasture. Once to the wall, turn left up the river. The trail closely parallels the river until you reach the Tower area 21 miles upstream. Once the two or three spots at the trailhead are filled, extra vehicles must be parked in some other legal spot, usually along US 89 in town.

Begin accessing the river at any point beyond the fenced field. The first few hundred yards of the river here are subject to Montana regulations. About another half mile of river 2 miles upstream from Gardiner, from just above to just below the mouth of Bear Creek, also is outside the park. The eddy pool known as the "Big Swirl," 3.25 miles upriver, is about the practical limit for a day trip.

Tributaries: The major tributaries in this section are Blacktail Deer Creek (site 86), Hellroaring Creek (site 87), and Bear Creek (site 88). The other tributaries are trivial streams without significant fish populations, though their outlet areas can produce excellent fishing in late June or early July during the cutthroat spawning run. Cottonwood Creek and the 200 yards of the Yellowstone River centered on its outlet are closed until July 15.

86. Blacktail Deer Creek and Blacktail Lake (see map on page 196)

Description: Blacktail Deer Creek is a small, fairly fast stream in open terrain. The lower end of the creek is a very steep drop down to the Yellowstone. The key features are the pools and undercut bank areas. The adjacent Blacktail Lake is usually referred to locally as "Shaky Lake" because of the bog areas around it, particularly on the south side near the Grand Loop Road. The best part of the lake is the deeper

Blacktail Lake is known by locals as "Shaky Lake" because of the boggy spots around its shoreline.

western end nearest the road. The creek fishes best in July and into August. The lake is best in June and then again after mid-September. In recent years the lake has been closed until sometime in July to protect nesting birds and rare plants. Check locally for the current opening date.

The fish: The Blacktail Deer Creek drainage is populated primarily with brook trout. The fish in the creek typically run 5 to 9 inches. Blacktail Lake usually will produce fish in the 10- to 14-inch range but has on occasion turned out fish in excess of 22 inches.

Flies and lures: The best flies for Blacktail Deer Creek are medium-size attractor patterns such as the Royal Coachman Trude or Royal Wulff. Hoppers are useful in August. A Prince nymph is as effective as anything in a wet fly. Blacktail Lake is a good place for small bright streamers such as the Joffe Jewel and still-water patterns like damselfly nymphs or Woolly Buggers. In lures, try a Mepps, Vibrax, or Little Cleo in the lake. Blacktail Deer Creek is very small and not well suited to the use of any but the lightest of spinning lures.

Special equipment: A float tube may prove useful on Blacktail Lake.

86a. Blacktail Trailhead

Drive east from Mammoth 6.9 miles or west from Tower Junction 11.9 miles on the Grand Loop Road to Blacktail Deer Creek. Two trailheads access the main body of Blacktail Deer Creek, one on each side of the road. Take the north trailhead, which parallels the creek as it drops down to join the Yellowstone. The trail is typically 200 to 300 yards west of the stream and 4 miles long. Pick your stretch and fish in whichever direction is appropriate for your method. The south trailhead is the best for reaching the upper part of Blacktail Deer Creek. After the first mile, the farther up the creek you get, the smaller the fish become.

86b. Blacktail Lake

Blacktail Lake is on the Grand Loop Road 6.4 miles east of Mammoth or 12.4 miles west of Tower Falls. Take the obvious set of anglers' tracks from the parking area to and around the west end of the lake. The north shore opposite the highway has much firmer footing than the boggy area near the road. Use a float tube to fish in the spring hole on the southwest corner of the lake.

87. Hellroaring Creek

Description: Rising in the Absaroka-Beartooth Wilderness and flowing south into Yellowstone National Park, Hellroaring Creek was named by a party of prospectors on their way to the rumored strikes at what became Cooke City. The party was working their way up the Yellowstone River in largely unexplored country. Each day they sent a scout ahead to check the route for the next day's trip. The scout described the next major tributary crossing as a "Hellroarer," and so it became Hellroaring Creek. This is an apt description for most of the creek.

The stream's middle section just outside the park is in a mountain basin. It features a gentle gradient and world-famous elk hunting. There are two lakes in the Hellroaring drainage that are of interest to anglers, Charlie White and Carpenter. Both are small lakes with partially timbered shorelines. The creek will fish well in July and August. The lakes are at their prime during the first month after the spring thaw, which usually means the last week of June and into July. The lower portion of the creek is in Yellowstone National Park, so park regulations apply. Outside the park the angler is subject to Montana regulations.

The fish: The principal fish in the Hellroaring drainage are cutthroat and cutbow trout. Occasionally, what appears to be rainbow or, more often, a nonhybrid cutthroat will turn up. The lower section of Hellroaring Creek gets a spawning run of cutthroat out of the Yellowstone and will produce fish up to 16 inches long in July. The fish in the two lakes will more often run in the 10- to 14-inch range, while the creek fish are more typically 6 to 10 inches in length, but with a larger average size in the lower part of the creek and in the meadow section.

Site 87

0 2 4
Miles

N

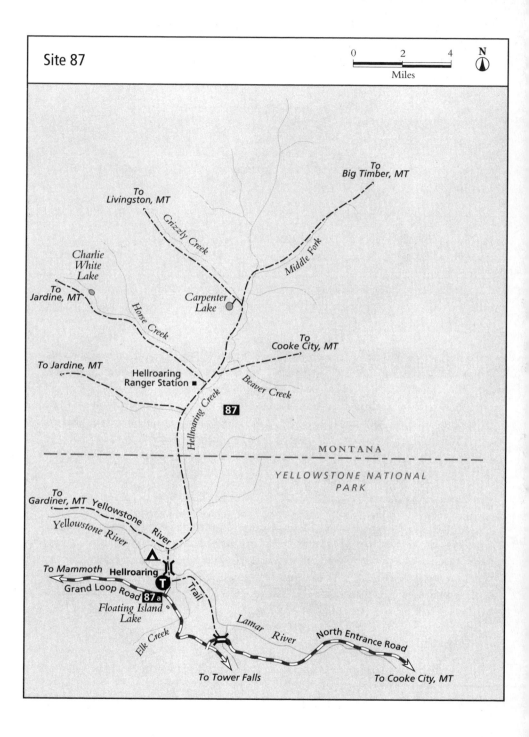

To Big Timber, MT

To Livingston, MT

Grizzly Creek

Middle Fork

Charlie White Lake

To Jardine, MT

Carpenter Lake

Horse Creek

To Cooke City, MT

To Jardine, MT

Hellroaring Ranger Station

Beaver Creek

Hellroaring Creek

87

MONTANA

YELLOWSTONE NATIONAL PARK

To Gardiner, MT Yellowstone

Yellowstone River

River

To Mammoth Hellroaring

Grand Loop Road

87a

Floating Island Lake

Elk Creek

Trail

Lamar River

North Entrance Road

To Tower Falls

To Cooke City, MT

Flies and lures: In the creek, Royal Wulffs, Stimulators, Royal Coachman Trudes, or other attractor dries, and wets such as the Prince nymph, are usually all that is required in the way of flies. As with most small streams with a steep gradient, lures should be kept small and should have just moderate action; try a Panther Martin or Cyclone spoon.

A Muddler Minnow, Woolly Bugger, Scud, or damselfly nymph, in addition to the dries, will prove useful on the lakes. The spin fisher should try a Li'l Jake's or Mepps.

Access: All access to Hellroaring Creek is by foot or horseback, as it is a true wilderness stream.

87a. Hellroaring Trailhead

To reach the only practical day-trip access to Hellroaring Creek, take the Grand Loop Road east from Mammoth 15 miles to the Hellroaring Trailhead. Look sharp to the left upon passing the trailhead sign, as the access to the parking area is obscured on the opposite side of the road. If you are approaching it from the Tower Junction side, you come around a bend and can easily spot the road after traveling 3.8 miles east of the junction.

From the trailhead it is 2 miles to lower Hellroaring Creek. The first mile is a steep descent of 600 vertical feet that you must climb again at the end of the day. About 1 mile of creek is readily available. There are backcountry campsites here, near the mouth of the creek. The Yellowstone River Trail continues through to Gardiner, and the Hellroaring Trail heads up the creek into the wilderness. Pack trails come into the Hellroaring basin from all directions. For detailed trail descriptions, it would be best to consult the Gallatin National Forest trail map. For our purposes, the important thing to note is that it is at least a full day's hike just to get into the middle part of the creek from any access point.

88. Bear Creek Drainage

Description: Bear Creek is a steep mountain stream rising north of Gardiner on the flanks of Sheep Mountain, Monitor Peak, and Ash Mountain. It flows south through a narrow, timbered canyon until it reaches Jardine, Montana, where it picks up its largest tributary, the North Fork. The timber gives way to sagebrush, but the creek remains in a steep narrow valley. Knox Lake, sometimes listed on older maps as Castle Lake, is very near the headwaters of Bear Creek. The main stem of Bear Creek fishes well from early July through August. Knox Lake is at its best from ice-out to the end of July.

The fish: The lower part of Bear Creek is mostly inhabited by rainbow and cutbow trout, though any of the fish of the Yellowstone River can be found here on occasion. The farther up the stream you get, the higher the proportion of brook trout. The last of the cutthroat are found at some point above Jardine. In the lower section of the creek, the fish run 7 to 14 inches. That average shrinks as one goes upstream.

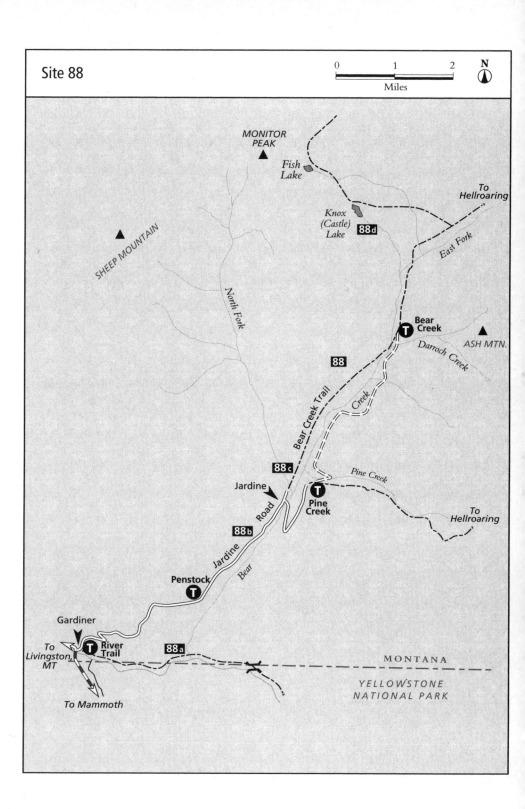

Site 88

0 1 2
Miles

N

MONITOR
PEAK

Fish
Lake

To
Hellroaring

Knox
(Castle)
Lake

88d

SHEEP MOUNTAIN

East Fork

North Fork

Bear
Creek

88

ASH MTN.

Darroch Creek

Bear Creek Trail

Creek

88c

Pine Creek

Jardine

Pine
Creek

To
Hellroaring

88b

Jardine Road

Bear

Penstock

Gardiner

MONTANA

River
Trail

88a

To
Livingston,
MT

YELLOWSTONE
NATIONAL PARK

To Mammoth

The tributary streams such as the North Fork, Pine Creek, and Darroch Creek are either fishless or nearly so, primarily due to their small size. Knox Lake fish are brook trout in the 7-inch class.

Flies and lures: If I could not catch fish on a Royal Coachman Trude or a Prince nymph on most summer days, I would quit and go home. As with most small, steep water, lures should be kept small and have moderate actions. Try smaller Rooster Tails or Kamlooper spoons. Knox Lake is a prime candidate for the Joffe Jewel or Renegade in flies; a Mepps or Cyclone should do the job in a spinning lure.

88a. Mouth of Bear Creek

The mouth of Bear Creek is most easily accessed by going up the Yellowstone River Trail from Gardiner. Take the Jardine Road in Gardiner and turn right on White Lane. The trailhead is 50 yards east on White Lane, between the church and the campground. There is limited parking at the trailhead, so vehicles must be left along US 89 in town. The trail crosses the mouth of Bear Creek 2 miles east of Gardiner. Fish upstream.

88b. Jardine Road

Take the Jardine Road, which joins US 89 across from the Exxon station in Gardiner. The road climbs up out of town via what is known as "Z Hill" and reaches Bear Creek's valley 3.2 miles north of Gardiner. At this point the road is several hundred feet above the creek. In the next 2.4 miles, the canyon floor rises to meet the road in Jardine. There are no formal trails to the stream, and what you see, a steep bunch grass and sagebrush slope, is what you get. Take whichever pullout and game track that heads you toward the section of stream you want to fish.

88c. Bear Creek Trail, Jardine

In Jardine the main Bear Creek Road turns right and crosses the creek. Stay on the west side of the creek for 0.4 mile to take the forest trail up Bear Creek from its confluence with the North Fork in Jardine. The main part of Bear Creek is still a satisfactory mountain stream for some miles yet. Since the road going to the upper reaches is well up on the hillside above Jardine, this trail represents the best access for the next mile or so. Pine Creek, a trivial stream, enters Bear Creek from the east 1.5 miles above Jardine. The Pine Creek Trailhead is an entry point for the backcountry trail network that goes east into the Hellroaring drainage 7.9 miles north of Gardiner.

88d. Knox Lake

Take the Bear Creek Road from Jardine to primitive USDA Forest Service campsites and a trailhead just above Darroch Creek. Timber Camp is 10.1 miles north of Gardiner. Bear Creek Camp is 11.2 miles north of Gardiner, and the trailhead to Knox Lake and upper Bear Creek is at the end of the road 11.5 miles north of Gardiner. A casual look at the map suggests to people heading for Knox Lake that going straight up Bear Creek is shorter and therefore an easier way to get there. This is not so, as the creek is in an extremely steep and timbered canyon with a lot of deadfall. Even though it is a hike of 3.5 miles, the trail to Knox Lake is the easy way to get there.

89. Gardiner Townsite

Description: Gardiner sits on benches about 60 feet above the river that cuts through old glacial till. The banks of both the Yellowstone and the Gardner Rivers—the two rivers meet here—are steep and strewn with boulders and brush. Moving along the riverbanks is work. The Yellowstone is class II whitewater. Shoreline pockets, a few riffle corners, and the confluence of the Gardner with the Yellowstone are the key waters for the angler. Because this site straddles the boundary of the park, it is imperative that you know which side of the line you are on so that you are aware of which set of regulations apply. Those portions of the water that are outside of the park offer year-round angling opportunities.

The fish: The main stem of the Yellowstone holds an eclectic mix of fish; cutthroat, whitefish, cutbow, rainbow, brown, and even an occasional brook trout are present. While all are wild populations, only the first two are native. The ratio of rainbows to other species is higher in this section than in any location above or below this point. On balance, these fish are reasonably willing to be caught and are present in good numbers. As with most wild populations, there is a full range of sizes. The cutthroat here seldom exceed 18 inches, but occasional browns or rainbows reach ten pounds. The average fish runs 9 to 14 inches.

Flies and lures: The most effective flies are attractor dries such as Trudes and Stimulators, stonefly patterns and hoppers in season, and midges during the winter. Bead-head Stone, Prince, and Hare's Ear are all useful nymph patterns. The Woolly Bugger and Muddler are top streamer patterns. Leading lures include the Panther Martin, Thomas Cyclone, and Mepps.

Access: Between private property and the steepness of the banks, access to the Yellowstone is restricted in this area. You can scramble down to the river under either end of the highway bridge and work upstream or down. The park boundary comes down to the river at the southwest corner of town near the school. Follow the boundary down to the river and then work upstream or down. Alternatively, walk down the old railroad grade from the school and fish back upriver. A 100-yard foot access cuts through the national park to the mouth of the Gardner River at the east end of Park Street. This street is almost universally referred to in Gardiner as "Front Street" because it straddles the park boundary. It is only built up on one side and faces south into the park. It is practical to carry kayaks, canoes, or rafts to the Yellowstone here. Be sure to park on the south side of the street; the other side is all private residential parking.

Tributaries: The only tributary in this section is the Gardner River (sites 96, 102, and 104).

Site 89

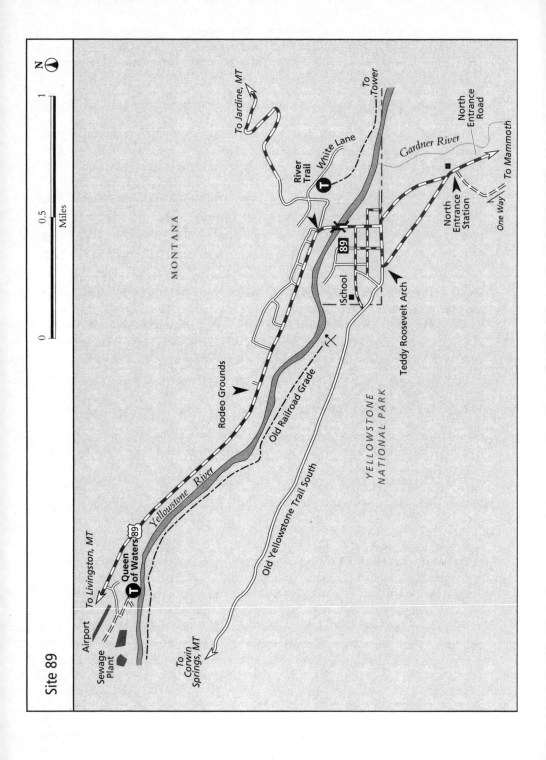

Airport

Sewage
Plant

To Livingston, MT

Queen
of Waters 89

To
Corwin
Springs, MT

Yellowstone River

Old Yellowstone Trail South

Old Railroad Grade

Rodeo Grounds

MONTANA

89

School

YELLOWSTONE
NATIONAL PARK

Teddy Roosevelt Arch

River
Trail

White Lane

To Jardine, MT

To
Tower

Gardner River

North
Entrance
Station

North
Entrance
Road

One Way To Mammoth

N

0   0.5   1
Miles

90. Yellowstone River, Gardiner to Corwin Springs

Description: This 7-mile section of the Yellowstone River is fast, with numerous rapids separated by flatter sections. The upper part from Gardiner to McConnell Access is almost continuous class II whitewater in a steep cut 30 to 75 feet below the main valley floor. The banks are mostly big rocks and willow brush with a few cottonwoods and juniper. Below McConnell the banks are only about 15 feet high, and the valley opens out a bit to afford views of Electric Peak and Devil's Slide.

The angler should fish shoreline pockets and the riffle corners at the heads of flatter pools. Technically, the river is subject to Montana regulations, but if you have come through the park on the west side of the river above Reese Creek, it is wiser to stay within the park regulations.

The Yellowstone is usually unfishable due to spring runoff during May and June. July hosts one of the West's major salmonfly hatches. Any day that the temperature is above freezing may be a fishing day the rest of the year.

The fish: The Yellowstone holds a mix of fish. In this section cutthroat, whitefish, cutbow, and rainbow predominate, though browns and a few brook trout are also present. The average fish runs 9 to 14 inches, with the cutts topping out at around 20. On occasion, rainbows and browns turn up in the ten-pound class. Whitefish are common and typically are about 13 inches, though they may reach 22 to 24 inches from time to time. This is an excellent fishery due to a large population of moderately gullible cutthroat.

Flies and lures: The best dry flies are Royal Coachman Trudes, Stimulators, and hoppers during the summer, and smaller Royal Coachman Trudes and midges such as the Griffith's Gnat during the winter. Other good dry-fly patterns include the Parks' Salmonfly, Turck's Tarantula, and Chernobyl Ant. Bead-head Stone, Prince, and Hare's Ear are all effective nymph patterns. The Woolly Bugger and Muddler are top streamer choices. Leading lures include the Panther Martin, Spin-a-Lure, Thomas Cyclone, and Mepps. Montana allows bait fishing, but since the release of all cutthroat is required, it is best to stick to artificials.

Special equipment: The frequent rapids in this section make the water unsuitable for low-freeboard craft such as johnboats and relatively unmaneuverable ones such as float tubes. McKenzie-style drift boats or dories are the angler's best choice here.

Access: While access to this reach of the Yellowstone generally is excellent, it is complicated by the presence of a considerable amount of private land. As a rule of thumb, if there is a fence between you and the river, somebody owns it, and you will be trespassing if you climb through or over that fence. Once on the river Montana law allows use of the area below the ordinary high-water mark. I will discuss access to the east side of the river from US 89 first, then describe access to the west side of the river.

Looking down the Yellowstone River to the town of Gardiner.

90a. Queen of Waters Access

The Queen of Waters access is at Airport Road, 1 mile north of Gardiner or 52.5 miles south of Livingston, Montana. This is the first place on the river that trailered boats can be launched. Note that unlike most river access sites, there are no signs identifying this one. Take Airport Road west across the end of the runway and head toward the hangers, passing by the first left, which goes to the waste transfer station. Take the second fork, which zigs left down the bank past the Gardiner sewerage plant and to a parking area about 25 feet above the river. The boat ramp itself is just a steep cut in the bank, angled upstream. The bottom of this ramp is mostly loose gravel that is capable of trapping a vehicle. It is wise to keep your driving wheels on the hard pan at the top of the ramp and skid the boat the rest of the way. While no problem early in the season, late-season launches here underscore why we sometimes think of this as the kamikaze boat ramp. If on foot, fish either up or downstream from this point. Most of the 2 miles of water from Gardiner to below the McConnell Access is publicly managed, so there are no access difficulties except the physical in getting along here.

Sites 90–95

0 2 4 Miles

N

To Livingston, MT

Yankee Jim Canyon

Yankee Jim Access

Slip and Slide Creek

89

91d

95

Slip and Slide Ponds

91c

Old Yellowstone Trail South

Rigler Ranch

OTO Ranch

Cedar Creek

94

Cedar Creek Road

91b

Mol Heron Creek

Bassett Creek

Royal Teton Ranch

Corwin Springs

Cinnabar Creek

Cinnabar Access

90e

91a

Corwin Springs Access

93

90d La Duke Spring

Mol Heron Road

Cannibal's Corner

90c

Little Trail Creek

Mol Heron Creek

McConnell Access

Old Yellowstone Trail South

90b

Queen of Waters Access

90a

Gardiner

MONTANA

90f

Reese Creek

92
Sportsman's Lake

YELLOWSTONE NATIONAL PARK

Gardner River Road

92b
To Specimen and Fawn Pass Trailheads

▲ ELECTRIC PEAK

Cache Lake

Mammoth

Sportsman's Lake Trail

92a
To Glen Creek Trailhead

To Norris Junction

To Tower Junction

90b. McConnell Access

Drive 2.2 miles north from Gardiner or 51.3 miles south from Livingston to find the McConnell Access, an improved boat-launch area with a pit toilet. This is a day-use area; camping is not allowed. McConnell is the most popular access for starting float trips in this section of the river. The east side of the river is owned by various public agencies from this point back into Gardiner. Private land begins about 100 yards downriver, so fish upstream if on foot.

90c. Cannibal's Corner

Park in the large pullout under the trees where the US 89 right-of-way intersects the river 4 miles north of Gardiner or 49.5 miles south of Livingston. Take the path at the west end of this parking area down to the river to access an excellent, if rugged, section of riverbank. The name derives from a locally notorious murder that took place in the 1970s.

90d. La Duke Spring Area

Adjacent units of Forest Service and state land run for 1.3 miles, starting 4.7 miles north of Gardiner. This section begins with the Devil's Slide scenic pullout, continues with the La Duke Spring Picnic Area, and concludes with the Corwin Springs Access. There are also a couple of intermediate parking spots. Toilet and picnic facilities are available at La Duke, but there is no boat launch.

90e. Corwin Springs Access

The Corwin Springs Access is just 6 miles north of Gardiner or 47.5 miles south of Livingston. This site is popular as a swimming beach and campsite even though it is unimproved. Sand that can trap even a four-wheel-drive vehicle makes this marginal as a boat launch. The entire stretch of river from Devil's Slide to the Corwin Springs Access is worth fishing.

90f. West Side Access

On the west side of the river, the whole 4-mile reach from Gardiner to Reese Creek is in Yellowstone National Park. The river is seldom more than a couple of hundred yards from any of several pullouts along Old Yellowstone Trail South. Park your vehicle, cross over to the river, and fish in either direction. Closer to Gardiner, use the old railroad grade to minimize climbing hills. The west bank of the river from the mouth of Reese Creek north to the Cinnabar Access is private land, and therefore is not very available. It is 8.2 miles from Gardiner to the Corwin Springs Bridge via Old Yellowstone Trail South.

91. Yellowstone River, Corwin Springs to Yankee Jim Canyon
(see map on page 209)

Description: Flowing northwesterly, this 5-mile stretch of the Yellowstone River has the least gradient in the whole area. The valley itself is defined by the constric-

Loading the dories at the McConnell Access.

tion of Cinnabar Mountain at its upper end and Yankee Jim Canyon at its lower end. The valley bottom is mostly private land divided between a single large holding on the west side and numerous small subdivided tracts on the east side. The seasonal pattern in the area of high and muddy water in May and June holds here as well. The banks are fairly open but often are covered by steep loose cobble or are lined with willow. Besides the usual shoreline pockets, anglers should concentrate their attention on the riffle structures, which include several major gravel bars, a couple of big eddy pools, and the outlet areas of two large tributaries, Mol Heron and Cedar Creeks.

The fish: Cutthroat, whitefish, cutbow, and rainbow dominate this section of the river. Browns are more common here than in the section above Corwin Springs, and brookies may still put in an appearance. The bread-and-butter fish is the 13-inch cutthroat, with most falling between 9 and 15 inches. Browns of more than ten pounds have turned up, as have rainbows nearly as large. Most whitefish are around 13 inches, but the odd "stoneroller" may hit four pounds. This is an excellent reach of river.

Flies and lures: The long season and variety of water types mean that just about any freshwater fly or lure may produce results at some time. Due to the catch-and-release rule for cutthroat, I recommend artificials, but Montana does allow the use of bait. Effective flies to use here are attractor dries such as Royal Coachman Trudes or Stimulators, stonefly patterns and hoppers in season, and midges during the winter. Bead-head Stone, Woolly Worm, and Hare's Ear head the list of useful nymph patterns. The Woolly Bugger and Zonker are good bets in streamers.

Leading lures include the Panther Martin, Thomas Cyclone, and Mepps. In some of the more structured runs, a Rapala is worth a shot.

Special equipment: The high percentage of private land along the river gives the floater a distinct advantage. McKenzie-style drift boats or dories are the angler's best choices. This reach poses no extraordinary navigational hazards, so johnboats, canoes, rafts, and small pontoon-style boats can be useful here.

Access: Remember that crossing somebody's fence without permission is trespassing. Because it is more complicated, the west bank of the Yellowstone is discussed first in this section.

91a. Cinnabar Access

Driving 46.7 miles south from Livingston or 6.8 miles north from Gardiner on US 89 brings you to Corwin Springs. Turn west onto Cinnabar Road, which crosses the river here on an old iron-truss bridge, which is scheduled to be replaced with a modern bridge in 2006 or 2007. The west end of the bridge is on Forest Service land. Turning left again, back toward Gardiner on Old Yellowstone Trail South, brings you in 0.3 mile to the Forest Service's Cinnabar Access. This is a good launch or retrieval point for floats to Yankee Jim or from the Gardiner area. The access has tables and a toilet. Forest Service land provides a total of 1 mile of public land on the west bank from 0.3 mile below to 0.7 mile above the bridge.

91b. Mol Heron Creek

Old Yellowstone Trail South continues, turning right after crossing the old bridge and heading down the valley. The road comes to a three-way fork 0.6 mile north of the Corwin Springs Bridge. The far left tine is the Cinnabar Basin Road that ascends Mol Heron Creek, and the center tine is a private access road for the Royal Teton Ranch, so take the right-hand tine, which is the Old Yellowstone Trail South. The road crosses Mol Heron Creek 1.4 miles north of the Corwin Springs Bridge. Park here to walk 50 feet down Mol Heron to the Yellowstone.

91c. Yankee Jim Canyon

The closer you get to the Forest Service boundary at the head of Yankee Jim Canyon, the worse the road gets. A major mud hole in the road 5 miles north of the Corwin Springs Bridge can trap a light vehicle whenever the road is wet. The last few hundred yards above the canyon are on Forest Service land, which provides a useful access on the otherwise isolated west side of the river 5.3 miles north of Corwin Springs Bridge.

91d. East Side, Check Station to Yankee Jim Access

A full mile of public land begins with the Montana Fish, Wildlife & Parks game-check station 11.2 miles north of Gardiner or 42.3 miles south of Livingston on US 89. Use any of several pullouts on the west side of the highway for pedestrian access to the Yellowstone between the check station and the next access point. The Yankee Jim Access is located alongside US 89 41.2 miles south of Livingston or 12.3 miles north of Gardiner. This is the end point for our discussion and for floats originating near Gardiner or Corwin Springs. The Yankee Jim Access is developed with a boat ramp, toilet, and picnic tables.

Tributaries: Mol Heron Creek (site 93) and Cedar Creek (site 94) are the only significant tributaries in this reach. Also of interest to anglers are Slip and Slide Ponds on the Rigler Ranch (site 95). Mol Heron starts in Yellowstone National Park at Sportsman's Lake (site 92). Other small streams such as Slip and Slide and Joe Brown Creeks are trivial and often dry.

92. Sportsman's Lake *(see map on page 209)*

Description: Sportsman's Lake, at the head of Mol Heron Creek, offers fishing in a high-mountain-lake setting, made more attractive by the presence of Yellowstone National Park backcountry campsites. Parts of the area around the lake were heavily burned during 1988; the burn was heaviest around the western end of the lake. The best water is around the inlet and outlet. The lake lies just under 8,000 feet, so ice-off may not occur until well into June. The month following the thaw is the best time to fish the lake. The Bear Management Plan restricts travel in the Gallatin Range to designated trails and recommends a minimum of four people per party.

The fish: Sportsman's Lake is populated by cutthroat, mostly in the 8- to 12-inch range.

Flies and lures: Hare's Ear and Prince nymphs, Scuds, and Woolly Buggers are the most effective fly patterns. Try Mepps or Li'l Jake's when spin fishing.

Access: Sportsman's Lake can be accessed from either the Gallatin Range to the west or the Gardner River to the east. No public access to Sportsman's Lake exists by ascending Mol Heron Creek. Using this route requires permission from the private landowner and also entails several miles of bushwhacking on a long-abandoned trail.

92a. Sportsman's Lake/East

Take the Grand Loop Road 4.9 miles south from Mammoth to the Glen Creek Trailhead. The Glen Creek Trailhead is 16.7 miles north of Norris Junction. Take the Glen Creek Trail west from the trailhead 2 miles to the junction of the Fawn Pass and Sportsman's Lake Trails. Sportsman's Lake is 12.7 miles off the road, and the trail crosses the main spine of the Gallatin Range. This is not suitable as a day hike.

92b. Sportsman's Lake/West

Drive 26.2 miles north from West Yellowstone on U.S. Highway 191 or 57.1 miles south from Four Corners to the Specimen Creek Trailhead. Take the Specimen Creek Trail east 2 miles to its junction with the Sportsman's Lake Trail, then follow the latter 9 miles to the lake. This 11-mile trek is by far the easiest approach to the lake.

93. Mol Heron and Cinnabar Creeks *(see map on page 209)*

Description: Mol Heron Creek and its tributary, Cinnabar Creek, are steep mountain streams in narrow canyons. They start on the flanks of the Gallatin Range along the park's northern boundary and flow north to the Yellowstone River. Only the upper couple of miles of Mol Heron are in the park, so Montana regulations generally apply. The banks are tree-lined or overhung with brush. Prime waters in these streams are the pockets and pools formed around the boulders and deadfall that litter the streambed. July and August are the best months to fish these waters.

The fish: These waters are dominated by cutthroat and cutbow, the latter primarily found in Cinnabar Creek. The fish are small, seldom exceeding 10 inches, except in the lower canyon of Mol Heron where fish up to 14 inches are possible.

The Yellowstone as it runs through Yankee Jim Canyon.

Flies and lures: Attractor flies, both wet and dry, such as Royal Wulff, Royal Coachman Trude, or Prince nymph are effective here. Spin lures such as a size 2 Panther Martin or small Cyclone work well. Once inside the park, artificials are required. Cinnabar Creek is really too small for effective lure fishing.

Access: From Corwin Springs cross the bridge to Old Yellowstone Trail South. After going straight ahead from the bridge, the road bends right toward the north. The Cinnabar Basin Road is the far left fork of a three-way branching 0.6 mile north of the Corwin Springs Bridge. The far right branch is the Old Yellowstone Trail south to Yankee Jim Canyon. The middle branch is a private road for the Royal Teton Ranch. Cinnabar Basin Road meets Mol Heron Creek where its canyon meets the main valley, about 0.9 mile past the fork. Most of the land is private, but there are corners of National Forest Service land that intersect the road and creek. Good access to the creek is provided by the road for 1.2 miles to the confluence with Cinnabar Creek. This lower canyon section is by far the most fishable part of Mol Heron. The Cinnabar Basin Road forks to the right and ascends Cinnabar Creek, while the Mol Heron Road continues up Mol Heron Creek to its public end on Royal Teton Ranch property 3 miles farther up the creek. Permission is required to fish or transit ranch property. The same is true for Cinnabar Creek, which is also almost exclusively on private land. Given that the fish are tiny there, little is lost by giving this water a pass.

94. Cedar Creek (see map on page 209)

Description: Cedar Creek rises on Monitor Peak and runs southwest about 5 miles to join the Yellowstone River. Like most tributary streams in Montana, much of its water is used to meet heavy irrigation demands, but unlike some it is almost never completely utilized for this purpose, so the creek remains significant as a cutthroat spawning stream. However, it is generally not fishable at that time due to both water conditions and access issues. The extreme headwaters are not useful due to small size and steep gradient. The middle reach of the stream flattens some through a more open pasture area. There is a steep pitch through a miniature canyon just above the headgate area where the creek enters the Yellowstone's valley. The pasture area is the most accessible and fishable section. The best time to fish here is July.

The fish: The lower section hosts a cutthroat spawning run. These fish come in during June and leave by mid-July. The fry mostly run out to the river during August. There is so little water the rest of the summer that there is little in the way of a resident fish population. Above the headgates the creek holds midget brookies, but it will never be famous.

Flies and lures: Dave's Hoppers, Royal Coachman Trudes (fished either as dries or wets), and Prince nymphs are the only flies required. The stream is really too small for lure fishing.

Access: Drive 9.3 miles north from Gardiner or 44.2 miles south from Livingston on US 89 to the Cedar Creek Road. The road goes east up the creek to the old OTO Ranch on Forest Service land. The Forest Service has a locked gate on the road and a trailhead area 0.5 mile from US 89. Walk the remaining 0.7 mile to the meadow area and fish upstream. The lower end of Cedar Creek is private property.

95. Slip and Slide Ponds (see map on page 209)

Description: The Slip and Slide Ponds are impoundments on private property managed as a fee fishery by the owner. Slip and Slide Creek, which supplies the water for these ponds, is not a fishery. The banks of both ponds are fairly open, with patches of brush. The lower pond is small, though a float tube can be useful there. The upper pond is truly tiny and in a hillside bowl.

The fish: The main lower pond has produced some excellent rainbows and browns. The upper pond holds what the owner describes as "kokanee/rainbow hybrids," actually probably kamloops.

Flies and lures: Woolly Buggers and damselfly nymphs are the best fly patterns. Rapalas and Mepps are good lure choices.

Access: Call Slip and Slide Ranch, listed in the Gardiner phone book, to make arrangements to fish these ponds. Take US 89 north from Gardiner 11 miles or 42.5 miles south from Livingston to the ranch drive.

The Gardner River Drainage

Both the Gardner River and Gardiner, the North Entrance to Yellowstone National Park, take their name from mountain man Johnson Gardner, who trapped the area around 1830. The spelling for the town may have been derived from the way Jim Bridger pronounced Gardner's name, and until 1959 the river also appeared on maps as "Gardiner." Fitting our image of the trapper, the river is a rough-and-tumble stream rising on Electric Peak and other mountains of the Gallatin Range. Running southeasterly through Gardners Hole, the river picks up a number of tributary streams. Turning abruptly onto a northerly course, the river drops through the Sheepeater Canyon, over Osprey Falls, past Mammoth and the park headquarters, and enters the Yellowstone River at Gardiner.

Mileage points: Mileage points for the Gardner drainage are found at Norris, Tower, and Mammoth Junctions on the Grand Loop Road. For the North Entrance Road, they are at Mammoth and the North Entrance Station at Gardiner.

96. Upper Gardner River

Description: The headwaters of the Gardner are a complex network of streams originating on the east flank of the Gallatin Range. They all converge at the Indian Creek Campground 8.7 miles south of Mammoth. The Gardner itself rises on Electric Peak and flows generally southward, only becoming a substantial stream after joining with Fawn Creek. Downstream from Fawn Creek is Gardners Hole proper, where old, long-abandoned beaver ponds shaped the ground. The river is very crooked, with small pitches over modest cobble into deep, sandy-bottomed pools. The high banks are lined with heavily browsed scrub willow. On picking up Indian Creek about 0.5 mile above the Seven Mile Bridge, the river abruptly changes character. The bottom becomes larger cobble and bedrock. The banks are still grass and scrub brush.

In the Gardners Hole area, the most interesting water is found where the pitches enter the pools and along the cut banks. The structural pockets around boulders produce the best results in the lower section. This area fishes well from the end of the spring runoff in early July until about the end of August. Fall fishing is generally poor.

The fish: This section sports a large number of small brook trout. Most fish are in the 5- to 8-inch range; you should not expect fish larger than about 10 inches.

Flies and lures: It's a very bad day that a #12 or #14 Royal Coachman Trude will not produce fish. Other effective patterns include Wulffs, hoppers in season, Prince nymphs, and Renegades. Keep the lures on the small side, and look to Mepps or Cyclones for your best results. This is a great section to use ultralight fly or spin tackle. The main stem of the Gardner is open to worm fishing by children under twelve years of age.

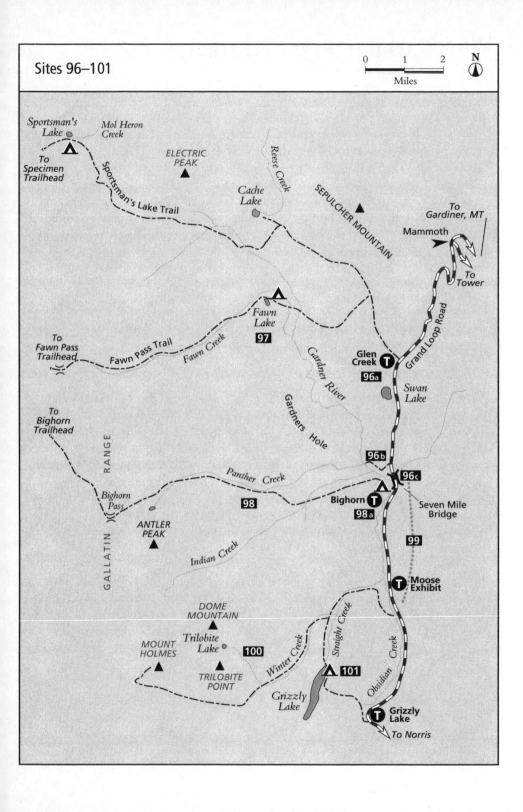

Sportsman's Lake

Mol Heron Creek

ELECTRIC PEAK

Reese Creek

To Specimen Trailhead

Sportsman's Lake Trail

Cache Lake

SEPULCHER MOUNTAIN

To Gardiner, MT

Mammoth

To Tower

Fawn Lake

Fawn Pass Trail

To Fawn Pass Trailhead

Fawn Creek

97

Gardner River

Glen Creek **T**

96a

Grand Loop Road

Swan Lake

To Bighorn Trailhead

R A N G E

Gardners Hole

96b

96c

Panther Creek

Bighorn Pass

98

Bighorn **T**

Seven Mile Bridge

ANTLER PEAK

98a

99

G A L L A T I N

Indian Creek

Moose Exhibit **T**

DOME MOUNTAIN

Straight Creek

Obsidian Creek

MOUNT HOLMES

Trilobite Lake

100

Winter Creek

TRILOBITE POINT

101

Grizzly Lake

Grizzly Lake **T**

To Norris

96a. Upper Gardners Hole

To fish the upper end of Gardners Hole, stop at the Glen Creek Trailhead pullout 4.9 miles south of Mammoth or 16.7 miles north of Norris Junction on the Grand Loop Road. The pullout is on the west side of the road opposite the Bunsen Peak Trailhead. Bushwhack straight west over the first ridge to hit the Gardner. Fish in either direction, but ask yourself why you did this other than to avoid people, as the fish are just 6-inch brookies.

96b. Gardners Hole, Main Section

To fish the main part of Gardners Hole, take the Grand Loop Road 7.7 miles south from Mammoth or 13.9 miles north from Norris Junction. A gated and locked service road enters the Grand Loop Road from the west. Park off the roadway here, but take care not to block either the highway or the service road. Walk 0.5 mile on the service road to the Gardner near the confluence of Indian and Panther Creeks. An anglers' trail parallels the Gardner upstream through Gardners Hole. Fish in either direction.

96c. Seven Mile Bridge

Stay on the Grand Loop Road and park in the pullout on the west side of the road just south of the Seven Mile Bridge to fish the Gardner between the bridge and the confluence with Indian Creek. Walk north across the bridge and fish upstream. Seven Mile Bridge is 8 miles south of Mammoth or 13.2 miles north of Norris Junction.

Tributaries: The principle tributaries in this section are Indian and Panther Creeks (site 98), Obsidian Creek (site 99), and Fawn Creek. Fawn Lake (site 97) is also of interest. Winter Creek (Site 100) and its tributary Straight Creek (site 101), which flows through Grizzly Lake (site 101), are tributaries to Obsidian Creek.

97. Fawn Lake

Description: Fawn Lake is a small pond bordered by a marsh zone that is, in turn, partially protected by timber to the south and west. Fawn Creek and a backcountry campsite are just to the north of the lake. The lake produces best right after ice-off and then again late, just before freeze-up; ideally the lake should be half-frozen. Most of the year the fish will be unreachable due to prolific weed growth in the lake. The Bear Management Plan suggests a minimum party of four and restricts off-trail travel in the Gallatin Range.

The fish: Fawn Lake is populated by brook trout. Unlike most brookie water, this pond has been known to produce fish in the 22- to 24-inch range.

Flies and lures: This is a fine place to try the Joffe Jewel. Being a lake, it is also a good spot for Scuds or damselfly nymphs. Mepps, Panther Martins, Cyclone spoons, or Li'l Jake's are good choices in lures.

Special equipment: This is a very small pond a long way off the road, so I don't recommend hauling a float tube in here unless somebody else is going to carry it.

Access: Drive 4.9 miles south of Mammoth or 16.7 miles north of Norris Junction on the Grand Loop Road to the Glen Creek Trailhead. Take the Glen Creek Trail 2 miles to the Fawn Pass Trail and then the Fawn Pass Trail an additional 3 miles to Fawn Lake.

98. Indian and Panther Creeks (see map on page 218)

Description: These streams rise on the east flank of the Gallatin Range. Initially separated by Antler Peak, they flow east toward their junction with the Gardner, just up from the Indian Creek Campground. The most fishable sections of Panther and Indian Creeks are very similar and only separated by 100 yards where they join the Gardner. They are in open terrain with a mix of scrub willow and sage along the banks. Their bottoms are more cobbled than the Gardners Hole section of the Gardner, but the key features remain the heads of pools and undercut bank margins. As you ascend either creek, another feature, minidams created by deadfall, becomes increasingly common. Eventually the streams become too small to retain much interest. For practical purposes, the good fishing here will be in July or August only.

The fish: The fish are numerous but small brook trout that seldom exceed 8 inches in length.

Flies and lures: These streams are waters where a basic attractor pattern such as a #14 Royal Wulff or Royal Coachman Trude dry, or a Renegade wet, should be all that is required. Hoppers may be useful in late July or August. This water is so small that lures must be kept in the ultralight range. Try a size 0 Mepps, a size 2 Panther Martin, or a 450 Kamlooper spoon. Both of these streams are on the list that allow children under 12 to use worms.

Access: Head south from Mammoth on the Grand Loop Road 7.7 miles to a service road entering the highway from the west. Find the service road 13.9 miles north of Norris Junction. Park out of traffic and walk 0.5 mile in on the service road to the diversion structure for the Mammoth water supply. This low dam lies directly between the confluences of Panther and Indian Creeks with the main stem of the Gardner. Cross the dam and fish up either creek.

98a. Bighorn Pass Trail

To fish the upper sections of either creek, stay on the Grand Loop Road to the Indian Creek Campground road 8.7 miles south of Mammoth or 12.9 miles north of Norris Junction. Take the campground road, cross Obsidian Creek, and park at the Bighorn Pass Trailhead. Walk in on the Bighorn Pass Trail, which parallels first Indian Creek and then crosses over to ascend Panther Creek. (By the way, the Indian Creek Campground is one of the smaller and more congenial campgrounds in the park.) Off-trail travel is restricted and a minimum party of four is recommended by the Bear Management Plan in the Gallatin Range.

99. Obsidian Creek (see map on page 218)

Description: Obsidian Creek joins the Gardner at the Seven Mile Bridge south of Mammoth. It flows generally north from its headwaters in the southern end of the Gallatin Range. The creek is effectively fishless above its confluence with Winter Creek 11 miles south of Mammoth. The productive lower section of Obsidian Creek traverses a willow flat and is slower than the Gardner. It is characterized by fairly deep pools with overhanging banks separated by small pebbly bars on corners. The heads of the pools and the undercuts are the best places to look for fish. July and August are the most productive months to fish this water. The roadside sign says, WILLOW PARK, LOOK FOR MOOSE—which is both good advice and a prudent warning.

The fish: The fish in Obsidian Creek are exclusively tiny brook trout.

Flies and lures: Besides the usual attractor dries repeatedly mentioned, this would be a good spot for a small bright streamer like the Joffe Jewel, a Prince nymph, or a Renegade. Keep the lures small. Good choices would be Panther Martins, Cyclones, or Vibraxes. This section is also available to children under twelve using worms for bait.

Access: Use any of the numerous pullouts between the Seven Mile Bridge, 8.4 miles south of Mammoth on the Grand Loop Road, and the Moose Exhibit pullout 10.9 miles south of Mammoth. The stream is in a willow swamp, so early-season fishing may require wading just to reach the creek. Once on the stream, fish in either direction. If coming from the south on the Grand Loop Road, the fishable section of Obsidian Creek begins at the Moose Exhibit 10.7 miles north of Norris Junction and ends at Seven Mile Bridge 2.5 miles farther north.

100. Winter Creek and Trilobite Lake (see map on page 218)

Description: Winter Creek rises on the flank of Mount Holmes in the Gallatin Range and flows first southeasterly and then northeasterly to its confluence with Obsidian Creek at the upper end of Willow Park. Along the way it picks up Straight Creek (site 101). The lower few hundred yards of Winter Creek are in fairly open ground, but as you go up the creek into its own valley, you get into an area heavily burned during the 1988 fires. The creek has a steeper gradient than Obsidian Creek, so the structure is more dominated by pools created by larger cobble and deadfall. July and August are the most productive times to fish.

Trilobite Lake does not appear to have an outlet to Winter Creek, though it lies very near the head of the creek. It sits in a bowl at 8,365 feet, surrounded by Dome Mountain, Mount Holmes, and Trilobite Point. The immediate shoreline is open, with timber a few yards back. The ice will be off the lake before the spring flood allows the repeated fords of Obsidian and Winter Creeks required to reach it. Fishing is best at Trilobite Lake in July and early August.

The fish: The fish in Winter Creek are small brook trout, mostly in the 6- to 10-inch range. Trilobite Lake fish are also brookies, but they are larger, 7 to 12 inches, with many around 10 inches.

Winter Creek flows through open country and burned timber.

Flies and lures: A Joffe Jewel, Prince nymph, or Renegade are good bets for wet flies. A smaller Royal Coachman Trude is my first choice in a dry, though in August a grasshopper pattern is also a reasonable place to start. This is really small water not well suited to spin fishing. If you try this method, keep the lures on the small side, say a #0 Mepps. Joffe Jewels, Skinny Buggers, and tan Scuds are productive choices for Trilobite Lake. The spin angler should try a Li'l Jake's.

Access: Take the Grand Loop Road south from Mammoth to the best access for fishing Winter Creek. Stop at Moose Exhibit, the last of the Willow Park pullouts, 10.9 miles south of Mammoth. Drive north 10.7 miles from Norris Junction to reach the Moose Exhibit pullout. This is within sight of the confluence of Winter Creek with Obsidian Creek. The obvious anglers' track intersects the Mount Holmes Trail 200 yards up Winter Creek. I would go to this point before beginning to fish upstream. The trail forks 2 miles up Winter Creek, with the western branch continuing up toward Mount Holmes and the left fork staying with Straight Creek toward Grizzly Lake.

The Trilobite Lake Trail forks off the Mount Holmes Trail 3 miles up Winter Creek from its confluence with Straight Creek. A couple of backcountry campsites near the trail junction provide a base area. Take the Trilobite Lake Trail the final 2 miles to the lake. The 7-mile total puts Trilobite Lake outside day-hike range.

101. Grizzly Lake and Straight Creek (see map on page 218)

Description: Straight Creek is only relatively straight. Flowing north along the east flank of the Gallatin Range, it is a small stream in a flat-floored, incised valley. The heavy timber of this area was intensely burned in 1988. Some of the valley floor was and remains a marshy meadow. The most interesting feature is Grizzly Lake, which is larger than many park ponds. It is 200 to 300 yards across and over 1 mile long. A backcountry campsite near the northern end of the lake lies near its outlet. The south end of the lake is an open, marshy valley. July and August are the best times to fish, though Grizzly Lake will produce as soon as the ice is off in early June.

Wind whips up small whitecaps on Grizzly Lake.
NATIONAL PARK SERVICE PHOTO

The fish: The fish in Grizzly Lake and Straight Creek are all tiny brook trout. Those in the lake may reach up to 12 inches on occasion, but 7 to 10 inches is more the norm.

Flies and lures: Try a #14 Royal Wulff in a dry or a Prince in a wet. Grizzly Lake is a good place to try a Joffe Jewel. The creek is really too small for spin tackle, but the lake is large enough and then some. Because the fish are small, the lures should be kept on the small side. Try a Kastmaster or Li'l Jake's.

Special equipment: The only thing wrong with hauling a float tube in here, other than the 5-mile round-trip, is that there is no payoff: The fish are dinky.

Access: The best access to this water is provided by the Grizzly Lake Trail. Drive 15.1 miles south of Mammoth or 6.5 miles north from Norris Junction on the Grand Loop Road. Stop at the Grizzly Lake Trailhead, which is a small pullout only large enough for two or three vehicles, about a mile south of Obsidian Cliff. If you get to Roaring Mountain (coming from Mammoth), you have gone about a mile too far. Grizzly Lake is 1.8 miles from the road over a modest ridge involving less than 400 vertical feet of climbing. From the outlet of Grizzly Lake, the trail loops down Straight Creek to meet the Mount Holmes Trail and then back to the Grand Loop Road near Apollinaris Spring. From this end it is over 4 miles to Grizzly Lake.

102. Gardner River, Sheepeater Canyon Reach

Description: The 6 miles of the Gardner from the Seven Mile Bridge downstream to its confluence with Lava Creek is in the Sheepeater Canyon. The 100-foot-high Osprey Falls is halfway through the canyon. Above the falls the river is in a steep-walled trench cut through the lava rock that forms the bulk of the central plateau area of the park. Below Osprey Falls the river is in a slightly more open V-shaped valley. Throughout this reach the Gardner runs fast over a boulder-strewn bed. The pockets of slower water above and below these rocks and the occasional downed tree are the best places to look for fish. Most of the area was heavily timbered before the 1988 fires. The standing timber and deadfall challenges the caster and hiker. Fishing in this section is best in July and August.

The fish: At the head of the Sheepeater Canyon, the fish are all brook trout. Some rainbows are added below the first couple of cascades formed by the river dropping into the canyon. Osprey Falls blocks upstream movement of browns, cutthroat, and whitefish, all of which are found in the lower section of this reach. Rainbows and brookies predominate close to the falls, but the balance shifts toward browns and rainbows as you go downriver. Below Osprey Falls the fish tend to run 6 to 12 inches. Above the falls a prolific crop of fish range between 4 and 10 inches, with most of the larger ones being rainbows.

Flies and lures: Above Osprey Falls Royal Coachman Trudes are as good a pattern as any. Below the falls the salmonfly hatch takes place as the water clears toward the end of June. Match the hatch. Thereafter, go back to the attractor patterns such as the Royal Coachman Trude or Royal Wulff dry and Prince nymph wet. Small

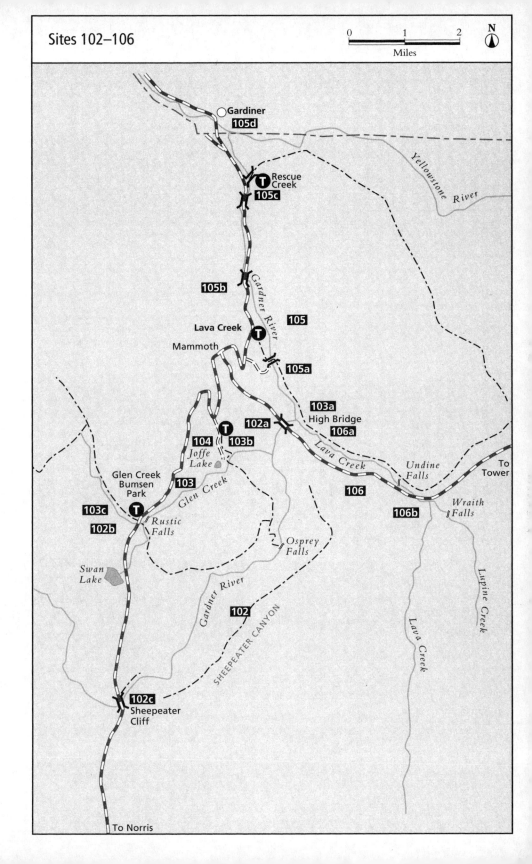

Sites 102–106

0   1   2
Miles

N

Gardiner
105d

Rescue
Creek
105c

105b

Gardner River

Lava Creek **105**
Mammoth
105a

103a
High Bridge
106a

104 **103b** **102a**

103 *Joffe Lake*

Glen Creek
Bumsen Park

Glen Creek

Lava Creek

Undine
Falls

To
Tower

103c **106**

Rustic
Falls **106b** *Wraith Falls*

102b

Swan Lake

Gardner River

Osprey Falls

102

SHEEPEATER CANYON

Lava Creek

Lupine Creek

102c
Sheepeater
Cliff

To Norris

Yellowstone River

Panther Martins, Cyclone spoons, or Kamloopers are good choices in spin lures. This section is open to children under twelve who wish to use worms for bait.

102a. High Bridge

The best access for the lower end is found at the Sheepeater Canyon Bridge, usually known as the High Bridge, located 1.6 miles east of Mammoth on the Grand Loop Road. The High Bridge is 16.5 miles west of Tower Junction on the Grand Loop Road. There are parking areas at both ends of the High Bridge. If your intent is to fish the Gardner upstream from the bridge area, it is probably best to park at the west end. If you plan to go farther upstream closer to Osprey Falls before starting, the east end parking is better. Obvious angler and animal trails point you in the right direction.

102b. Bunsen Peak Road

The upper end of the Bunsen Peak Road is found where the Grand Loop Road breaks out of Golden Gate onto Swan Lake Flat 4.9 miles south of Mammoth. The trailhead is 16.7 miles north of Norris Junction. The trail is a dirt two-track usually closed to motor vehicles. A 2-mile walk southeast from this trailhead brings you to the west rim of Sheepeater Canyon. A very steep and rugged scramble down into the canyon puts you onto a seldom-fished section of the Gardner populated by small but enthusiastic rainbows and brookies.

102c. Sheepeater Picnic Area

The upper section of Sheepeater Canyon is reached by taking the Grand Loop Road south from Mammoth 8.2 miles or north from Norris Junction 13.4 miles to the Sheepeater Picnic Area access road. Go east 0.2 mile on the access road to the picnic area. Fish either up or downstream. Take the anglers' trail down the river to get into the canyon area below the Sheepeater Cascade. The hike from the canyon rim to the river gets more difficult as the canyon deepens downstream. Get below the third cataract to locate the area where rainbows are possible.

Tributaries: There are two substantial tributaries in this reach, Glen Creek (site 105) and Lava Creek (site 106). One little lake of interest, Joffe Lake (site 104), discharges to Glen Creek.

103. Glen Creek (see map on page 225)

Description: Glen Creek drains the south side of Mount Sepulcher. It flows southeast until it reaches Golden Gate, where it turns to the northeast and leaps off the plateau over Rustic Falls. While the fishable upper part of the creek is in an open meadow of moderate gradient, the lower end of Glen Creek is extremely steep and rugged. The upper part of the creek is only a couple of feet wide but is made fishable

The Gardner River flows through Sheepeater Canyon.

by small pools protected by high, grassy banks. Glen Creek joins the Gardner about 0.5 mile above the High Bridge. Glen Creek's only substantial tributary is the Swan Lake Outlet, which joins Glen Creek just above Rustic Falls. In stark contrast, this stream is several feet wide, sporting a very flat, spring-creek-like appearance. Late June, July, and early August are the best times to fish this water.

The fish: For practical purposes, Glen Creek is exclusively a brook trout fishery, though other species may show up near its mouth. The fish in the lower section are uniformly tiny. They are a bit larger in the upper section, and the Swan Lake Outlet can occasionally turn out fish up to 14 inches long. Swan Lake itself is only about 3 feet deep and therefore is without fish.

Flies and lures: For most of Glen Creek, there is little point in trying anything other than an attractor such as a Royal Wulff. The flat spring-creek-like nature of the Swan Lake Outlet makes for very selective fish that often demand tiny nymphs and midge-type dry flies, along with a perfect presentation. With the exception of the Swan Lake Outlet, Glen Creek is too small to fish effectively with lures. The spinning angler should try the smaller sizes of Mepps or Cyclones on ultralight tackle in the Swan Lake Outlet.

103a. High Bridge

The best way to reach the lower end of Glen Creek is to take the Grand Loop Road 1.6 miles east from Mammoth or 16.5 miles west of Tower Junction. Park at the west end of the Sheepeater Canyon (High) Bridge. Use the anglers' tracks and game trails that head upstream from the bridge. Glen Creek joins the Gardner 0.5 mile south of the bridge. Fish up Glen Creek.

103b. Bunsen Peak Loop

The north end of the Bunsen Peak Loop provides another access to the lower section. Go south 1.3 miles on the Grand Loop Road from Mammoth to the residential service road on the outside of the first hairpin turn. Find the southeast corner of the housing area, park, and walk in on the Bunsen Peak Loop. A 0.5-mile hike brings you to Glen Creek a bit over 0.5 mile above its confluence with the Gardner. Fish in either direction.

103c. Glen Creek Trail

Taking the Grand Loop Road 4.9 miles south from Mammoth brings you to Glen Creek at the Golden Gate where the long climb onto the Yellowstone's central plateau breaks out onto Swan Lake Flat. Take the Glen Creek Trail to the west. This trail ascends Glen Creek for more miles than it is fishable. Take the Bunsen Peak Trail to the east for access to the Swan Lake Outlet. The trailhead is 16.7 miles north of Norris Junction.

The high-banked pools of upper Glen Creek are fishable.

The Joffe Jewel was named after Joffe Lake in the Gardner Drainage.

104. Joffe Lake (see map on page 225)

Description: Joffe Lake is a tiny L-shaped pond. The steep south shore is heavily timbered, while the remainder is more open. It will usually fish well from ice-off in early June through September.

The fish: The fish in Joffe Lake are brook trout, typically 8 to 10 inches long. Some years the average size will creep up to about 12 inches, with some in the 14-inch class.

Flies and lures: This is the pond for which the Joffe Jewel was named. Other still-water patterns such as scuds and damselfly nymphs work well here. A basic spoon such as the Cyclone is a good lure to try. Anglers under twelve years of age are allowed to use worms.

Special equipment: Joffe Lake is so small that virtually all of it can be reached from shore, but with its south side timbered to the water's edge, a float tube may be useful.

Access: Take the Grand Loop Road 1.3 miles south from Mammoth. The access is 20.3 miles north of Norris Junction. Joffe Lake is accessed by a service road leaving the Grand Loop Road on the outside of the first hairpin turn just south of Mammoth. The road is identified only by a small sign saying "residential area." Drive past the housing for seasonal employees and the giant pink cement-block maintenance garage. The paved drive changes abruptly to a dirt two-track road. Follow it 0.9 mile directly to Joffe Lake.

105. Lower Gardner River (see map on page 225)

Description: The remaining 5 miles of the Gardner, from Lava Creek down to its confluence with the Yellowstone, present a lot of opportunities to the angler. The riverbank is often composed of large boulders with a fringe of willow or sage punctuated by an occasional cottonwood or juniper. The steep, rough terrain makes the Gardner a very physical stream to fish. The river itself is characterized by the pockets formed by the numerous boulders making up the riverbed. These pockets are the key fishing areas, though there are some pools and more conventional riffle corners, particularly in the few places where the gradient flattens. The park boundary runs exactly through the mouth of the river, leaving it entirely within the bounds of Yellowstone National Park.

When the season opens the Gardner is usually unfishable due to spring runoff. About the end of June, the water will have dropped and cleared enough to make fishing practical. In the fall spawning browns move into this section from the Yellowstone River, so fishing holds up until the season closes. There are no fishable tributaries between Gardiner and Lava Creek. Slide Lake was at one time stocked with rainbows, but the stream feeding it is too steep for upstream migration from the Gardner and too small at the inlet to permit spawning. This population died out in the early 1970s.

The fish: The lower 5 miles of river are populated by a mix of browns, rainbows, cutthroat, cutbows, whitefish, and brook trout. The proportions change with the season and the reach of river, with the upper section holding far fewer browns and more rainbows. The resident fish in the Gardner are mostly 7 to 14 inches, but the fall run of browns are more often in the 16- to 20-inch range and have been known to exceed nine pounds.

Flies and lures: As the river clears toward the end of June, the lower Gardner produces a substantial stonefly hatch followed by a string of caddis hatches. This makes stonefly nymphs, say a Brooks' Stone or Woolly Worm, the most effective early flies, followed by adult patterns such as an Elk Stone or Stimulator, and then attractors such as the Royal Trude or Wulff patterns. As the season advances, the average size of your fly should shrink until the fall browns hit. They are seldom interested in surface flies, so stonefly or big attractor nymphs such as a Prince are a good bet. Late summer also brings out grasshoppers.

Because of the steep gradient of the Gardner, the spin fisher should stick to lures with moderate actions; for example, flat spoons like the Cyclone or

Kamlooper and narrow blade spinners such as the Panther Martin or Rooster Tail. Children under 12 years old may use worms.

105a. Incinerator/Lava Creek Trail

The Lava Creek Trailhead is opposite the Mammoth Campground 3.75 miles from the North Entrance Station. From here a trail descends to a footbridge across the river. The trail goes up the Gardner River and then Lava Creek as the northern branch of the Howard Eaton Trail. Go another 0.2 mile, turn left into the Mammoth School access road, and hold to the left past the school on the service road down the hill to the "Incinerator," a storage yard and waste transfer station. At this point you are only 100 yards from the footbridge, but overnight parking is only allowed back up at the trailhead. Take one of the anglers' tracks on either bank up or down the river. The school access road is 1.1 miles and the Lava Creek Trailhead is 1.3 miles north of Mammoth Junction.

105b. Forty-fifth Parallel Bridge

Drive north 2.4 miles from Mammoth or south 2.6 miles from the North Entrance Station to the Forty-fifth Parallel Bridge. The North Entrance Road crosses the river twice in the 1.9 miles between this bridge and the Rescue Creek Trailhead. Throughout this section the road is adjacent to the river, with numerous parking spots available. Use any one of them that isn't already occupied. "Chinaman's Garden," located just downstream from the second bridge, is one of the few moderate-gradient sections of the river. Use the downstream parking area just south of the bridge to work either up or downstream on either side of the river. A sign here identifies this as the Forty-fifth Parallel. The large parking lot on the upstream side is the access for "Boiling River," a popular swimming hole.

105c. Rescue Creek Trailhead

You will find the Rescue Creek Trailhead on the river side of the North Entrance Road 0.75 mile past the North Entrance Station from Gardiner. The trailhead is 4.3 miles north of Mammoth. The footbridge here gives access to the east side of the river even when it is otherwise unfordable. Fish either up or down on either side of the river.

105d. Town

Access the mouth of the Gardner from the east end of Park Street in Gardiner. Park on the south side of the street along the iron fence and take the trail passing behind the pump house down to the river. Fish upstream on the west side of the river. After midseason the water will allow wading across the mouth, enabling the angler to work upstream on the east side of the river as well.

The Gardner River.

Lava Creek flows from the Washburn Range into the Gardner River just east of Mammoth.

106. Lava Creek *(see map on page 225)*

Description: Rising on the northwestern flank of the Washburn Range in the north-central part of the park, Lava Creek flows north and then west to its junction with the Gardner just east of Mammoth. The lower section is in a deeply incised, steep canyon with timber on the south side and more open slopes on the north. The fish in this section are found in the pockets formed around the many boulders of the creek bed. This section heads with a series of steep cascades and Upper and Lower Undine Falls. Above the falls Lava Creek has a more moderate gradient, and the prime fishing spots are pools formed around the many deadfall tree trunks. A mostly fish-less tributary called Lupine Creek joins Lava Creek from the east 1 mile above the falls. This section of Lava Creek is mostly in a timbered valley, much of which was burned in 1988. Satisfactory fishing is available in the lower section of the creek from July through October. The upper section fishes best in July and August and is very poor thereafter.

The fish: The lower couple of miles of Lava Creek carry a mix of rainbows, browns, cutthroat, cutbows, brooks, and even an occasional whitefish, but with the proportions skewed toward rainbows and cutbows. Above Undine Falls the population is exclusively brook trout. The fish in the lower section may run up to 13 inches, but above Undine Falls they are all small, seldom exceeding 8 inches.

Flies and lures: As with most high-gradient mountain streams, the fish in Lava Creek are not particularly selective. The standard attractor dries and wets, such as a Royal Coachman Trude or Prince nymph, will do fine. Because the water is so small, lure fishing is difficult and should be restricted to only the lightest of tackle.

106a. High Bridge

The lower end of Lava Creek is best reached from the Sheepeater Canyon Bridge, usually referred to as the High Bridge, where the north leg of the Grand Loop Road crosses the Gardner 1.6 miles east of Mammoth. The bridge is 16.5 miles west of Tower Junction. Park at the east end of the bridge and take the game trails north, down into the canyon of Lava Creek. This lower section is in a deep canyon downstream of Undine Falls.

106b. Upper Lava Creek

Go 4.2 miles east of Mammoth to the large Undine Falls pullout to view the falls or fish up the creek in this area. Half a mile farther on, the Grand Loop Road crosses the creek near where it comes down from the south. Fish in either direction from the picnic area at the bridge. A farther 0.5 mile east of this bridge is the Wraith Falls Trailhead, 5.1 miles from Mammoth, which can be used to access the upper portion of the stream. A cautionary note here: Wraith Falls itself is on Lupine Creek, and there is no formal trail ascending Lava Creek. Wraith and Undine Falls parking areas are respectively 13.7 and 14.6 miles west of Tower Junction on the Grand Loop Road.

Resources

SOURCES AND ADDITIONAL READING

Part of the pleasure of preparing this book was the opportunity it afforded me to review some of the latest releases and to revisit some old friends. Some of the sources listed below are about fishing, and some are about the country of Yellowstone National Park. In no way should it be taken as a complete list.

Brooks, Charles E. *Fishing Yellowstone Waters*. New York: Lyons & Burford, 1984. Focuses on the big-name waters with emphases on his "home" waters of the Madison, Gallatin, and Henry's Fork drainages.

Haines, Aubrey. *The Yellowstone Story*. 2 vols. West Yellowstone, Mont.: Yellowstone Library and Museum Association, 1977. The best general history of Yellowstone National Park available.

Hughes, Dave. *The Yellowstone River and Its Angling*. Portland, Ore.: Frank Amato Publications, 1992. Hughes's book overlaps this guide in scope. It is a beautiful photo-essay on the Yellowstone River from its sources to east of Billings, Montana.

Reese, Rick. *Greater Yellowstone: The National Park & Adjacent Wildlands*. Helena, Mont.: American & World Geographic Publishing, 1991. Look at this for a wonderful photo-essay on the Greater Yellowstone ecosystem and contemporary management issues.

Russell, Osborne. *Journal of a Trapper*. Lincoln, Neb.: University of Nebraska Press, 1965. An incredibly literate diary of a mountain man's travels through Yellowstone country and the West during the 1830s.

Schneider, Bill. *Hiking Yellowstone*. Helena, Mont.: Falcon, 1997. This is a must-have book for anyone wishing to seriously explore Yellowstone's backcountry. It gives far more detail on the trails of Yellowstone than I could include in this guide.

Staples, Bruce. *River Journal—Yellowstone Park*. Portland, Ore.: Frank Amato Publications, 1996. Half of this publication is devoted to the Cascade Corner and Snake River sections of Yellowstone National Park, and the remainder concentrates on the big-name waters.

Varley, John D. and Paul Schullery. *Freshwater Wilderness: Yellowstone Fishes & Their World*. West Yellowstone, Mont.: Yellowstone Library and Museum Association, 1983. This excellent review of the fishes of Yellowstone has been out of print for some years, but I am informed that a new edition is in the works and should be available soon.

Whittlesey, Lee H. *Yellowstone Place Names*. Helena, Mont.: Montana Historical Society Press, 1988. All the place names that appear in this guide were checked against this reference. Anglers have names for places that have never made it to the list of official names, and I have used those when appropriate. The other sources for names are the official Geological Survey maps. In at least one instance, older copies of some maps have a name misspelled. To the best of my ability, my text is correct, but errors should be assumed to be mine.

AGENCIES

One of the many complexities of the Greater Yellowstone ecosystem is the plethora of agencies holding some level of authority over one or more of its components. The list that follows is limited to those agencies with authority over the federal public land or fish discussed in this guide. They should be looked upon as sources of information as well as governing authorities who issue and enforce rules.

Federal Agencies

Yellowstone National Park, P.O. Box 168, Yellowstone National Park, WY 82190. The park headquarters is at Mammoth Hot Springs. Boat, fishing, and backcountry campsite permits can be purchased at the Albright Visitor Center. Backcountry campsite permits are available at most of the visitor centers and ranger stations in the park. Fishing permits are generally available at the visitor centers and ranger stations throughout the park, except for the entrance stations. Fishing permits are also available from a number of commercial vendors both inside and outside the park. Main park switchboard: (307) 344–7381; backcountry office: (307) 344–2160. Website: www.nps.gov/yell.

Grand Teton National Park, Moose, WY 83012. The main park switchboard is (307) 739–3300. Grand Teton National Park boat permits and backcountry campsite permits are available at the park headquarters. Wyoming fishing licenses are available from many vendors. Website: www.nps.gov/grte.

Gallatin National Forest, P.O. Box 130, Bozeman, MT 59715. General information may be secured from the supervisor's office at (406) 587–6701. It is better to contact the district offices discussed below to secure maps and permits. Website: www.fs.fed.us.gallatin.

Bozeman Ranger District, 3710 Fallon Street, Box C, Bozeman, MT 59715; (406) 587–6920.

Gardiner Ranger District, P.O. Box 5 (U.S. Highway 89), Gardiner, MT 59030; (406) 848–7375.

Hebgen Lake Ranger District, P.O. Box 520 (U.S. Highway 191), West Yellowstone, MT 59758; (406) 646–7369.

Bridger-Teton National Forest, 340 N. Cache Drive, Jackson, WY 83001; (307) 739–5500; www.fs.fed.us.btnf. The Jackson Ranger District office shares this location with the forest headquarters.

Jackson Ranger District, P.O. Box 1689, Jackson, WY 83001; (307) 739–5400.

Targhee National Forest, P.O. Box 208, St. Anthony, ID 83423; (208) 624–3151; www.fs.fed.us/r4/caribou-targhee.

Ashton Ranger District, P.O. Box 858, Ashton, ID 83420; (208) 652–7442.

State Agencies

The headquarters offices of the various state wildlife agencies are good places to secure general information and copies of the regulations. As a general rule, their regional offices are closer to the ground and better able to answer detailed questions. For convenience's sake, it is easier to purchase licenses from one of the large number of commercial vendors authorized by each state.

Idaho Fish and Game Department, P.O. Box 25, Boise, ID 83707. General fishing information is available at (800) 275–3574 or by visiting fishandgame.idaho.gov.

Upper Snake Region, 1515 Lincoln Road, Idaho Falls, ID 83401; (208) 525–7290.

Montana Department of Fish, Wildlife & Parks, 1420 East Sixth Avenue, Helena, MT 59620; (406) 444–2535; fwp.mt.gov.

Region 3, 1400 South Nineteenth Street, Bozeman, MT 59715; (406) 994–4042.

Wyoming Game and Fish Department, 5400 Bishop Boulevard, Cheyenne, WY 82006; (800) 842–1934; gf.state.wy.us.

Regional Fisheries Supervisor, P.O. Box 67, Jackson, WY 83001; (800) 423–4113. Regional Fisheries Supervisor, 2820 State Highway 120, Cody, WY 82414; (800) 654–1178.

CONSERVATION ORGANIZATIONS

There are literally dozens of conservation organizations that have some level of interest in Yellowstone National Park, its fish, and the surrounding area. The ones I have selected have the most consistent presence.

Federation of Flyfishers, 502 South Nineteenth Street, Bozeman, MT 59718; (406) 585–7592; www.fedflyfishers.org. This grassroots membership group has several local affiliate clubs in the region. Its primary focus is on fly fishing as a sport and the conservation of the resources that make it possible.

Greater Yellowstone Coalition, 13 South Wilson Avenue, Bozeman, MT 59715; (406) 586–1593; greateryellowstone.org. A regional membership group with field offices in Wyoming and Idaho, GYC is the only organization with a specific focus on the integrity of the Yellowstone ecosystem.

National Parks and Conservation Association, 1776 Massachusetts Avenue NW, Washington, DC 20036; (800) 628–7275; www.npca.org. The NPCA is a national advocacy group for national parks.

Northern Plains Resource Council, 2401 Montana Avenue, Suite 200, Billings, MT 59101; (406) 248–1154; northernplains.org. A grassroots organization with several community-based affiliate groups on the northern rim of Yellowstone, NPRC has maintained a focus on water quality issues as part of its work.

Trout Unlimited, 1500 Wilson Boulevard, #310, Arlington, VA 22209; (703) 522–0200; www.tu.org. Focused on protecting and enhancing cold-water fisheries and their watersheds, TU is a membership organization with several local chapters in the Yellowstone region.

The Yellowstone ecosystem is under intense pressure from several directions. It is not possible to overemphasize how important it is for those of us who care about the future of the Yellowstone fishery to be active members of one or more of these organizations.

ABOUT MAPS

A guide book without maps would be a pretty poor thing, rather equivalent to film without a camera. I consulted many maps while writing this guide. The principle source of map data is the United States Geological Survey. All the maps are based on USGS topographical maps. A frequent map user is aware of the constant tension between the desire to capture the detail of the ground on the one hand, and the need to end up with a manageable size on the other hand. It is unfortunate, in my estimation, that USGS decided to eliminate the 1/62,500 scale, 15-minute map series. The 7.5-minute series maps at 1/24,000 scale are very difficult to handle in the field because of their size and number. Below are the maps that I think you will find the most useful. The listing presents, in order, the title, publisher, scale, and other useful information.

Mammoth Hot Springs (NW part of Yellowstone National Park plus border area), Trails Illustrated, 1/83,333, folded plastic, revised 1993, includes backcountry campsites and 1988 burn-area information.

Old Faithful (SW part of YNP plus border area), Trails Illustrated, 1/83,333, folded plastic, revised 1994, includes backcountry campsites and 1988 burn-area information.

Yellowstone Lake (SE part of YNP plus border area), Trails Illustrated, 1/83,333, folded plastic, revised 1997, includes backcountry campsites and 1988 burn-area information.

Tower/Canyon (NE part of YNP plus border area), Trails Illustrated, 1/83,333, folded plastic, revised 1994, includes backcountry campsites and 1988 burn-area information.

Yellowstone National Park, USGS, 1/125,000, folded waterproof, based on the 15-minute maps surveyed in the 1950s.

Yellowstone National Park, Trails Illustrated, 1/168,500, folded plastic, revised 1994, includes information on the areas burned in 1988.

I also consulted many other maps for particular information or to guide the preparation of the maps for this book. The USGS 1/250,000 scale maps are handy for a broad appreciation of a large area but are not satisfactory on the ground. The USDA Forest Service produces maps for each of the national forests that are particularly helpful in sorting out the forest roads that are numbered and named on the maps but sometimes inconsistently identified on the ground. The Forest Service maps are available from the district offices listed above. Many commercial vendors carry some or all of the USGS and Trails Illustrated maps.

VENDORS

There is a vast range of shops in the communities surrounding Yellowstone National Park that cater to various aspects of angling and backcountry adventure. I have not even touched the world of horsepack outfitting. I think it would be possible to produce a sizable book just by cataloging the commercial operations. The vendors appearing below should be taken as a sample, not a definitive list.

Maps

USGS Information Services, Box 25286, Denver, CO 80225; (800) 872–6277; fax (303) 202–4693.

Many of the other vendors carry USGS and other maps.

Fishing Tackle and Guide Services

Aune's Absaroka Angler, C. Scott Aune, 754 Yellowstone Avenue, Cody, WY 82414; (307) 587–5105; fax (307) 587–6341.

Henry's Fork Anglers, Mike Lawson, P.O. Box 487, St. Anthony, ID 83423; (800) 788–4479; henrysforkanglers.com; e-mail: henfork@srv.net.

Jack Dennis Outdoor Shop, Jack Dennis, 50 East Broadway, Jackson, WY 83001; (307) 733–3270; www.jackdennis.com.

Jacklin's Fly Shop, Bob Jacklin, 105 Yellowstone Avenue, West Yellowstone, MT 59758; (406) 646–7336; jacklinsflyshop.com.

Montana Troutfitters, Dave Kumlien, 1716 West Main Street, Bozeman, MT 59715; (406) 587–4707; www.troutfitters.com; e-mail: mttrout@gomontana.com.

Parks' Fly Shop, Richard Parks, P.O. Box 196, Gardiner, MT 59030; (406) 848–7314; www.parksflyshop.com; e-mail: richard@parksflyshop.com.

Other Specialties
Northern Lights Trading Company, 1716 West Babcock Street, Bozeman, MT 59715; (406) 586–2225; www.northernlightstrading.com. Technical camping equipment, maps.

Yellowstone Association, P.O. Box 117, Yellowstone National Park, WY 82190; (307) 344–2293; www.yellowstoneassociation.org. The association formerly operated under the name Yellowstone Library and Museum Association. The Yellowstone Association is a nonprofit organization that works in cooperation with the National Park Service. It acts as a publisher and distributor of educational material, particularly books and maps. The association also sponsors the Yellowstone Institute, which conducts classes on a wide range of topics in and around Yellowstone. The institute can be contacted by mail at the same address and by phone at (307) 344–2294.

Index

About the Author

Richard Parks lives in Gardiner, Montana, where he owns and operates the fly shop his father, Merton, established there in 1953. Richard's fishing experience derives from growing up behind the counter, at the tying bench, and on the streams of Yellowstone National Park. He has run the family store and guide service ever since his father died in 1970.

Richard is active in professional and conservation associations. He has served as president of the Fishing Outfitters Association of Montana and chairman of both the Northern Plains Resource Council and the Western Organization of Resource Councils. He is also a lifelong member of Trout Unlimited and the Federation of Flyfishers. He co-authored *Tying and Fishing the West's Best Dry Flies.* His fly shop is featured on the Web at www.parksflyshop.com.